Fresh Eyes to READ the BIBLE

Book 1

Fresh Eyes to READ the BIBLE

Book 1

Biblical Steps for Growing in Faith

Chung DuckYoung

Haggai Books

Unless otherwise indicated, Scripture is taken from the King James Version of the Bible.

Haggai Books

Printed in the United States of America

ISBN: 978-89-953885-4-9

Sincere thanks
to those members of Jayu Church
who have put all their prayers and endeavors together
as one body
to introduce this title to believers worldwide.

CONTENTS

PREFACE 9

INTRODUCTION 13

PART ONE
YOU WILL GET FULL IF YOU EAT

1 Misguided Faith 21
2 Mine is Only What I Experienced 28

PART TWO
BIBLICAL STEPS FOR GROWING IN FAITH

1 Are the Scriptures the Word of God? 33
2 Arrangement and Order of the Scriptures 38
3 Old Testament Period 41
4 New Testament Period 47

PART THREE
DETAILS OF MAJOR STAGES

1	Stage of Genesis	—Creation	69
2	Stage of Old Testament	—Legalistic Faith	85
3	Stage of Matthew	—Repentance	103
4	Stage of Synoptic Gospels	—Following Jesus	171
5	Stage of John	—Born Again	201
6	Stage of Acts	—Baptism with the Holy Spirit	231
7	Stage of the Epistles	—Life of the Born Again	271
8	Stage of Revelation	—Confirmation of Born Again	291

*TABLE 300
OF BIBLICAL STEPS FOR GROWING IN FAITH

PREFACE

I must admit that I do not have substantial knowledge or ideas to share with others which would merit authoring a book. However, I have undergone many hardships in my life and when I reached the end of my tether, I met God. Since then, my eyes have been opened to a whole new world. I am not able to keep to myself those amazing experiences that have occurred during my walk with God. The need to tell my good news made me start writing this book.

Here in this book, I will proclaim Jesus Christ. However, when I was just a church-goer without meeting God, I told nobody to believe in Jesus since I myself was really not sure about the existence of Jesus or God. Naturally, before I met God, I had no prior knowledge that Jesus was God. But, when I met God, I came to know that Jesus was God as described in the Scriptures. I will tell of my experiences of Jesus as they happened to me.

The Jesus that I am going to mention goes beyond the traditional doctrinal frameworks of the churches. He is not Jesus who was made by men according to their misunderstandings of the Scriptures, but He is Jesus, the God of truth. I recommend this title to Christians who desire to know the true Jesus, as well as to those seekers who are eager to find the truth. Any one who is thirsty for the truth will find the way to the truth through this title.

This title has two major pillars. The first pillar is the teaching that reveals the true meaning of the Scriptures; the second is the testimonial confessions of faith I acquired through meeting with God. These two parts correspond to the way and to walking with God: the two essential factors for growing in faith. If we over-emphasize either one of them at the expense of the other, then our faith will be incomplete and will fail.

There are many books available today that teach the Scriptures in depth, and we can easily find other books that provide testimonial experiences of walking with God. However, it is difficult to find books that encompass the profound and true meaning of Scripture, which ultimately is the way to heaven, *and* the testimony of walking with God personally.

Of course, testimony of walking with God can be personal and subjective, but its relevance is not limited to the one testifying. Rather, this testimonial confession is common to all of us since it is based on God. Paul's experience of meeting Jesus as recorded in the Scriptures is, in fact, his personal confession. Nevertheless, it is God's word.

As for the way; the way to heaven is Jesus Christ Himself. And the way to heaven is the step for growing in faith, which is also the step of being born again and salvation. So, if you understand and actually walk in the way with God, at the end of the journey you will be in heaven. You are then born again and saved as a man with faith, who has the power to love his neighbors as himself; as Jesus did.

However, as there are many ways that lead us astray, it is vital to know the right way when it comes to the way to heaven. Please remember! What the Scripture is saying may be different from what you currently understand concerning the way, faith, love, born again, salvation, kingdom of God, *et cetera*.

This book will reveal the right and biblical way of following the order of the Bible's books. Every serious reader will be able to find the right way through this text.

God gave us, the believers, all the good promises in this world through Jesus. However, as we have failed to understand the right way described in the Scripture, we are now lost in the darkness. Arise! And walk in the right way. Let us all meet in heaven!

May the grace of our Lord fill you and all who will read this book.

Chung DuckYoung

INTRODUCTION

Getting a Guide Map

You may have experienced feeling lost in the complex passageways of the transfer subway station. Wandering here and there, it may have seemed difficult to find the way out. You would have been glad to find a guide map to indicate the right way out. Luckily, there are guide maps in many places in the subway station.

The guide map shows the location of entrances, exits, transfers, and other various facilities. Thus, it is possible to find the way through and out of the subway station. The guide maps are very useful for those who get lost in the subway station.

Like a guide map, this book will show the way of truth, that is, the way to the kingdom of God. You may feel that you have never known this way clearly; therefore, you have been feeling uneasy and perplexed. This book explores scriptures and explains events which correspond to every step as we progress on the way of truth. As such, this book will work as an important guide map, like the guide map in the subway station, for those who seek the way of truth.

Reading the Guide Map

Once you find the guide map in the subway station, you must

spend some time studying it if you want to apply it. This means that you need to comprehend the map to get the vital information: location of desired final exit, passageways that lead to the exit, the landmarks and facilities that you will encounter as you progress on the way. This process is inevitable if you want to find your way out of the subway station.

One must remember, however, that understanding how to find the way out is only part of the process. One must leave the guide map location and actually walk all the way to the exit. At this stage in this analogy, we can see our inclination to teach others about the way to exit, forgetting that we ourselves have not actually experienced walking to the exit.

If we are hooked on the satisfaction of teaching others and are pleased with the flattery from others for our good knowledge, then we ourselves will not be able to reach the exit after all. Understanding but not applying the map is a danger for all those who study the map.

In a spiritual sense, this book will show the way to truth. As with the guide map in the subway station, one may need to spend considerable time in study to understand the way that this book reveals.

The contents of this book invite the reader to a world that is totally different from the existing world. Sometimes, the reader may be unable to grasp or understand all that the book explains. One may wonder, "What on earth does it mean?" But if you keep on reading it carefully, you will see and understand the way to the kingdom of God.

However, as mentioned in the subway map scenario, once you understand the way to truth, it is tempting to think that you have already passed along the way; you may then wish to teach others. You may even receive praise or recognition as one who knows the truth and the way to the truth well.

But one thing is clear: you have not actually passed along the way. It is a completely different thing to understand the way of truth and actually to pass along that way. The difference between these two things is the difference between non-truth and truth, death and life, the world and the kingdom of God. Do not confuse these two things while walking the way of truth. You must actually go the way of truth. Let us not forget this.

Knowing the Current Position

If you understand the guide map, then you must locate your current position on the map. Only then, you can decide the proper directions to follow. Thereafter, you can march on toward the exit without losing direction in the real world.

If you do not locate your current position on the map, there is no connection between the real world and the guide map to guide you on your way. In this case, the guide map is detached from your reality, the real world, and it will be useless to you, no matter how accurate it is.

This scenario is exactly the same in your walk to the way of truth. This book, if you can understand it correctly, will serve as the guide map that shows the way to truth. When you understand the way to truth through this book, then you have to locate the current position of your faith. If you do not locate your current position correctly, then you will be lost even though you have a good understanding of the map—even this book.

The Pharisees in the days of Jesus, for example, could not reach the truth because they misunderstood their current position in terms of their faith. They misjudged themselves and believed that they had already reached the truth as they had been worshiping God and were not like the Gentiles. Even though Jesus pointed out that they were lost in darkness repeatedly, they did not listen and behaved as if they had already come to the truth.

They deviated from the way to truth because they had failed to correctly identify their current in faith the Bible and through the word of Jesus.

For us, knowing our current position is both easy and difficult.

It is easy because all one needs to do is to apply the faith-growing process given in this book. Conversely, it is difficult because one must admit that one's past efforts and zeal in Jesus were legalistic and in vain. No one can reach the truth if he does not locate his current position on the map accurately.

In order to know your current spiritual position you have to check whether you have met the living Jesus in your life personally. It is so simple. Those having met Jesus live by the grace of God; others, having not yet met Him, live under the law.

We generally think that if a man attends church and confesses Jesus as Savior then he has met Him and has received Him. However, as a matter of fact, he may not have met Him at all. Like the Pharisees, this is an example of failing to establish one's current position.

If one wants to meet Jesus, one must truly repent. Here, true repentance means that through your life experiences you come to realize that you are a sinner. I describe this true repentance in detail later in this book.

A Bright World

Let us get back to the passageways of the subway station. Once you know your current position on the guide map, you can set your direction to the destination, the exit. As you keep walking on, you will approach the exit. No step is in vain. Finally you will come out of the dark subway passageways and walk in the bright world. Now, you can assuredly and accurately explain and guide others who get lost in the dark underground to the exit.

So it is with the way of truth. When you locate your current position on the spiritual map drawn by this book, Jesus will lead you to the way thereafter. What is needed here is a walk that is focused on the destination. You must be following His guidance at all times. This is right Christian living. The time will come when you arrive at the exit, the kingdom of God.

Those who complete this journey are in a position to lead

others in the way they have walked. The Scripture, if we understand it correctly, calls the leading of others to the kingdom of God as 'loving your neighbor as yourself.'

This book will show you the whole process in which a man is born, walks the way of truth, and ultimately conveys the way to others. I hope we can walk through this process within our lifetime.

PART ONE

YOU WILL GET FULL IF YOU EAT

1

MISGUIDED FAITH

"You'll get full if you eat." This would seem to be a very natural statement, and it embarrasses me to write it down. However, this natural law is totally ignored when it comes to believing in Jesus. We wrongly think that if we believe in Jesus, God Almighty or Jesus will make us full even if we do not eat. Does God operate in this way? I would like to challenge you about incorrect or misguided faith by looking into this most fundamental problem of faith.

Faith Without Thinking

As one sows, so shall he reap. No one can violate this principle of God. Of course, God follows it, too. It is obvious that the Scriptures, the word of God, are also recorded based on this principle. However, we often ignore the principle God established when we believe in Jesus. For example, we believe that if we fervently pray and satisfy Him, Jesus will make tomatoes grow in the field where we have planted potatoes. The Scriptures do not say so.

> Be not deceived; God is not mocked: for whatsoever a man soweth, that shall he also reap. For he that soweth to his flesh

> shall of the flesh reap corruption; but he that soweth to the Spirit shall of the Spirit reap life everlasting. [Galatians 6:7-8]

These verses tell us the natural principle that each person will reap what he has sown. That is, they tell us that we should sow soberly to the Holy Spirit because if we sow to the flesh, we cannot reap everlasting life—even if we pray for it sincerely. What is reaped is already determined by what is sown.

However, we wish to reap good by any available means, instead of thinking about what we are actually sowing at present. Why don't we want to acknowledge what we are sowing? It is because it annoys us to think about this. We are inclined to pray to God as follows, "All I can do is to trust in You, so please lead me to the kingdom of heaven," or "I will only believe in You, and please allow me Your blessing and everlasting life."

Faith grows in you and no one can do this for you. Even Jesus cannot do it on your behalf. For example, Jesus leads us to bear fruit, but He does not gather fruit from another tree and hang it on us when we bear no fruit. We must bear the fruit ourselves.

Our lives belong to us, and we should have serious thoughts about our lives. If we believe without thinking, it is like walking along the road with our eyes closed. We need to think and think again. Our souls will open eyes when we think.

The Laws of Nature Versus the Concept of Give and Take

"You will get full if you eat."

And, "I will give you money if you eat."

Let's examine the differences between these two propositions. In the first, the act of eating and the result of getting full are one. If we eat, we will all get full without any exception. This is the law established by God and the order of nature. Therefore, the sentence "You will get full if you eat" can be rewritten, as "God will make you full if you eat." Nobody raises any objection to God on the fact that we will get full if we eat. No one murmurs to God about the fact that we will feel hungry if we do not eat. It is because the first sentence shows the order of nature as set out by God.

However, the second sentence "I will give you money if you eat" is very different from the first. It may be used by parents to persuade a child who will not eat. In this case, the act of the child eating is separated from the result of receiving money. These two acts are not connected by the laws of nature, but they have a temporary give-and-take relationship that is artificial.

So, the parents can give the child money (if they change their mind), even though he does not eat. Or if they do not give the child money, neighbors can accordingly blame them as follows: "Why didn't they give him money and have therefore made him so angry?"

The fundamental difference between the two sentences is as follows. For the first one, the condition and the result are one, combined according to the laws of nature. There is no margin for intervention by human beings or even God Almighty. Therefore, no one complains about the result. However, for the second one, the condition and the result are separated so the result can be changed as and when the parents change their mind. For this reason, if the parents go too far, people will blame or murmur against them.

Misunderstanding About the Thought, "You Will Enter the Kingdom of God if You Believe in Jesus"

So to which of the two sentences discussed above do the Scriptures relate? The Scriptures are the words of absolute truth, so the statement "You will get full if you eat" is most closely related to the truth of Scripture. However, we tend to understand the Scriptures along the lines of "Jesus will give you money if you eat."

The whole content of Scripture might be summarized as a single sentence: "We will enter the kingdom of God if we believe in Jesus." This sentence is a statement of the truth. It has a unified structure, a necessary condition and the result. The statement shows that if we believe in Jesus, we will naturally enter the kingdom of God as a direct result. There is no margin for inserting self-will between the condition of believing Jesus and the result of entering the kingdom of God.

This relationship is totally different in nature to the statement that "I will give you money if you eat," which is used when we make a contract or a transaction. Nevertheless, many of us understand the Scriptures according to the give-and-take paradigm whereby if we believe in Jesus, God will cherish us, and in return, He will give us entrance into the kingdom of God.

When we are mistaken in this manner, we will murmur against God if He casts out those who did not believe in Jesus on the Day of Judgment, saying "How come He burns them up with unquenchable fire, even though they have sinned?"

However, the judgment of God is of the order of natural law, just as we feel hunger when we do not eat. God does not work according to the give-and-take paradigm that men rely on.

Obedience and Blessing Versus Disobedience and Curses

I will quote a verse from Deuteronomy Chapter 28 in order to demonstrate that we tend to understand the Scriptures as explained above.

God promises blessings to us who believe in Jesus. But the blessings may not be immediately realized. There are conditions that we must fulfill in order to get those blessings. After we do this, He will bless us. Note the promise in the following verse.

> And it shall come to pass, if thou shalt hearken diligently unto the voice of the LORD thy God, to observe and to do all his commandments which I command thee this day, that the LORD thy God will set thee on high above all nations of the earth: [Deuteronomy 28:1]

This verse is telling us about the blessing we will receive if we observe and do all His commandments. Consider the following statement: "If you keep the commandments of the LORD, all blessings shall come to you."

This is a truth statement, in which case the condition and the consequence are to be construed as one. In general, however, we consider obedience to God and the subsequent blessings separately. In other words, we recognize the words according to the give-and-take paradigm such as "I will give you money if you eat."

This is an incorrect understanding. The above verses are written based on the principle that God's blessing is included in obedience, and it naturally comes after the obedience. They are one. We will be blessed if we obey to God.

Let us look further at Deuteronomy:

> But it shall come to pass, if thou wilt not hearken unto the voice of the LORD thy God, to observe to do all his commandments and his statutes which I command thee this day; that all these curses shall come upon thee, and overtake thee. [Deuteronomy 28:15]

Here we see that God will destroy us if we disobey Him. Those who separate the disobedience and the curse will also murmur against God. We may say, "How could He do that?" I have seen many people, having left the church after reading verses like these, thinking to themselves that a God who curses His people cannot be a God of love.

God Who Judges No Man

I will rewrite the statement "You will get full if you eat" in the manner of Deuteronomy 28, as follows: "He who eats, I will make him full! And he who does not eat, I will make him starve to death!" This sentence includes an expression of the will of God who makes the man starve, but as a matter of fact, God talks about the ordinary course of nature that everybody is aware of. There is nothing mysterious about it.

God does not additionally chasten or curse us even though we disobey Him. Disobedience and curse are one; hence, disobedience has the curse inherent in itself. Obedience and disobedience depend on the exercise of free will by individuals. Therefore, if we choose disobedience, we simultaneously choose the curse. If we disobey God but wish to be blessed by God, it is nonsense similar to wanting to get full without eating anything.

God does not forcibly push disobedient people into hell. Those who enjoy a life of disobedience and live such a life meet the results caused by having chosen disobedience. It is the same as sowing potatoes. If we sow potatoes, it immediately follows that we shall reap potatoes. The result cannot be changed for any reason whatsoever. God does not judge a man after having seen the result. The result itself is the judgment of God.

Further, some people may accuse God for having made the curse. In fact, the blessing can only be a blessing with the existence of the curse. It is a principle of nature. Likewise, being full cannot be defined without the concept of hunger. As such, the curse is essential, but it is prudent for us to avoid the curse by obedience.

A God of Public Justice?

Some people think of God as a judge, and they introduce the concept of public justice in order to rationalize God's judgment. They understand God as He who, for the sake of public justice, punishes unbelievers even though He may not have to. For instance, if a king's son breaches the law, the king can forgive him without putting him into jail. But for the sake of public justice, the king puts his son into jail according to the law. They think of God's judgment in a similar manner.

However, this thought implies that God may allow those who sowed potatoes to reap tomatoes, but He also may allow them to reap the potatoes, considering public justice. This is not a correct understanding of the truth.

The judgment about not believing in Jesus is already determined when we do not believe in Him. God does not seek to control the result. If we believe in Him, He only works and allows us to reap the result of believing in Him. Conversely, if we do not believe in Him, He then works and allows us to reap the result of not believing in Him. He cannot allow other results; in that case, He would no longer be God. He will not exercise any additional judgment beyond the order of nature in days to come. Therefore, it is fundamentally wrong to think of God as He who judges for public justice.

We are condemned already if we do not believe in Jesus, and we are saved already if we believe in Him. The results are already determined, depending on what we do in the present.

Jesus said:

> He that believeth on him is not condemned: but he that believeth not is condemned already, because he hath not believed in the name of the only begotten Son of God. [John 3:18]

Say good-bye to misguided faith!

2

MINE IS ONLY WHAT I EXPERIENCED

The Difference Between Knowledge and Experience

I would like to tell you one thing that will help you to understand this book. It is about experience. "You will get full if you eat" is a true statement. We can say it to others. However, to know the fact that we will get full if we eat is one thing; to actually eat and get full is quite another. The former is knowledge and the latter is experience. We do not actually get full without action, even if we have knowledge of it. However, we are already full if we experience it. Therefore, the experience means everything in this case.

Let us assume that someone does not agree with our saying that we will get full if we eat. He questions us as follows, "We really get full if we eat? No kidding, I don't think so." What if we force him to agree by saying, "What are you getting at? Just listen to us because we are right!"

If a man argues like this we will think that he is not in his right mind. That is because the truth in the statement "You will get full if you eat" is a matter of experience, not a matter of mere knowledge. Even if we succeed in persuading him to agree with us, he will never get full if he does not experience it, i.e. eat. Therefore, it will be meaningless to try to make him agree with us through argument.

Nevertheless, we frequently do this meaningless thing in an attempt to preach Jesus. Sometimes we force others to believe in Jesus, and sometimes we threaten them. But believing in Jesus and being saved is a matter of personal experience, not of knowledge. So, it is useless to seek to threaten people into believing in Jesus.

Do we perhaps do this based on the following passage from Romans?

> That if thou shalt confess with thy mouth the Lord Jesus, and shalt believe in thine heart that God hath raised him from the dead, thou shalt be saved. For with the heart man believeth unto righteousness; and with the mouth confession is made unto salvation. [Romans 10:9-10]

Here, to confess with the mouth does not refer to a verbal expression of our decision to believe in Him. If any one understands these verses in Romans as a matter of choice, it proves that he has never experienced Jesus. As he has no experience meeting Jesus, he misunderstands Jesus as He who saves him according to confession with the mouth.

Here, the confession indicates the experience of a person in meeting Jesus as his personal Savior. In other words, when experiencing Jesus as his Savior as Peter and Paul did, he can then confess Him as Lord and Savior. The confession in the Scriptures refers to the real experience. This will be described later in detail in the section "Baptism with the Holy Spirit."

Believing in Jesus Is a Question of Experience, Not Knowledge

As believers, we might have abundant knowledge about Jesus through hearing sermons, studying the Bible, sharing testimonies, *et cetera*. However, that knowledge about Jesus cannot save us from the sin. In order to believe in Jesus, we need to meet Jesus in person in our lives, and be guided by Him to salvation.

1 John begins as follows:

> That which was from the beginning, which we have heard, which we have seen with our eyes, which we have looked upon, and our hands have handled, of the Word of life. [1 John 1:1]

John met Jesus, the Word of Life. Apparently, he saw with his eyes, and his hand touched Him physically. However, by this verse, John does not mean that he saw Jesus with his eyes and thrust his hand into His side like Thomas. Jesus cannot be known and believed in through knowledge and/or bodily contact.

The above verse speaks of the spiritual experience in which John met Jesus in his life and became one with Him by receiving the Holy Spirit. Thus, the intangible word of life became tangible in John personally. John was a real believer through his *experience* of Christ.

This necessity of experience is applicable to us in the same way as it was for John. Those having the spiritual experience of meeting Him, know Him as He is and only they can truly believe in Jesus.

In summary, the Scriptures are written according to the laws of nature rather than the give-and-take paradigm of men. Second, believing in Jesus is a question of experience, not knowledge.

PART TWO

BIBLICAL STEPS FOR GROWING IN FAITH

1

ARE THE SCRIPTURES THE WORD OF GOD?

Evidence That the Scriptures are the Word of God

It is said that the twenty-seven books of the New Testament currently used in churches were officially approved as canons at the Council of Carthago in A.D. 397. We accept and read them as the word of God without question. In your Christian life, you may come to know more about the establishment of the canonical Scriptures. At this point in your learning, you might falter in your faith in the Scriptures. If you had been vaguely thinking that the Scriptures fell from the sky, were brought by an angel, or something similar, then you may be surprised to know that it was men who compiled them.

Moreover, there were serious arguments during the establishment process over whether certain books should be included as Scripture or excluded. The process was entirely different from the way you might have envisioned. Furthermore, you may be discouraged by the notion that the Word of God has had so many opportunities for human intervention in its compilation.

You might ask, "Then, how could such Scriptures be the word of God?" You might not have thought about this matter deeply, but let's think about it together. Is there objective evidence that the Scriptures are the word of God? Where can we find this evidence?

Some people say that Scripture is the word of God since it is stated as such in the Scriptures. "Somewhere in 1Timothy or 2 Timothy," they might say. In 2 Timothy it says:

> All scripture is given by inspiration of God, and is profitable for doctrine, for reproof, for correction, for instruction in righteousness. [2 Timothy 3:16]

Indeed, this passage witnesses that all the scriptures are the word of God and inspired by His Holy Spirit.

However, if we insist that the Scriptures are the word of God because the Scriptures say so, there is an inherent flaw to that logic. Following that argument, any man could claim that his book is the word of God while writing it with his own ideas. In that case, the book could not be considered the word of God, even though the book declares it to be.

We Will Know When We Experience

Then, how can we know that the Scriptures are the word of God?

A lot of people try to prove that Scripture is the word of God, but this is quite fruitless. There is no way to prove it to others. Even if we are quoting from a well-known historian, a reliable archeologist, or a famous theologian, it is not possible. Even if we had the chance to meet the apostles or prophets who wrote the Scriptures and get their testimony that the Scriptures are the word of God, it would be fruitless, too.

Why? Simply because we who are listening to the testimonies have no way of ascertaining whether these testimonies are true or not. What they testify to is truth to them only, not necessarily to us.

In order for us to know that the Scriptures are the word of God, we should first meet God in our lives. Such experiences might include being moved by God while reading the Scripture or hearing God's voice speaking to us through the Scriptures. People having these kinds of experiences come to recognize that the Scriptures are not the ordinary words of men.

It is only through our individual experience of meeting God that we come to realize that the Scriptures are, indeed the word of God. We need to confirm with God by ourselves that the Scriptures are word of God. Quite reasonably, the word of God is only to be confirmed by God Himself.

Therefore, knowing Scripture as God's word is a matter of an individual experience of meeting God, not a matter of the will of a man to believe in God.

The Jews in the Bible did not deny that the Scriptures were the word of God. They believed the Scriptures as the word of God with greater confidence than anyone else. However, they believed that Scripture was God's word, not by experience, but by their own will and efforts based on religious traditions. These people were carnal believers. Even if carnal believers firmly believe Scripture is the word of God, they cannot get over their carnal inclinations.

When the Jews met Jesus, they expected bread from Him to fill the body, which was very natural for carnal people (Jhn 6:26). To their thinking, He would be God if He could feed them with bread, and He would be Satan if he could not. They told Jesus to give them loaves to eat and to set them free from the oppression of the Roman Empire—if He was really sent by God. However, their thoughts were carnal.

Jesus came to give spiritual bread, not physical bread. He came to give freedom of the spirit, not physical independence from the Roman Empire. Accordingly, Jesus ignored their requests, and they ultimately delivered Him to be crucified because they believed that He was not sent from God but was a blasphemer.

Likewise, if anyone confesses and believes the Scripture by his own will, without experiencing God, the god who will be formed in his heart will be a man-made god, not the true God. The Jews could not recognize Jesus, sent by God, since they had a man-made idol, not the true God, in their hearts. Surely, their idolatry led to the crucifixion of the son of God.

This attitude or phenomenon is, however, not limited to the Jews. We can find a lot of people around us, making resolutions to believe in Scripture as the word of God by themselves.

The truth is that they can only believe in and serve God through experiencing Him in their own lives.

No Double-Mindedness After Experience

Usually when somebody talks about unfamiliar words or new facts which we have little idea, we tend to believe in him thinking that he knows something special that we do not know.

For example, Biblical critics may say something like this:

"The Scriptures are fabricated by extracting articles from the Babylonian myths and editing them." Or,

"The contents in the Scriptures are similar to the teaching of Mithraism, a belief system the ancient Romans held before Christianity was spread."

Likewise, they may tell you,

"The Scriptures are not the words of God but the words of man that are artificially edited." Or,

"Since the Pauline faction gained ground during the redaction process, many epistles of Paul, who did not followed Jesus in the flesh, are included in the canons, and the epistles of Peter, who did follow Him, are pushed out." *Et cetera.*

However, when we come to know that the Scriptures are the word of God through the experience of meeting God, our faith will not be shaken—even when someone says something negative about the Scriptures. This is because we have experienced God while reading the Scriptures in the form of the Holy Bible. If the current Holy Bible had lost value as the word of God, God would not have spoken to us through these very books and verses.

Those who want to ascertain that the Scriptures are the word of God need to experience God first. Of course, such experience is individual and subjective. When God actually speaks to a person through Scripture and he has a subjective experience, Scripture then becomes the word of God to him.

The experiences are subjective, and all that the individual has undergone is his experience alone. If we wish to see that all the people accept Scripture as the word of God, they all must individually experience God. Then, they will have an objective belief in Scripture as the word of God, and they will never lose their confidence in Scripture.

2

ARRANGEMENT AND ORDER OF THE SCRIPTURES

Arrangement and Order of the Scriptures Are No Accident

The first book of the Scriptures is Genesis, but a table of contents is provided before Genesis. The table of contents displays the arrangement of the thirty-nine books of the Old Testament and the twenty-seven books of the New Testament, from Genesis to Revelation.

Considering the order of these respective books, we can feel that the books were not arranged by accident but that God has intervened in this arrangement and has controlled it. Even if someone is not familiar with the Scriptures, he will generally know that Genesis is written about the creation of man, woman, and all things. Revelation describes the second coming of Jesus, judgment, and the end times.

From this brief overview, we can easily guess that Scripture is arranged based on a certain order. As a matter of fact, this order represents the steps by which God leads us to salvation. Therefore, if we can understand this arrangement and order of Scripture, we will know the steps through which God will save us. We will be born again when we have completely undergone these steps.

Looking at the process in further detail, it will be easier to understand if we assume that there are milestones provided for us from Genesis to Revelation and that each of us walks following the steps and stages according to an order in Scripture. For instance, a baby who is born today will start walking from the book of Genesis, having the steps of sixty-five books set before him. A sixty year-old man, for instance, went through the stage of Genesis sixty years ago, He then began the Exodus stage and may have progressed on from there.

The current stage of development of faith in God is different for each person. Some people will die after having spent their lives in the Exodus stage, and very few people will die having reached the Revelation stage.

The actual steps of salvation, according to the order of Scripture, can be summarized as follows:

Our birth in the flesh (we are under the law as sinner)→ Repentance (we meet Jesus in our lives)→ Forgiveness of sin/Born again (Completion of Salvation)→ Baptism with Holy Spirit→ Life of the Born Again→ Death of Body (Confirmation of Salvation)

These steps will be dealt with in detail as we go on.

Faith and Salvation Are Not a Reward But Are Growth in Life

Throughout this book, the salvation steps will be interchangeable with the steps of growing in faith since they convey the same meaning.

When saying that we are saved, we are generally inclined to regard salvation as God's reward in response to the works of righteousness that we have done. It may be easy to think that God is saying, "That's a good job! You take salvation as the prize."

However, this is not what the Scripture says about salvation. The salvation presented in Scripture indicates a whole process in which new life is born into a person through Jesus. The new life that is born in this way matures in him. In other words, Biblical arrangement reveals the steps for him to know the way to the kingdom of God and to walk in that way. An individual's current position of salvation and his measure of faith correspond to the degree in which he walks in the way. This understanding about salvation and faith will greatly assist one in understanding Scripture.

As long as we understand salvation and faith in terms of a reward, many passages in Scripture will be difficult to understand. According to the concept of reward, we must struggle hard to make a big impression on God so as to be saved. The Jews, having understood salvation as a reward, strictly observed the law to establish their own righteousness so that they might stand before God on the square, but they only failed.

However, if we understand salvation according to the concept of the growth of life, the efforts of man gain no toehold in the climb to salvation. Man has no work to do during the life-growing process. What is required of him is only to grow.

He who gives the growth is not us but God. We are only to feel God's hand and follow Him with obedience, which will be our work, if we can call it work. Accordingly, salvation and faith are not of ourselves but are the gift of God as stated in Ephesians 2:8:

"For by grace are ye saved through faith; and that not of yourselves: it is the gift of God:"

Now, we will review the outlines of the respective books of the Scriptures, and we will see further how the order of the Scriptures matches with the steps that grow our faith.

3

OLD TESTAMENT PERIOD

Genesis

Genesis is the first book in Scripture. It is about the creation of man and the universe. It has records of the beginning of everything. However, Genesis is not only a book about the beginning, but it is also a book about completion. What beginning and completion am I referring to? It is about the beginning and the completion of our faith.

The whole outline of Genesis can be summed by the following sentences:

"God created man and woman to be fruitful and multiply. However, they sinned in the eyes of God, and He judged and destroyed them with water in the days of Noah. Then He called Abraham and established him as the father of faith. Through Abraham's descendants, God built a new nation of Israel to be fruitful and multiply."

Therefore, Genesis is about the creation and the completion of the nation of Israel, and here, the Israelites symbolize those of us who now believe in Jesus. Spiritually speaking, they could be called 'Faith in Us.'

The core message of Genesis is that God destroys the old man, the source of sin, and gives us a new life based on faith. Here, the generation before Noah, who was destroyed by the flood, symbolizes our old man while the Israelites, who are descendants of Abraham, symbolize the new birth of life through faith, the new man.

We must go through the process of destroying the 'old man' who belongs to the world and building up the 'new man' in order for us, born of the flesh, to be born again in the spirit. This is not only the salvation that frees us from sin, but it is also the completion of creation of the new man that God intended. In other words, it is the process of creation in which God breaks down our old man and makes a new man. This is the theme of Genesis, as well as of the whole of Scripture. Genesis, therefore, can be considered as a summary of all the Scripture.

One thing, the Old Testament is a record, mostly about the history of the Israelites. However, for a full comprehension of Scripture, we need a thorough understanding of the spiritual context which connects the records with us who are living today. Only then can God's words become living words that change and affect us today. If we miss this spiritual meaning of the Scriptures, we will question:

"So, what has the creation of the nation of Israel got to do with me?" Or "What does Jesus, who once came to this world 2,000 years ago, have to do with me now?"

When we have the spiritual meaning of Scripture, we will realize that the records about the history of Israel are also about each one of us. To read more about this, refer to the section "Each of Us Are Adam," in Part Three, Chapter One, Genesis Stage—The Creation.

For us at least, Scripture is not a history book of the Israelites. The records of the Scripture, for an analogy, are pictures produced by the endoscope, which show unseen inside of all human beings. So the Scripture is a direct record of all of us.

Let us examine the thread of Genesis in the spiritual sense. We generally view salvation as restoring the fallen Adam to his former state when he was in the Garden of Eden.

This understanding is, however, mistaken. Salvation does not follow the steps of 'creation of Adam' → 'fall of Adam' → 'restoration of the Garden of Eden and of Adam.' Had this been the whole purpose, Christ would not have needed to come to earth because Adam would have fallen again, even if Christ had restored the Garden of Eden for him.

Please do not be surprised when I say that spiritually Adam is me. We will realize this truth bit by bit.

Jesus does not come just to restore Adam to his original state in Eden. His purpose is to give Adam the Spirit of Christ so that he may be united with Christ and have eternal salvation. Therefore, the steps of salvation in the Scriptures are 'creation of Adam' → 'fall of Adam' → 'union of Adam with Christ.'

God foresaw Adam's fall in His plan and used it positively to support His creation. Therefore, God's creation of Adam is not completed in the Garden of Eden, but it is only completed when Adam meets Jesus Christ and become perfect after having fallen.

This issue will be discussed further and in depth in the parable of the lost son in the chapter "True Repentance."

We all begin life in the fallen state. Since it is an unavoidable phase in our creation, we do not have to be disappointed; we do not have to despair or blame others for our circumstances. Our aspiration in this life is not to return to the pre-fall state of Adam, but it is to be united with Christ which is the way we should go in this life.

Genesis indicates the time when God created each of our souls; it is the beginning of the existence of me. In the faith-growing steps, the Genesis stage corresponds to the point when one's soul was created in Eden. This stage, however, is forgotten in our memory as it happened out of time and space.

Exodus

The book of Exodus begins with the story of Israelites. Having been fruitful, they leave Egypt under the leadership of Moses.

If we consider Genesis as the general synopsis of the whole Bible, we can then say that Scripture substantially begins from Exodus forward. In fact, Exodus is the stage where we are born, the beginning of ourselves in this world.

The background of Exodus is a wilderness, which is not a good place to live. The wilderness is filled with fiery serpents and scorpions; it is barren and hard. Such characteristics match the stage of Exodus as we grow in faith. When each of us is born and begins life, the background of our life is the wilderness, that is, this world. This world can be symbolized as the wilderness; it is barren and hard to live through.

We disobey God while we believe in this world's ways, just as the Israelites disobeyed God in the wilderness (Hbr 3:15-18). You may think this statement is wrong since it says that the believers are disobedient to God. However, often we are not able to hear what the living God says, even when we believe, and this results in disobedience.

"Are we hearing from the living God while believing?" God communicates with us through all things, using every means, but we have no idea of it at all and cannot hear Him; hence, we cannot obey God even if we want to. Our disobedience towards God is biblical considering that the Israelites, who symbolize believers, disobeyed God in the wilderness. And it is true.

God led the Israelites by day in a pillar of cloud and by night in a pillar of fire while they were passing through the wilderness after the exodus from Egypt. Canaan was the destination. Likewise, He leads us with the word from the day we are born in this world.

What was Canaan for the Israelites is the kingdom of God for us. Just as the Israelites, led by Moses, advanced towards the land of Canaan through the wilderness, in this world we also make way towards the kingdom of God, being led by the law.

We are created in the Genesis stage, and after having eaten from the tree of the knowledge of good and evil, we are given birth in this time and space, the world of the flesh. For each of us, we then step into the Exodus stage of growing in faith.

Leviticus, Numbers, and Deuteronomy through Malachi

These books are about the law, offerings, and prophecy. They describe forgiveness of sin through sacrifice after violating the law. Here the offering represents repentance in the present day. The law controls all the life of a man before Jesus comes into his life; this corresponds to the Old Testament period.

The Pentateuch (including Genesis, Exodus, Leviticus, Numbers, and Deuteronomy) and the books of History speak about the law, and the books of Prophets talk about the prophecy of the coming Messiah, the Christ, who set us free. The books prophesy the Messiah who is to come since they were written before He came. The Old Testament, therefore, is God's word that is written about Jesus yet to come, and it is called the 'Law' or the 'Law and Prophets' in Scripture.

The Beginning of the New Testament Period Differs from Person to Person

As mentioned above, everyone begins his or her life in the Exodus stage when he or she is born in this world. The Genesis stage is the creation of our spirits in the Garden of Eden, and the Exodus stage is the creation of our human flesh in this world. The beginning of the Exodus stage would be different as birth dates differ individually. Our birth time is the beginning of the Exodus stage for our growing in faith.

We can easily think that we who are living in contemporary times are living in the New Testament period because Jesus already came to earth 2,000 years ago. However, this is a big mistake because Jesus starting the New Testament time 2,000 years ago does not have any direct relationship with the present me. If the people who lived in the same generation as Jesus met Him, then the New Testament period could have been started by Jesus in that period. This is, however, not necessarily applicable to me now.

The New Testament period begins only when one meets Jesus here and in person. As I have shared in the chapter "You Get Full if You Eat," 'something' can be considered mine only when I experience it myself. Without this personal experience, 'something' shall only remain there, without any relationship to me.

Furthermore, we cannot assume that we have met Jesus because we have been attending church for a long time or have read the Scriptures many times. Although we live in the 21st century, people who have not personally met Jesus Christ are living in the Old Testament period.

We learn and know about Jesus in church, however, it cannot be equated with meeting Him. Until we have a personal experience of meeting Him, such learning about Jesus is simply a study of laws and prophesies that Jesus will come.

4

NEW TESTAMENT PERIOD

Repentance to Meet Jesus

When Jesus comes into the life of a man who has been living in the Old Testament period, he begins his New Testament period. However, a prerequisite for him meeting Jesus in his life is encountering John the Baptist. He was born six months before Jesus was born. As an adult, his workplace was a wilderness, and he preached,

"Repent ye: for the kingdom of heaven is at hand" (Mat 3:2).

The wilderness represents this world, which is indeed a difficult place to live in. John the Baptist symbolizes repentance. John cries repentance in the wilderness. What does this mean?

The nature of the world drives us to seek God and to repent to Him because of its harshness. So all mankind have the chance to meet John the Baptist in this life. This repentance, i.e., meeting John, means 'seeking God wholeheartedly' led by the bitterness of the world. This is the repentance and baptism by John the Baptist.

God will send Jesus Christ to us who already completed the repentance of John. Thus, we can meet Jesus and begin the New Testament period of the faith-growing steps.

However, most of us demonstrate the Pharisaic syndrome in

our Christian life; we think we believe in Jesus, but we have neglected the step of John the Baptist. If we do not meet John the Baptist, we cannot meet Jesus. However, not knowing this, we think that we meet Jesus in the church. In this case, we outwardly believe in Jesus, but we inwardly have a faith that is based on the law—like the Pharisees.

I consider this syndrome to be a kind of disease in the faith-growing process. Symptoms of this syndrome include boasting of self-righteousness, such as "I prayed long," or "I give tithes." This will be discussed again in this book when we talk about the Pharisees.

The repentance of John the Baptist and the receiving of Jesus do not mean that we repent of one or two sins that we ask God to forgive. The true repentance that the Scriptures refer to represents turning to God in total despair after giving up our earthly, carnal life. Having gone through repentance, one leaves all and follows Jesus. Peter is one of the disciples who was called by Jesus, and he repented in this way:

> When Simon Peter saw it, he fell down at Jesus' knees, saying, Depart from me; for I am a sinful man, O Lord...
> And when they had brought their ships to land, they forsook all, and followed him. [Luke 5:8, 11]

This repentance will be dealt with again under the heading Stage of Matthew—"Repentance" in Part Three.

The Gospels According to Matthew, Mark, and Luke

The Gospels according to Matthew, Mark, and Luke are called the Synoptic Gospels. The Four Gospels record what Jesus did, but Matthew, Mark and Luke are separately classified because they have many similarities in writing style and approach. The Gospel according to John is not included in the Synoptic Gospels due to above reason.

Faith in the stage of the Synoptic Gospels represents the faith of those who have just met Jesus in their lives and have forsaken all to follow Him. These are people called by Jesus.

Four Kinds of Fields in the Parable of the Sower

Within the process of growing in faith, the order of the four Gospels in the Bible matches the gradual progress of the four kinds of fields appearing in the parable of the Sower (Matthew, Chapter 13; Mark, Chapter 4; Luke, Chapter 8). This parable introduces four kinds of fields on which the seeds fall: the wayside, stony places, thorns, and good ground. Read the following verses of Matthew:

> And he spake many things unto them in parables, saying, Behold, a sower went forth to sow; And when he sowed, some seeds fell by the way side, and the fowls came and devoured them up: Some fell upon stony places, where they had not much earth: and forthwith they sprung up, because they had no deepness of earth: And when the sun was up, they were scorched; and because they had no root, they withered away. And some fell among thorns; and the thorns sprung up, and choked them: But other fell into good ground, and brought forth fruit, some an hundredfold, some sixtyfold, some thirtyfold. [Matthew 13:3-8]

The field refers to our heart. The seed means the word of God. Hence, this parable speaks about four kinds of fields that receive the seeds as a representation of how we react when the word of God falls on our heart. In other words, the same seeds of the word are sown to the heart, but they produce different results according to the condition of our heart.

The state of the heart can change. The heart, which was a way side at one point, is not a way side forever. When we initially receive the Word of God, our heart remains in the 'way side,' but as God works, the Word takes root in the ground, shoots buds, and grows little by little. In this way our hearts progress from 'way side' to 'stony places' to 'thorny ground' and finally to 'good ground.' The first three types of field typically do not bear fruit. Only the good ground bears fruit.

The process of the development of a person's faith through the three types of field matches the order of the revelation of God's word in the Synoptic Gospels: Matthew, Mark, and Luke. However, the fruit God desires is produced only in the 'good ground,' which corresponds to the faith of the Gospel of John (the fourth Gospel) according to the order of the Bible. In other words, we will have faith corresponding to the good ground that produces much fruit when we reach the stage of the Gospel of John in the faith-growing process. It is also a reason for the Gospel of John being identified separately to the Synoptic Gospels, which bear no fruit.

🗁 Different Statements by Thieves

I will now look, from a different standpoint, at the gradual faith-growing process as it corresponds to the Four Gospels.

When Jesus was crucified, two thieves were also crucified with Him, one on the right hand side and the other on the left. The Synoptic Gospels record the attitudes of the thieves towards Jesus as follows:

> The thieves also, which were crucified with him, cast the same [insults] in his teeth. [Matthew 27:44]

> Let Christ the King of Israel descend now from the cross, that we may see and believe. And they that were crucified with him reviled him. [Mark 15:32]

> And one of the malefactors which were hanged railed on him, saying, If thou be Christ, save thyself and us. But the other an-

swering rebuked him, saying, Dost not thou fear God, seeing thou art in the same condemnation? And we indeed justly; for we receive the due reward of our deeds: but this man hath done nothing amiss. And he said unto Jesus, Lord, remember me when thou comest into thy kingdom. [Luke 23:39-42]

When reading these passages, we can find that Matthew and Mark record that the two thieves who were on either side of Jesus reviled Him, but Luke records that one of them repented. We are not sure whether both the thieves reviled Him or only one of them.

Unbelievers sometimes disparage that Scripture lacks consistency after finding such different records from the Gospels, but we Christians cannot find any appropriate counter argument against them. Some attempt explanations such as, "The respective Scripture writers quoted different documents," but all the attempts including this explanation fail to clarify the different interpretations of the same incident.

We should consider this problem from the viewpoint of steps for growing in faith. A person having faith in the Matthew or Mark stage walks with Jesus but has not yet repented perfectly. The old man/Adam is still alive. For this reason, we find no repentant thief in Matthew and Mark, and the perfect repentance is only recorded in the Gospel of Luke.

This is in line with the faith-growing steps that matches the order of the books of the Bible.

Two Kinds of Repentance

There are many stories of repentance in Luke, such as the prodigal son, the conversion of Zacchaeus, and repentance of Peter. These stories appear here as the book of Luke precedes the faith-growing stage of the Gospel of John; that is, Luke corresponds to the eve of the born again stage as a new man.

We can read many records of repentance in the book of Luke

since it shows the transition from focusing on the things of this world to seeking things in heavenly places and turning our lives around fundamentally. This is repentance.

The stage of John the Baptist is provided just before the stage of the Gospel according to Matthew begins. Since John the Baptist symbolizes repentance, the stage of John the Baptist represents the time of repentance in the salvation process.

Some of you may be confused by these last statements because I described the stage of Luke also as repentance. Now let me explain this to you.

We will meet Jesus after having repented at the stage of John the Baptist, and we will meet/receive the Holy Spirit after having repented in the stage of Luke. Jesus and the Holy Spirit's coming indicate this process happens after the respective stages of repentance. In other words, a person is pregnant with a new life by receiving Jesus according to the repentance of John the Baptist, and the person gives birth to the life by receiving the Holy Spirit according to the repentance of the stage of Luke.

Pregnancy and delivery are the same in that they indicate the time when a new life appears. Since appearance of a life can be considered as the time of pregnancy or as the time of delivery, pregnancy and delivery carry the same meaning in this context. Likewise, the repentance of John the Baptist and the repentance of Luke represent the situation just prior to the appearance of the new life, thereby implying the same thing.

Otherwise, we can describe the stage of John the Baptist as the beginning of repentance, and the stage of Luke as the completion of that repentance.

The Gospel According to John

Looking at the Gospel of John, we find that it gives us many spiritual feelings. John looks easy to read, but actually, it is quite difficult to interpret. A person in the faith-growing stage of John has been released from the bondage of the law, has been perfectly united with the life of Jesus, and has had his old man crucified on the cross; he has received a new life by the resurrection of Jesus in him. He now has been born again. Let us read the following verses from John:

> But as many as received him, to them gave he power to become the sons of God, even to them that believe on his name: Which were born, not of blood, nor of the will of the flesh, nor of the will of man, but of God. And the Word was made flesh, and dwelt among us, (and we beheld his glory, the glory as of the only begotten of the Father,) full of grace and truth. [John 1:12-14]

Those who are in the stage of John have received Jesus. In this instance, 'received him' represents the oneness in which Jesus, after having been crucified and risen, comes again on the bodies of saints as the Holy Spirit and abides in them forever. Those who live together with the Lord forever are the sons of God who are led by the Spirit of Christ. This is very different to the traditional Christian view that we will be sons of God simply by confessing the Lord Jesus with our mouth.

In the stage of the Synoptic Gospels, people having met Jesus leave all and follow Him, but they are not yet completely born again. However, they will be born again in the stage of John thanks to the works of Jesus during the Synoptic Gospels stage. We will be full of grace and truth as Jesus, who is the Word, will come on us again as the Holy Spirit and will abide in us with our bodies as His temple. That is His eternal place to abide.

If anyone of us wants to be full of grace and truth, we should increase in faith to the stage of John. If you begin walking from Genesis and then continue walking to reach the stage of John, Christ comes into you. Then, you will be a son of God, being full of grace and truth.

The person who is in the stage of John corresponds to the 'good ground' in the parable of the sower. He bears fruit and brings forth, some thirty, some sixty and some a hundredfold. The stage of John matches the good ground and brings forth fruit while the three previous fields produce no fruit. When one's faith has increased to this stage of John, God is well pleased with him and blesses him. The born again man is bringing forth fruit.

Therefore, the stage of John represents the born again time in the steps for growing in faith.

Acts

Acts describes the process by which early churches are established and the gospel is spread to all nations by the Spirit of Jesus. The person having faith according to this stage has received a new life in the stage of John, and he is then baptized with the Holy Spirit to testify to the gospel of Jesus Christ with great power. This person may have required great effort to talk about Him in the past, but preaching the gospel has now become part of his life, so he does it automatically and naturally.

If we wish to preach the gospel of Christ in this way, we should be initially born again through the stage of John and be baptized with the Holy Spirit in the stage of Acts, and then God will use us as evangelists. The entire record of Acts shows preaching the gospel with power, which is only allowed to those who have grown into this stage of faith.

Even if a person having faith in the stage of Leviticus in the Old Testament period prays diligently, "My God, allow me your Holy Spirit and let me preach the gospel with power as recorded in Acts!" God will not answer him because his faith has not yet increased that much. However, when he has undergone all the faith-growing stages and has increased to the stage of Acts, he will be naturally baptized with the power of the Holy Spirit. He will manifest the power for raising up the dead and casting out the devil.

In Acts 20, when Paul tried to go up to Jerusalem, people around him pleaded with him not to go there because of the risk to his life. However, he approached Jerusalem saying that he was ready to die for preaching the word of God:

> And now, behold, I go bound in the spirit unto Jerusalem, not knowing the things that shall befall me there: Save that the Holy Ghost witnesseth in every city, saying that bonds and afflictions abide me. But none of these things move me, neither count I my life dear unto myself, so that I might finish my course with joy, and the ministry, which I have received of the Lord Jesus, to testify the gospel of the grace of God. [Acts 20:22-24]

While reading the above passage, the hearts of Christians vigor burn within them, and they make a resolve to increase their fighting spirit; however, this resolve only lasts for a short while.

What is the reason for this? It is because their faith has not yet increased to the stage of Acts. We cannot acquire Paul's ardor to preach the gospel by trying to copy him and his attitude.

We can and will, however, preach the word of God with the power and passion of Paul when our faith has developed sufficiently and to the stage of Acts. Until then, we are to work according to the measure of faith that we have.

It is in this context that we understand the concept that "we will get full if we eat." We may try to mimic a full person while we are hungry, but such behavior has its limitations since we are, in fact, not full after all. God does not want us to behave like this. God wants us to eat and get full. Then, we do not need to mimic a person whose hunger has been satisfied; we are already full.

We read in Scripture that churches appear and the gospel is preached after the time of Acts. The church becomes a center of faith and worship. This realization is also applicable to each of us.

When a person is born again in the stage of John, he will be baptized with the Holy Spirit in the stage of Acts, and then he will enter the universal church as a member. He is no longer alone from that time, but he becomes a member of one body, the church, and preaches the gospel as a member of the church.

🗁 Even that which he has shall be taken away

The distinctive feature of those who are under the law is that they try to act whatever they hear about God. For example, if they hear that they cannot truly preach the gospel before reaching the stage of Acts, they will stop preaching as they used to do thinking that they will do so when they reach the stage of Acts. This is a legalistic response to the gospel. They should keep on preaching as they used to at their level of faith. If they stop, they are losing the existing faith.

Jesus speaks to them as follows:

> For whosoever hath, to him shall be given, and he shall have more abundance: but whosoever hath not, from him shall be taken away even that which he hath. [Matthew13:12]

The above verses warn us that if anyone who has ears to hear, hears the gospel and his soul receives new strength and his faith increases. However, if a man who has no ears to hear hears the gospel, he changes it into the law; thus he will encounter the danger of losing the deed of legalistic faith that he already has.

What does 'legalistic faith' mean?

In a word, legalistic faith is the 'faith of the believer who believes in Jesus under the law.' You may say that 'believe in Jesus under the law' does not read fluently. Yes, maybe. However, the Jesus that you believe in now is not Jesus, but Moses, the symbol of law. So, it is reasonable that such faith is described as legalistic faith.

Legalistic faith is also 'fortune seeking faith.' This fortune seeking faith works as a motive for leading us to God for the first time. We also come to church to ask of God good fortune in this world. It is not wrong for us to pursue the fortune of this world, which is natural, divine providence, and God's program. God uses the fortune of this world as a decoy in order to call people in the world.

Those who lead a Christian life of seeking the fortune of the world provided by God are the persons having a legalistic faith. The decoy includes acquiring wealth, curing disease, spiritual gifts, solving problems, and church revivals, all of which are loved by people.

However, they do not realize that all of these things are no more than bait. Most of those who lead a Christian life for a long time do not know this. They think that they have reached the utmost level of faith when having received such fortune from God. So they make a confession about the good fortune that they have received. However, they have not yet begun to experience true faith.

Anyway, this decoy, although it is not the final blessing that God wishes to give us, plays an important role up to a point. Without it, nobody will have reason to come to church. Also, we should keep this fortune desiring faith because we will even lose the opportunity of contacting the true gospel if we do not come to church.

Faith that depends on this decoy enters into a new phase when we are fully caught on the hook of God, and then we begin to understand and develop true faith.

🗁 Gospel is Not What We Should Do; It Is What Grows

The gospel is the life of Jesus itself, not a command to follow. The statement "The person having reached the stage of Acts will truly preach the gospel" means that such a person does so quite naturally and without feeling compelled to do so. It is neither a command to preach nor a holding back from preaching. It speaks of the fact that the person who has a faith that has increased to such a level can preach the true and powerful gospel.

Therefore, if we are not yet able to do so, we should know that we have not yet increased to the stage of Acts. If you desire to preach as such, you should hope to grow to be a man having the faith of the stage of Acts. The Lord will then lead you to that way.

This book was written for that purpose. That is, this book shows us the final target of faith toward which we should make progress. This book makes us hope for real faith, and it shows how to fulfill what we are hoping for. This is the way God makes us grow. He encourages us to have hope by showing us the way, and He gives it to us.

If you are now preaching at the elementary level, do not stop. It is appropriate for you to do so. An elementary school student must learn mathematics that fits his level. He cannot learn mathematics at the college level. While it looks sophisticated and smart, he will not understand this advanced level. Both elementary and college mathematics are, at the end of the day, simply mathematics. The mathematics for both students is the same, in spite of their different levels, and the mathematics for the elementary school student is a prerequisite for college level mathematics.

It is good for the elementary school student to learn elementary mathematics and the college student to learn college level mathematics.

Accordingly, continue preaching, ministering, and leading a Christian life as you did in the past while believing in Jesus. Keep in mind that your past Christian service is not everything. The preaching, ministering, and Christian life that belong to a different level will be given to you in the future after you have read this book. Hope for them. The Lord will let you know what to do when the time has come and you have grown up. All levels of faith are needed. Keep the faith you have now.

🗁 Stage of Acts Is the Stage of Baptism with the Holy Spirit

The stage of Acts represents the stage of baptism with the Holy Spirit in which the Holy Spirit is poured out on the born again man who receives a new life.

Scholars have different opinions about the definition of baptism with the Holy Spirit. Anyway, baptism with the Holy Spirit is quite different from spiritual gifts, such as healing, speaking in tongue, prophesying, visions and so forth, which may be given even while he is under the law. Baptism with the Holy Spirit means the Holy Spirit abides in the born again man forever, and it is the fulfillment of Immanuel (God is with us) begun by Jesus.

Baptism with Holy Spirit is given to the person who is born again by Jesus only and as such he is under grace.

You will not mix up the terms describing the Holy Spirit hereinafter if you understand this. I will further explain the baptism with the Holy Spirit in detail in Part Three.

🗁 Acts, the Sequel to Luke

Acts is the second book in the Bible authored by Luke. Acts begins as follows:

> The former treatise have I made, O Theophilus, of all that Jesus began both to do and teach, Until the day in which he was taken up, after that he through the Holy Ghost had given commandments unto the apostles whom he had chosen. [Acts 1:1-2]

Here, the 'former treatise' indicates the gospel of Luke. So, if the Scriptures were to be arranged in consideration of the fact that Acts is the sequel to Luke, the order will be Luke, Acts, John, Romans. Therefore, the current arrangement in the order of Luke, John, Acts, Romans can be seen as God's intentional intervention.

God's inclusion of John between Luke and Acts has a spiritual meaning. The overall flow of Luke is about repentance that has not yet born fruit. The flow of Acts is about preaching the gospel to others, which means sharing fruit with other persons. It is, therefore, natural to provide the context of bearing fruit between the two. For this reason, God allowed John to be inserted between Luke and Acts.

When a person reaches the stage of John and becomes born again, he enters a new stage of preaching the gospel to his neighbors. The new stage covers the stages from Acts to Revelation. Therefore, we should be born again first if we desire to be able to preach the true gospel to our neighbors.

Romans

Romans is a very precious epistle as it summarizes the teachings of Jesus Christ, that is, the truth of Christianity.

The New Testament includes many epistles written by Paul. Romans is not the earliest one recorded by him according to chronological order. Most scholars agree that 1 Thessalonians is the first epistle written by him. However, it is not a coincidence that Romans is positioned where it is, that is, the position after Acts, since it pulls the fundamental truths of Jesus Christ together in a most systematic way.

From the viewpoint of growing in faith, the born again person who was baptized with the Holy Spirit began fervently preaching the gospel in the Acts stage. Now in the Romans stage he will be getting his words or argument logically organized in order to effectively communicate the gospel to others.

The church faith-growing steps are the same. The anointed build a church and minister with ardor, and in the stage of Romans, they theoretically establish the words that will become the featured mission or focus of the church; such as teaching, preaching, or ministering.

In the faith stage of Romans, an individual receives his own logic for preaching the gospel to others.

1 Corinthians, 2 Corinthians, and Other Epistles

1 Corinthians, 2 Corinthians, and other epistles are given to establish the church and the faith of members of the church.

From Romans to Jude, these stages collectively would be called the Epistles stage of faith.

After having established their understanding of the word in Romans stage, those in the Epistles stage preach the gospel to their neighbor. To preach the gospel is to love them. This is the fulfillment of what the Scripture says: "Love your neighbor as yourself" (Mat 22:39).

They received the love (*agape* in Greek) of God from heaven, and with that same love, they love their neighbors. They are those who have the power to love, and this love flows through sharing the gospel. The many churches established by Paul are the outcome of his love attained in his faith-growing steps.

A lot of people say that Christianity is the religion of love, and they try to love neighbors, but not many people know what 'loving your neighbor' actually means. We human beings who are born of the flesh have no love of God within us. When we are baptized with the Holy Spirit, the love of God comes upon us. Only then will we have the power to love our neighbors.

Consider Jesus' saying that love is all and everything of the Scriptures.

> Then one of them, which was a lawyer, asked him a question, tempting him, and saying, Master, which is the great commandment in the law? Jesus said unto him, Thou shalt love the Lord thy God with all thy heart, and with all thy soul, and with all thy mind. This is the first and great commandment. And the second is like unto it, Thou shalt love thy neighbour as thyself. On these two commandments hang all the law and the prophets. [Matthew 22:35-40]

Jesus says in Matthew that all the law and the prophets depend on our loving God and loving our neighbor. The law and the prophets represent the whole contents of Scripture. Jesus says that the 'love of neighbor' and the 'love of God' are one by saying "the second is like unto it" while speaking about the commandment of love in Matthew 22:39.

We try to love God with all our hearts, with all our souls, and with all our minds, but we cannot do so. To love God in this way, we need to meet Jesus first in our life. Jesus will form in us the 'love of God' by giving us the Holy Spirit in progressive stages. When we have the 'love of God', which is Holy Spirit, we will be able to love our neighbors naturally. This is the reason Jesus said, "The second is like unto it." We will be able to love our neighbors, which is the stage of Epistles, in our faith life, when we receive the 'love of God' first, which is the stage of John and the Acts.

In that case, we will become one with God who is love, and then we also are love itself. In this sense, love is being, not doing. Love loves. Thus, we will love everything, anytime, anywhere. Love is not innate in us from the time we are born, but it is to be acquired through Jesus during our lifetime.

James speaks about faith having works, and the epistles of John beseech us to love one another. All of the other epistles basically mention loving our neighbor. Even if a man having the faith of the Old Testament period tries hard to love according to this love commandment, he cannot. The love John refers to is not the love produced by our own efforts, but it is the love that comes from God.

When we are born again, we will have the love of God. Then, love will flow out from us. John and other writers of the epistles talk about this acquired love.

This faith in the stage of Epistles, starting from Romans, represents the life of the born again man who has received the love of God and then loves his neighbors as himself. We should long for this life.

Revelation

Revelation is the last book of the Scriptures and indicates the time when the born again man has reached the final stage in which God's will is fulfilled. In the stage of Revelation, the born again man stands before God after finishing the life of love in this world with glory. In this stage, his faith is finally confirmed, and his life is justified before God.

The stage of Revelation is the confirmation of the born again faith.

Apostle Paul's Growth in Faith

The faith-growing steps of the apostle Paul follow the arrangement of the books of the Bible. Consider his life as it relates to the order of Scripture.

Paul was thoroughly educated in the Scripture and Jewish religion, and he did his utmost to live by the Scripture (Gal 1:14). Because of his exceeding zeal, he could not ignore those who, he thought, did not believe in God in the correct way. So, he tried to shut them up in prison (Act 9:1-2). However, absurdly, the people whom he tried to put in prison were Christians sincerely believing in the same God. Paul had the blind faith of the Old Testament period at that time.

Paul met Jesus on his journey to Damascus (Act 9:5), thereby starting his journey of faith in the New Testament period. He started the New Testament period when he first met Him, and his faith increased to the stage of John after he went into Arabia and stayed there for three years (Gal 1:17-18). He then received the Holy Spirit to have the faith in the stage of Acts, and he built churches and preached the gospels to others in the stage of the Epistles. He ended life in the faith of the stage of Revelations.

What stage of faith have you reached among the sixty-six books of the Bible? If you have not yet met Jesus in your personal life, you are still living in the Old Testament period, even if you live as a Christian in the time after Jesus.

PART THREE

DETAILS OF MAJOR STAGES

We will now look into the important stages of the faith-growing process: repentance, being born again, baptism with the Holy Spirit, and the intermediate parts in between these defining milestones.

Part Three will cover very important theological subjects and will provide clear answers to historical questions in relation to the Scripture and Christianity. Part Three will constitute the core of this book.

While reading, some people may think that this text is hard to accept in some parts or may feel that it is difficult to understand. If so, this discomfort means that the reader is not fully ready to read this book. However, if he continues to read, the book will work to help faith grow anyway. To understand this influence, consider an illustration from glass cutting. When cutting glass, one draws lines on the surface with a glass-cutting knife in the desired direction. In this instance, no superficial changes appear initially, but the glass will break when a shock is applied to it.

The contents of this book are like the sharp instrument. Although one cannot understand it while reading right now, it will draw the invisible line of truth on the heart. You may feel nothing has changed. However, when an opportunity comes, you will be carved by the lines made in your heart.

Therefore, pour sincere effort into reading this; it will be rewarding.

1

STAGE OF GENESIS — CREATION

Creation of the Heaven and the Earth Is the Creation of Me

The Scripture begins with Genesis. It is the beginning of all things. "In the beginning God created the heaven and the earth," so Genesis 1:1 starts. In general, we understand this passage to mean, "In the beginning God created the material universe as we see it." Undeniably, yes.

However, we will go deeper into Genesis 1:1. Each of us was born in the world several decades ago. From birth we experience and observe the world that we are born into. The world represents heaven and the earth as found in Genesis.

Heaven and the earth already existed even before I was born and was conscious of them. However, at that time, the heaven and earth did not exist for me. I was in a state of 'nothingness' in which I could neither see nor touch heaven or earth. However, when I was born and became conscious of heaven and earth I could observe and experience them.

By my birth, the heaven and the earth became real for me. They came into my world. Therefore, that is the time of the creation of the heaven and the earth for me. Accordingly, the creation of the heaven and the earth in Genesis represents the time of creation and the time of birth of each individual.

The passage "In the beginning God created the heaven and the earth" therefore means, "In the beginning God created me." By that creation, my individual life began. Hence, the word is applicable to all human beings, and it is fulfilled when each person is created in Eden. This is the Genesis stage when we, our spirits, are created in Eden.

Thereafter we proceed to be born into the current world where we are living. This is the Exodus stage of our faith. So the spirit is created in Eden and body in flesh is created in this world.

The spiritual subject of the book of Genesis is the creation of man and the Israelite nation, while that of Exodus is the marching towards Canaan. Reaching Canaan is the symbol of entering into the kingdom of God—achieving salvation. At the Genesis stage, we see creation, but at the Exodus stage, we see the necessity of salvation. It means that sin has intervened between the Genesis and Exodus stage. We who are born in the world now are sinners who need salvation. How we come into this world as sinners will be explained under the title "No Inheritance of Sin Committed by Adam."

Flow of the Scripture

Scripture tells us about our salvation, and Genesis Chapter 1 can be regarded as the summary of the Scripture.

Genesis Chapter 1, verse 1 reads that God created the heaven and the earth. As explained, this creation means the creation of a man—each of us individually. Genesis 1:2 describes the falling away of the man created in Genesis 1:1:

"And the earth was without form, and void; and darkness was upon the face of the deep. And the Spirit of God moved upon the face of the waters."

This is the status of the mind of a man who has fallen and is in darkness and chaos. Such a man is entirely ignorant of the truth—even God. This is quite natural, since he fell and left God. The darkness is the structural chaos and void that people cannot escape nor overcome at all by themselves.

For the darkness, God sends the light: And God said, "Let there be light: and there was light" (Gen 1:3). This means that God sent the light—Jesus as Savior—for the fallen man. And through the light God creates the fallen man in the image of God for six days (Gen 1:27). Further, after completion of the creation of man, God rested on the seventh day.

To sum up, God creates the man. The man falls, so he is in the darkness. God sends the light, i.e., Jesus, to save him. After due process, the man is re-born according to image of God, and thus God completes His creation of man and rests.

This is an overview of the flow of Genesis Chapter 1:1-2:3 as well as the whole Scripture, which is the process of salvation of mankind.

Adam's life represents us in this process. When Adam was created in Eden, he was sinless (Gen 1:1), but he sinned by eating from the tree of the knowledge of good and evil. He was forced to get out of Eden, facing darkness (Gen 1:2). And when he meets Jesus, his sins start to be forgiven by Jesus (Gen 1:3-31), and he was given born-again life on the seventh day (Gen 2:3).

No Inheritance of Sin Committed by Adam

I would like to talk about one of the most important theological topics. That is inheritance of the sin committed by Adam. We all surely have the following queries: "How was the sin committed by Adam passed down to me?" Or, "What is the relation between the sin of Adam and my sin?"

Referring to Genesis Chapter 3, Adam and the woman were tempted by the serpent. They ate of the tree of knowledge of good and evil, which God forbade, and they were sentenced as follows:

> Unto the woman he said, I will greatly multiply thy sorrow and thy conception; in sorrow thou shalt bring forth children; and

> thy desire shall be to thy husband, and he shall rule over thee. And unto Adam he said, Because thou hast hearkened unto the voice of thy wife, and hast eaten of the tree, of which I commanded thee, saying, Thou shalt not eat of it: cursed is the ground for thy sake; in sorrow shalt thou eat of it all the days of thy life; Thorns also and thistles shall it bring forth to thee; and thou shalt eat the herb of the field; In the sweat of thy face shalt thou eat bread, till thou return unto the ground; for out of it wast thou taken: for dust thou art, and unto dust shalt thou return. [Genesis 3:16-19]

As we know, this sentence on disobedience is not only applicable to Adam and the woman, but it is also substantially applicable to all people everywhere—generation after generation. In addition, Scripture points out that we are born as sinners. How does the disobedience of Adam, who ate of the tree of knowledge of good and evil, possibly make us, who are born in the present time, sinners? This issue seriously troubles many believers in Jesus.

Until not so long ago, theologians have explained that the original sin is inherited through the blood of Adam. It is the heredity of sin. However, that theory is not really accepted nowadays. Instead, the covenantal representation is accepted as an established theory.

According to the covenantal representation, when Adam, as the representative of all people, covenanted with God, we were also obliged to observe the covenant. Therefore, when he violated the covenant by eating forbidden fruit, we also violated it. For example, this reasoning means that if the President of Korea, as representative of the Koreans, accepted a treaty with the US President, then all Koreans would also be obliged to keep the treaty, even though they did not sign it themselves.

However, 'sin' or 'being a sinner' is a totally different matter from what can be represented by a treaty between two nations. It is something like eating food, the individual has to consume his food himself.

If we apply the covenantal representation theory of inheritance of Adam's sin, we are saying the following nonsense: "A group of hungry people elected a representative, and he ate food on their behalf. Therefore, all people ate the same as well." Obviously, the covenantal representation theory cannot be the proper explanation for the inheritance of Adam's sin.

Considering that it is Adam who ate of the tree of the knowledge of good and evil, why do his descents have to be born as sinners?

The answer is that Adam and his descendants have the same nature and attributes as human beings. The record that Adam ate of the tree of the knowledge of good and evil is ours, too; we have the same sin nature as Adam. The Adam in Scripture indicates each of us individually. So the sin of Adam is imputed to us because but each of us sinned individually as Adam did. I will explain further.

Each of Us Is an Adam

All the people after Adam have the same nature as Adam. In other words, all mankind is the same in this world (Act 17:26). So, all nations are represented by one man, Adam. The Hebrew word *Adam* is not only a proper noun representing the first man Adam, but it is also a common noun indicating a man. Hence, no meaning will be changed or lost if we replace the word Adam with our own name. That is, each of us is an Adam.

We ate of the tree of the knowledge of good and evil, and we left the Garden of Eden following Adam's way. The coming out of Eden physically is that we are born in the flesh here in this world. In other words, Eden is heaven where God is with us, but in the time-space world where we currently live, God is not with us. As Adam was sentenced by God for his transgression, so are we, and we have been leading a hard life here in this world.

It is not true that Adam sinned and his sin was passed down to all mankind as is generally believed. Instead, each of us is an

Adam. This being the case, it is inappropriate to blame Adam for the eating from the tree of the knowledge of good and evil. Adam himself is 'earlier me' or 'yester-me' before being born again.

Of course, we have never eaten of the tree of knowledge, and we have no memory of having stayed in the garden of Eden. But no matter what we say, we ate it. When the same punishment of disobedience is given to us as was given to Adam, it means that we disobeyed as he did. Where there is smoke, there is fire.

All mankind ate of the tree of knowledge and must leave Eden as Adam did. Now we, as an Adam and as one mankind, might possibly wonder, "Why did Adam have to eat of it?" I will explain this topic more in the section entitled "True Repentance" in which you may find the answer to this most fundamental question.

🗁 Fathers Have Eaten Sour Grapes and the Children's Teeth Are Set on Edge?

Now let us get back to the sin inheritance issue. Due to the education provided to us in the past, we think that we are born to be sinners because Adam ate of the forbidden fruit as a representative of us. Alternatively, we are born as sinners after Adam ate of it, and his sinful nature is passed down to us. In short, we understand that the original sin of Adam is passed down to us, one way or the other. But is this biblical thinking?

No. Ezekiel says as follows:

> The word of the LORD came unto me again, saying, What mean ye, that ye use this proverb concerning the land of Israel, saying, The fathers have eaten sour grapes, and the children's teeth are set on edge? As I live, saith the Lord GOD, ye shall not have occasion any more to use this proverb in Israel. Behold, all souls are mine; as the soul of the father, so also the soul of the son is mine: the soul that sinneth, it shall die. [Ezekiel 18:1-4]

According to Ezekiel, the Israelites were being ridiculous to say that the fathers' actions were to blame for the children's teeth being set on edge. They would never say this if they had known what they were saying.

The Israelites indicate not only the people of Israel in history, but they also represent those who now believe in Jesus. The Scripture is written through the medium of the old Israelites, but it spiritually reveals the nature of all human beings. As a human being, we should know that the Scripture are ours, applicable to each one of us.

Then, if the Israelites represent us, how could we say such a ridiculous thing as this proverb? Apparently, it is our thought that we, the descendents of Adam, taste the bitters of life since he ate the forbidden fruit. This is ridiculous thought like a proverb that "The fathers have eaten sour grapes, and the children's teeth are set on edge." If Adam ate the fruit, then he is the one to face the consequence, not his descendents. However, we accept this kind of oxymoron and take it for granted as natural. This proverb is prevalent in Christian society.

God will prevent us from believing in Jesus based on this kind of quack proverb. The verses of Ezekiel were written thousands of years ago, but their true meanings were hidden until now. When their true meanings are revealed, the words will be fulfilled, and now the time has come.

God says that each soul is of Him as the soul of Adam is of Him. It is not true that our souls are born by fleshly reproduction while Adam's soul is directly created by God. As God directly created Adam, He directly created each of us too. In this sense, it is not correct to say that we are the descendants of Adam. Instead, we, each of us, are an Adam. Just as Adam has a one-to-one relationship with Him, we also have a one-to-one relationship with Him.

Since God directly created each of us through the same creation process as Adam, there is no room for the sin of Adam to be imputed to us. Clearly, the soul who has sinned takes responsibility for his offence. We all disobeyed in eating from the tree of knowledge as Adam did, and we consequently came to this world. We did all of these things of our own choice, so we must accuse ourselves, not Adam.

By One Man

Ezekiel states definitely that there is no inheritance of sin as explained. However, many of us refuse to understand it in this way. The reason for the refusal may come from Romans, Chapter 5. Paul wrote in Romans, Chapter 5 that by one man sin entered into the world. This verse states the sin inheritance indeed.

Due to the strong influence of this passage from Romans, we tend to interpret the Ezekiel verses otherwise. However, in fact, the understanding we should correct is about Romans, not about Ezekiel.

Read the following verses from Romans:

> Wherefore, as by one man sin entered into the world, and death by sin; and so death passed upon all men, for that all have sinned:(For until the law sin was in the world: but sin is not imputed when there is no law. Nevertheless death reigned from Adam to Moses, even over them that had not sinned after the similitude of Adam's transgression, who is the figure of him that was to come. But not as the offence, so also is the free gift. For if through the offence of one many be dead, much more the grace of God, and the gift by grace, which is by one man, Jesus Christ, hath abounded unto many. And not as it was by one that sinned, so is the gift: for the judgment was by one to condemnation, but the free gift is of many offences unto justification. For if by one man's offence death reigned by one; much more they which receive abundance of grace and of the gift of righteousness shall reign in life by one, Jesus Christ.) Therefore, as by the offence of one judgment came upon all men to condemnation; even so by the right-

> eousness of one the free gift came upon all men unto justification of life. For as by one man's disobedience many were made sinners, so by the obedience of one shall many be made righteous. [Romans 5:12-19]

Many of the statements in these verses may sound as if all mankind subsequently became sinners since Adam, the one man, ate the forbidden fruit in disobedience to God. But the true meaning is not so. If we know it, we will realize that these verses are all in line with the verses of Ezekiel about sour grapes.

The above verses of Romans mean the following: Adam is a prototype who shows the nature of all mankind. Therefore, just as he ate of the tree of knowledge, all men ate and will eat in the same way. In other words, all mankind after Adam individually ate of the tree of knowledge.

There is no need to record the cases of all men in Scripture because Adam reveals the nature of all. Accordingly, the record of the disobedience of Adam is that of each individual born in this world. If Adam had not eaten of it in the Scripture, we, who are having the same nature, would not have eaten. When Adam ate of it, it shows that all mankind were to eat. What he did is what each of us would do. He only preceded us as a prototype of us. For this reason, Paul says, "Wherefore, as by one man sin entered into the world."

The dictionary definition of prototype is "someone or something that exemplifies a type." Considering this definition, the statement of 'all the other men are damaged by one man' is another expression of the thought that 'the one man and all the other men have the same nature and attributes.' Therefore, by one man all men are dead means truly that the one man and all men have the same nature and attributes. After all, if Adam, the prototype, is a sinner, so is all mankind.

The next statement: "so death passed upon all men, for that all have sinned" is interpreted in the same context (Rom 5:12). That is, it means that death passed upon all men since all men have sinned since they are the same as Adam. Thus, Adam's sin was not inherited by us, but we have sinned of our own volition. I shall give an example.

A Prototype (Greek: *Typos*)

Let us assume that there are ten students who will win an honor prize in school. Not all of them need to step onto the stage to get the prize; only one is chosen to step on the stage to receive the prize. In this instance, there is no difference between the nine students and the one on the stage in terms of qualification for wining the prize. The only difference between the two groups is whether they stood on the stage or not. Those who have not stepped onto stage have the same qualification for the prize.

In this case, the student on the stage is the prototype of the other students as far as the qualification for the prize is concerned. The relationship between Adam and all mankind could possibly be explained with this example.

When the student on stage receives a prize, the others not on the stage receive the prizes at the same time (although the prize receiving action is actually done by only one student). In this instance, the prize is not inherited nor passed down from the student on the stage to those students standing aside. The nine students individually receive the prize simultaneously in the same fashion as the student on stage does.

Now let us lay this example over Adam's eating of the tree of knowledge. The one student on stage is Adam, the receiving of the prize is equivalent to eating of the tree of knowledge, and the nine students standing aside are all mankind. Therefore, the verse "by one man's disobedience many were made sinners" would mean that since one student standing on the stage received the prize, the nine students standing aside also received it in the same way (Rom 5:19).

Here is another example. Let's consider a bean growing. There was the first bean at the beginning of time, it shot out buds, grew a stem, blossomed, and bore fruit. The record of the growth process for this one bean will be sufficient because all beans thereafter will undergo the same process. Therefore, if the first bean grew buds, today's beans will shoot buds as well. The first bean was the prototype of all beans that will come.

When Adam, the first man, ate of the tree of knowledge, his action was to be followed by all human beings to come. Adam is the prototype of all human beings. So, doubtlessly, by Adam, one man, we ate of the forbidden fruit. This is how we inherited the sin of Adam, if we are to say 'inherited.'

From Adam to Moses

A little deviation from the inheritance of Adam's original sin will enable us to go a little bit further to explore the features of men who belonging to Adam.

Read the following verse:

> Nevertheless death reigned from Adam to Moses, even over them that had not sinned after the similitude of Adam's transgression, who is the figure of him that was to come. [Romans 5:14]

We can find no record of men having eaten of the tree of knowledge after Adam. However, as death reigned over Adam after he ate of it, death reigned over all men from Adam to Moses. It means that Adam and men from Adam to Moses have the same nature as Adam.

'From Adam to Moses' does not indicate a certain period in history. If so, we would not be included because we were born long after Moses, and this passage would seem to have no relevance to us. Here, Moses symbolizes the law, not Moses, in Bible history. Therefore, 'from Adam to Moses' represents a certain time span in our individual faith life. Adam indicates the time when we are born and our soul is created.

Then, when will be the time of Moses in our faith life? That is the time when we receive the law, as Moses is a metaphor for the law. When do we, the believers of Jesus, receive the laws of God?

Do we think that we have nothing to do with the law as we believe in Jesus and live in the New Testament period? This is not so. We all have to go through the law period first to come to Jesus and God, regardless of our will. As we all know the laws are the commandments of God for us to keep.

We receive the laws when we come to church and confess Jesus as our Savior. Since then, we are to keep the commandments specified in the Old Testament, such as "do not murder," "do not commit adultery," "do not steal," "do not give false testimony," "honor your father and mother," and "love your neighbor as yourself."

On top of that, we receive from Jesus the commandments including "If someone strikes you on the right cheek, turn to him the other also (Mat 5:39)," "Anyone who looks at a woman lustfully has already committed adultery with her in his heart (Mat 5:28)," "Judge not (Mat 7:1)," and so on.

This way, we receive various laws when we start to believe in Jesus, and we make every effort to keep these laws in the church life. We might think that we are being led by Jesus, but in reality, we are led by Moses, the law.

Therefore, 'from Adam to Moses' indicates the period from the time when we are born to the time we believe in Jesus under the law in the church. So, in short, 'from Adam to Moses' means the period of one's faith being under the law. Paul says that those whose faith is positioned in this period belong to Adam and death reigns over them. Adam is the prototype of those people who are under the law.

When will we get out of the time of 'from Adam to Moses?' In other words, when will we finish our faith under the law in the church?

We can finish the period of the law by meeting the real Jesus in our lives—the living Jesus. Even if we go to church and believe in Jesus, we may not have met the living Jesus. Until we meet the living Jesus, we are staying in the period called 'from Adam to Moses' whereby death reigns over us.

As Adam is the prototype of those who are under the law, Jesus Christ is the prototype of those who are under grace. Here, we can find one thing in common; that is, both of them are a prototype of each group. In this sense, Paul says that Adam is the prototype of Jesus Christ who is to come.

When a man who belongs to Adam is born again, then he belongs to Jesus. Now, his prototype is not Adam, but Jesus Christ.

To avoid confusion, so far in this book Adam is described as the prototype of the following three cases: Firstly, of all mankind who are born. Secondly, of all the people who are under the law. Likewise, Jesus Christ is the prototype of all the people who are born again by grace. Thirdly, of Jesus Christ as explained in Romans 5:14 above.

Man and Woman

Adam and Jesus Christ are alike and different men. They are alike because they were human beings, different because one is man and the other is woman. In the spiritual sense, Adam is the woman who is to receive the seed of God, and Jesus Christ is the man who can give the seed of God. There will be an opportunity to explain this topic further in the section entitled "Being Born Again."

Adam is the prototype of those having the nature of sinning, and Jesus Christ is that of those having the power to love neighbors. All human beings born in the flesh belong to Adam at first. By going through the process of taking our cross as led by Jesus, we will then belong to Jesus Christ. This is the salvation or faith-growing process. When we belong to Jesus, being men spiritually, all of us have one thing common; the Spirit of Christ is inside of us. In this case, our prototype is Jesus Christ, no longer Adam:

> But ye are not in the flesh, but in the Spirit, if so be that the Spirit of God dwell in you. Now if any man has not the Spirit of Christ, he is none of his. [Romans 8:9]

Righteous Man Automatically?

> ...By the obedience of one shall many be made righteous. [Romans 5:19b]

The misunderstanding that the sin of Adam is inherited by us and we automatically become sinners brings forth another wrong idea that the righteousness of Jesus is inherited by us, the believers, and we automatically become righteous. That is, we think that if we confess Jesus as our Savior, we will be automatically saved, thanks to His obedience unto death. However, it is a very big error, on par with thinking that Adam's sin is inherited to us.

If we wish to be righteous and to belong to Jesus, we should meet Him in our current life and be led by Him to our own cross (Mat 16:24). Belonging to Jesus, therefore, is not a mere question of confessing Jesus as Savior with the mouth (i.e., there is no free ride for salvation).

By going through the cross of our own with Jesus, we would become truly righteous as Jesus is. Just as Adam represents the nature of those that belong to him, Jesus represents the nature of those that belong to Him. This means that the prototype and those that belong to him have the same nature. Thus, it is quite natural that we are as righteous as Jesus if we belong to Him.

There are two groups of people in this world. One group belongs to Adam and the other group belongs to Jesus. At the initial stage, we belong to Adam and act like Adam did. As Adam was disobedient to eat of the tree of the knowledge of good and evil, we were disobedient as well. Likewise, when Jesus Christ was obedient to God unto death, even death on the cross, it reveals that all the born again men would do the same.

Every one who comes to this world is an Adam and is to be

saved and born again as the one who belongs to Jesus.

This is the Genesis/Exodus stage in the process of growing in faith.

2

STAGE OF OLD TESTAMENT — LEGALISTIC FAITH

Stage of Old Testament

The books from Genesis to Malachi as a whole are called the Old Testament, and we should pass through this Old Testament stage as our faith grows. In detail, a man is created in the Genesis stage and born in human flesh in the Exodus stage. Thereafter, he continues the Old Testament stage of faith life.

Those that have not yet met Jesus Christ are in Old Testament period of their faith life. Their faith life is led by the law of God. What would this mean?

The Israelites who left Egypt entered the wilderness, and they were heading for Canaan under the leadership of Moses. God gave the Ten Commandments and various other laws to the Israelites through Moses. The Israelites, during the time of Moses, could not hear God, and they indirectly heard of the messages of God through Moses and tried to keep them. The Israelites in those days did not go directly to God.

As revealed above, those who are currently in the Old Testament stage cannot hear God directly. Instead, one might receive the will and commands of God in the church through pastors or evangelists playing the role of Moses. The characteristic of those who are under the law is that they hear what God says second hand.

The leader of the Israelites when they were leaving Egypt was Moses. However, the leader was changed to Joshua when they were entering the Canaan, which is the kingdom of God metaphorically. Moses is the sign of the law, and Joshua is the sign of Jesus Christ, the grace. This fact tells us that in order to enter the kingdom of God we need to be led by the law first, and after that, we will meet Jesus Christ, the grace, to enter the kingdom.

Law Comes First, Grace Comes Next

> For the law was given by Moses, but grace and truth came by Jesus Christ. [John 1:17]

Law and grace—it is a very heavy and difficult issue. What are they? What is the relationship between the two? I will start to explain with the question "What is the law?"

🗁 What is the Law?

The law is the word of God. The word of God is the expression and representation of God's mind, even God Himself. In general, we experience the word of God through Scripture. The law, the written word of God, has two meanings depending on how the reader reads it, although it is only one text. Consider the following dialogue in Luke:

> And behold, a certain lawyer stood up and put Him to the test, saying, "Teacher, what shall I do to inherit eternal life?" And He said to him, "What is written in the Law? How does it read to you?" [Luke 10:25-26 NASB]

In the above conversation with a lawyer, Jesus distinguishes what is actually written in the Scripture from what is read by an individual. What is written in Scripture is one thing, and how it reads to us is another. Of course, what is written is God and reveals God's mind, but how we read it depends upon our eyes, i.e., our being.

In our faith life, there is the first time span in which Scripture reads to us as commandments. And there is a second time span in which the Scripture reads as the mind of God. The second time span will not come to us unless we completely finish the first time span. Unfortunately, most current believers do not finish the first part and die without knowing and experiencing the second part of faith life.

If the Scripture reads to us as a set of commandments, we are under the law, if it reads as the mind of God, we are under grace. Thus, the Scripture naturally judges the readers as to whether they are under the law or under grace.

Anyway, the law, the written God Himself, can be read in two ways: First, it is the commandment of God that the reader must keep (Rom 2:13). Second, it is the mind of God to make the reader the being who can keep such commandments. Thus, it is grace, i.e., good tidings. For such a man, the commandments are being made perfect within him as the law is being written on his mind. And it works as spiritual food to him. Let us have an example to help our understanding.

"Love your neighbor as yourself."

This is the word of God. One text, but it can be construed in two different ways:

First, it reads to us as the law. In fact, all of us would read this word as such. In case we read it as the law, it is a simple and outright commandment: "Love your neighbor," full stop. So, ever since we first believed in Jesus and up until now, we have been pouring all our efforts into keeping this commandment. At first, we are to read God's word this way, as the law.

Second, it reads to us as the grace (good tidings) with which God will make us such men who can love our neighbors as ourselves. If we get to know this meaning through our experience, then we will be waiting for Jesus' guidance and will obey him in everyday life. Only by becoming one with God through the work of Jesus will we have God's mind and be able to love our neighbors. In this case, the law is made complete and fulfilled within us.

Here, we can know that the relationship of law and grace is not a matter of interpretation, but a matter of who is reading the Scripture. If the Scripture reads as the law, it is evident that the reader is under the law, being separated from God. To him all Scripture, even the sayings of Jesus in the New Testament, are the law. If the Scripture reads as grace, then the reader is under grace, being or becoming one with God. To him, all Scripture, even the sayings of Moses in the Old Testament, are of grace. Therefore, the law and grace can only be defined according to the state of the reader of the word of God.

Law and grace are terms which might be used to describe God, i.e., law is God or Grace is God. Then what is the difference between the two?

God is the same all the way, but God looks different to each person. If a man is separated from God, to him God is the law, and if a man is one with God, to him God is grace. Therefore, the definition of law and grace should be considered together with an individual man. In this regard, law and grace, even though they are the terms to describe God, in fact, actually indicate whether a man is separated from God or not.

Here, the law as the commandment will be addressed. The Israelites in Scripture represent us who believe in Jesus. When we come to church, confess Jesus as our Savior, and register ourselves as church members, then we become the Israelites described in Scripture. As the Israelites received the law, so we receive the law in church. The Israelites received the word of God in the Old Testament as the law, and we receive the word of Jesus as the law to keep in addition to what is specified in Scripture.

As we all agree, the words that Jesus spoke in the Scripture are not read to us as the gospel but as commandments. The words of Jesus are also commandments of God, written in letters for us to keep. In a word, the law represents the commandments of God and Jesus; these commandments tell us to do something or to avoid something.

🗁 Imperfect Law

God gave us many laws to keep through the Scriptures. Someone counted them from the Scriptures and they were 613 laws to keep. Be it many or less, we must strictly keep the laws, every last one. If we transgress even in a little one, we have transgressed and disobeyed the whole commandment of God. Even if we are forgiven sins through repentance each time, we have to labor and are heavily laden with keeping the laws. We will be lucky if we can keep the laws through such efforts—even if we work hard to that end. However, humankind has no such power to keep these laws from the very outset.

Because of this reason, the Scripture casts the law in a negative sense, even though the law is word of God:

"...The law worketh wrath" (Rom 4:15a)

"For as many as are of the works of the law are under the curse..." (Gal 3:10a)

"To redeem them that were under the law..." (Gal 4:5a)

"For the law made nothing perfect..." (Hbr 7:19a)

However, these passages do not mean that the law fundamentally has a negative aspect. As mentioned already, the law is the expression and representation of God's mind and as such, the law is God Himself and is holy: "Wherefore the law is holy, and the commandments are holy, and just, and good" (Rom 7:12).

The law itself is holy, but the man who read the laws as commands is not holy himself. If the holy law reads to a man as commands, it witnesses that he himself is not holy, and he is cursed under the law.

Every one is automatically under the law when they are born in the world, which is the providence of God. So it does not matter if we are under the law currently. However, we must keep in mind that it should be temporary for us to be under the law, and when the time comes, we should advance into the free world of grace.

Paul points out the imperfection of the law in the above verses, wanting us to see that no believer should be content with a faith life under the law.

The Way to Be Free from the Law

The law, the written commandments of God, will be included in God Himself when we meet God in person, not by letters.

For example, let us assume that a father going on a business trip has left a memo to his children saying, "Come home before 9:00 p.m." This is the law for children to keep. The law has no mercy and no exception. If they are one second late getting home, they have violated the established law. No excuses, no avoiding punishment, no nothing because they breached the law by being one second late.

However, if the father returns home to be with them, their situations will change. In case of getting home late, they can explain the reason why they might be late to the father, and he can adjust the homecoming time. Now the law of "Be back before 9:00 p.m." is included in the mind of father, who is present and living with them. The father then will teach children why they need to be back home by 9:00 p.m., and they will learn the mind of the father. Thereafter, their minds and the father's are one, and by understanding, they are freed from the law of "Be back by 9:00 p.m."

Likewise, if we are to be free from the law of God, we should meet God, the maker of the law, in our lives. Then, the law will be gone, and in another expression, it will become perfect within us. The one and only way to get out from under the law is to meet God. God, whom we meet in our lives, is Jesus. When we have received the Holy Spirit by meeting the living Jesus, then we will be single mindedly in tune with God and Jesus and will be freed from the law.

To be free from the law does not mean to be in a lawless state. Do not misunderstand. We cannot be free from the law by doing something. Jesus makes us free from the law. The law stage, the Old Testament stage in our faith life, is a prerequisite before we meet Jesus. When we believe in Jesus, we first face the law, and after that, we are to meet the living Jesus.

Therefore, if any one says, "The law is of no use because we are saved by faith," or "We must keep the law with thanks to Jesus since He saved us," then he is confessing that he never experienced salvation, law, faith, or grace; the speaker knows nothing.

Further, if anyone reads this book and makes a resolution that "I will read the Scripture as grace," it is a wrong attempt to be free from the law. Because that is also another type of doing something on his own. All they are trying to do is to be free by doing something by themselves which will result in lawlessness. Jesus is the One who makes us free from the law. So meet the living Jesus and follow Him in your life.

Please keep in mind that you are not yet allowed freedom if you are not conscious that you are walking with Jesus and communicating with Him. I lay emphasis on it again that freedom is to be given by Jesus, not by what we gain by our doing. The man made free by Jesus sees the word of God, the Law, not as the commandment to be kept, but as the grace of God.

Going further, the word of God has a shell that is the law and an inner part that is grace. We can touch the inner part, the grace, when we have passed through the shell, the law. The law comes first, and then the grace comes, but both of them are one. The Law leads the man who is in the Old Testament stage of his faith life, and grace leads the man who is in New Testament stage of his faith.

God Is Not Far from Us

"Did God pass away after having written the Scriptures?"

I am raising this question in order to enlighten those who are sticking to the meanings, be it deep or otherwise, of the Scripture. If we cling to studying the written Scripture, we come near to forgetting the living God.

We make a mistake in thinking that God stays far from us and that He never appears to us. It is not true. He walks with us, and He is speaking to us, even here and now. We cannot hear Him because we have closed our minds towards Him. The relation between God and us is interactive. Therefore, both parties should open their minds so as to communicate with each other.

The double gates of the elevator will be a good example for this interactivity. Passengers can get in or out of the elevator when both the outer door and the inner door are opened together. People cannot use the elevator when the inner doors are closed—even if the outer doors are opened wide.

The door of God's mind is open always to us. However, the door of our minds is shut to God always. That is the characteristic of the sinners who ate from the tree of the knowledge of good and evil. Thus, no communion with Him is available; darkness has come to us. The Lord says in Revelation 3:20:

"Behold, I stand at the door, and knock: if any man hear my voice, and open the door, I will come in to him, and will sup with him, and he with me."

As we see here, God never closed His door towards us, but we closed our doors to Him. As a consequence, no communication with Him has been possible. However, in this case, we mistakenly think that God does not answer our prayers and has left us. We become frustrated and dismayed.

Sorry! God does not leave us, but we have a false sense of this because *we* have left Him. We need to open our minds and receive Him, and then we will be able to communicate with Him.

Anyway, those who think that they are separated from God can receive the will of God only through the written words in the Scriptures and/or through other men indirectly. This is the faith of man who is under the Old Testament stage. People in the Old

Testament stage of faith live in darkness. Even though they do not retain God in their knowledge, He will not leave them alone. He leads them into the way of truth, all the time and everywhere. Of course, they cannot see God's hand, though.

I will share two testimonies with you that show how He leads those who are in the stage of the Old Testament of faith, blind toward the living God.

Accident of My Brand New Car

Several years ago, my left ankle was broken by accident, and I had to be in hospital for about three months. When I was about to leave hospital, I sold my nine year old non-automatic car. It is because, after being discharged from the hospital, I had to walk on crutches with a plaster cast on my left leg, and I could only drive an automatic car. Therefore, I bought a new one.

My previous car was giving me lots of trouble. Sometimes the engine stopped and the antifreeze pump burst. Therefore, I was often on pins and needles for fear of unexpected troubles that might come up while driving the car.

Now, however, I had a brand new car. My joy was exceedingly great because of that new car. I operated it very carefully and felt nervous that someone might scratch it in the night. I prayed to God as soon as it was delivered to me that no accident would happen to it. The Lord answered to me saying, "I got it."

However, when one month was not yet passed after I took delivery of it, I finished the Sunday morning service and parked the car before a supermarket in the neighborhood. I stayed in the car, and my wife went into the supermarket to buy something. Then I saw that a woman was backing her car towards mine so as to change her direction in front of the grocery store. The store manager came out and gave her hand signals for moving the car, but he only focused on making sure that his radishes weren't harmed by her car.

She kept on backing up her car, failing to see my car while she watched the store manager's signals to protect his radishes. Sitting in my car, I kept thinking that she would stop her car eventually, but surprisingly, she kept on backing towards me. I sounded my horn urgently, but alas, it was too late. Regretfully, the rear of her car crushed the rear door of my brand new car. I was totally dismayed when I looked at the crushed door of my most cherished car.

I bore a grudge against the woman who damaged my car, but I further blamed the Lord because He let this miserable accident happen to me after He had told me, "I'll keep it safe from accidents." I got angry at Him within myself for a while, and then I thought I heard a severe scolding voice in my mind saying, "Do you reproach God for this thing?" Then, I quickly repented.

Coming to my senses, I told her, "It's a new car, so I must have the crushed door changed with a new one instead of just having it repaired." I knew it could not be as good as the original one, even though I would have it replaced with a new one, but I had no other alternative. Anyhow, she was at a loss and felt sorry. I went my way after receiving her contact information.

The next day, I came to my office and called the car service center to learn the replacement cost of the rear door. The man said it would cost me three hundred and thirty dollars. I telephoned her about the expense, and she agreed to pay for it without any conditions. Not much time later, my wife phoned me. She asked me with an excited voice whether the compensation for the car accident was solved and whether I would receive full compensatory payment.

At that time, I instantly sensed the voice of the Lord in her excited voice. Within myself, I heard, "Why did you decide to receive money from her? Don't receive it." It seemed to me that the Lord was unhappy with my decision to receive compensation from her. But as it always was, God's voice was so subtle that I might ignore it anytime if I wanted to. It was very hard for me to accept that message as the voice of God because it was a matter of a substantial amount of money.

The conflict in my mind was long because it was not unjust money, and I thought there was no reason for the Lord to tell me to give up what I was due. If I made an error in decision, i.e., if it was not God's voice, then three hundred and thirty dollars might be wasted in vain, and so I confirmed it again and again.

Anyway, I thought it over and came to the conclusion that He always spoke to me in a small voice like this ever since He had come to me. It was such a small voice that I could immediately ignore it if my mind wavered a little. Therefore, I was finally convinced that it was the will of the Lord not to receive the money, and I made up my mind in that way.

After all, yes, it was God's voice, which I realized clearly a little bit later. If I had not been trained to hear the voice of the Lord all the while, it would have been impossible for me to abandon this big sum of money. Once I made up my mind, I felt easy because the conflict disappeared in my mind, but I was eager to know why He did not allow me to receive the money.

I attended the Wednesday evening service at the church and then went to the accident place at 9:00 p.m. to see the woman who damaged my car as promised. I arrived there before her; while I was waiting in the car, she appeared with her husband. Since it was raining outside and we could not find a suitable place to talk, I invited them into my car. Her husband sat on the front seat, and she sat on the rear seat. When they sat, I started by saying,

"I will not receive the repairing expense because God told me not to do so." I thought what I said about God and receiving no money might sound very strange to them. They were in a daze failing to understand accurately what I said. I continued,

"I want to talk with you because I want to know the reason why God forbade me." I imagined it was the plan of God to provide them with money because they made a vow to give offering of three hundred and thirty dollars to the church, or I guessed that they were poor so God had pity on them. I was so curious why God asked me not to receive. Then I asked them,

"Do you happen to attend church?" I asked the strangers a question about church while not knowing what their religions were. I had the boldness to ask because I knew God meddled deep in this car accident.

The man said that he was forty-eight years old, went to church when he was twenty years old, was involved in the choir, and left church three years later.

Hearing this, I knew why the accident happened. God loved him. So, He did not forget him, even though many years have passed since he left the church. God had made this precious opportunity to call him back to church again. I made clear to them that they had reached the time in their lives to think of church again. I told them that this minor collision was not a coincidence; it was the plan of God calling them back to church.

The man said, "Recently, my friends have asked me to come to church with them, but I haven't yet made up my mind." She added, "I was told that my friends were praying for me to lead me to church."

I talked about God with them in the car for about forty minutes. When we were almost finished, the man said that the circumstances were not coincidental, and she was sincerely thankful that I explained God in a way that was easy to understand.

She forcibly tried to give me the money, saying that they would feel guilty if she did not give me what she owed. I could not receive it, however, because God forbade me to. We played at tug of war for a while, and then I suggested an idea to her: "Why don't you keep the money with you and offer it to God as gifts when you go to church?" She replied, "Then, let's split it half, and you give half of it to your own church!" She counted the bundles of money to divide into two, gave me one of them, and kept the other one to herself. Also, she said she would surely go to church and offer the rest to God.

Then we parted. At that time, each of us praised God and saw the profound Providence and program of God.

I should like to emphasize again through this accident that

God never abandons us. God told me not to receive the money because it was the program and zeal of God desiring to call them back to church again. If God would have not told me differently, I would have just received the money and left them without saying a word about Jesus. However, since I declined their money, I could speak about Jesus and they could also open their minds to listen.

I truly hope they went to church after that according to the will of God. If they did not, they will have nothing to say to God when they stand before Him later.

Healing by a Shaman

I would like to share another testimony. In the past, while I worked for a company, I used to go to Singapore on business. At one time, I accompanied a group of producers of a broadcasting station to help them in Singapore so that they might collect news material smoothly. It was not usual for company staff to accompany a broadcasting crew, but I accompanied them due to their special request. I could send another staff member, but I determined to accompany them myself because I vaguely felt that the Lord had a plan for this trip.

They departed for Singapore via Bangkok, while I flew directly to Singapore, arrived there in advance, and met them at Singapore airport. That day, they shot many places under the guidance of a lady guide, a Korean, who was hired by our company to guide this crew throughout the itinerary.

The next day in the morning, we, the crewmembers and I, were waiting for the guide to arrive in the hotel lobby. Shortly afterwards, she came, and we exchanged "Good Mornings" with each other. Then, she told me lightly: "I woke up early in the morning, and I went to the Catholic church to pray to God." As soon as I heard this, I told her almost automatically, "Your faith can't grow rightly unless you meet with the living God, regardless of which type of church you are attending, be it Catholic or reformed."

In those days, I used to emphasize to believers that they must meet the living Jesus. I did not mean to move her greatly, but later she said she was substantially pricked in her heart by what I said.

During the itinerary, we had a chance to talk to each other in the rented bus, so I was able to get to know some of her background. She was a flight attendant. She got married to a Singaporean and lived in Singapore since having kids. Her husband was a branch manager of a European warehousing firm, and her family was well off and lived in plenty. But for some reason, to my eyes she looked gloomy all along while she was guiding us. She did have a reason, and I got to know this later.

I spoke with her from time to time about God. She wanted to hear from me how I met God after sending the crews back to Korea. She knew that the crews would be taking an earlier flight than mine, so there would be several hours to talk before my flight. However, I did not listen to her carefully because I thought it was just an empty compliment.

After the shooting schedule was all over, the crews left for Seoul, and I stayed back at the airport with her so as to board the later flight. She then said, "I told my husband that I would be late tonight. Would you please tell me the story of how you met God?" I was very glad that she wanted to hear about God whom I had met.

We walked to the coffee shop together on the second floor, and I talked to her for more than two hours about how I met God. Further, I conversed with her about how to believe in Jesus in the right way. As the dialogue progressed, she opened her mind and told me her story that she felt she could not talk about with others.

When she got married to a Singaporean man, she was very confident that she could lead him to church and that they would believe in Jesus together. However, he was not much concerned about going to church, so she had to go to church alone. Even though her first plan of leading her husband to the church was not achieved, she managed to get along, forgetting their differences since she could lead a wealthy life.

Not long ago, however, her daughter told her that her left knee ached, and she took her daughter to the hospital for an examination. The doctor said she had no problem, but the daughter's knee ache did not disappear, and she kept on crying with pain. She wondered if her daughter was stricken with polio, but she dismissed that possibility because her daughter had gotten a preventive shot for polio. However, the daughter kept on feeling pains in the left leg, and thereafter, her pain transferred to the right leg, and the daughter cried and cried out of pain. But she could not do anything for her daughter; she really was at a loss.

In the mean time, she needed to go on a trip to Australia on an urgent business matter, leaving the sick daughter in Singapore. While the guide was staying in Australia, her mother-in-law and her husband took the daughter to a spiritualistic medium for healing purpose. She, the Shaman, wrote a charm for the daughter, burnt it, mixed it with water, and had her drink it. Curiously enough, after she drank it, she was completely healed of her knee aches.

On hearing this after coming back from Australia, the guide was in great agony. It was good to hear that her daughter got well, but as a believer, she could never accept a healing by a spiritualistic medium.

"I can't agree to it. As a Christian, I cannot accept what they believe at all. But, why is it that my daughter is restored from the disease?" She was afflicted by these thoughts all along. She could not speak of this matter to anyone that she knew; she had to worry on her own. After that happened, she felt so small when she wanted to ask the husband to go to church, and her husband did not even pretend to hear her if she took the courage to ask.

I went to Singapore when she was deeply troubled with this problem. She was assigned to handle my team in the very nick of time, and she finally had a chance to talk to me about these things.

Hearing her full story, frankly speaking, I could not explain it all to her. I could only give her a general comment: "It was God's will to have your daughter healed by a spiritualistic medium." However, these words did not seem to help her much.

Considering this, I was about to be discouraged at my own helplessness. I was downcast because I used to shout loudly and with confidence, "You should meet God!" But in the end, I could not say anything helpful to someone who was eager to know God's mind. Soon after, however, the Lord started to give me unexpected thoughts in my mind, and I continued.

"God loves you, and He intentionally made this thing happen to bless you. You were leading a so-so faith life, and your faith could not grow, even if you thought you believed in God. So, He wanted to have your faith grow. However, since you were living a comfortable life, you would have talked back or would have given no heed if someone had advised you to be more eager to believe in God. God, knowing you, had to prepare a circumstance in which you would be willing to receive the word in your stony mind. He allowed your daughter to be healed through the spiritualistic medium, and He thus generated great agony and trouble in your mind. Accordingly, you went to the church early in the morning to know God further; you seriously sought Him. Now, when you are ready, He called me from Korea to Singapore to address God's mind to you."

Indeed, while I was talking about God, she was listening to me very seriously from the start to the end.

Through the miracle of the spiritualistic medium, God ploughed up the stony mind of the guide, and then He sent me to Singapore to sow the seed of the word. If the seeds fall on a mind that is like a stony field, the fowls come and devour them or the seeds cannot properly shoot their roots. The guide and I praised God after understanding the plan and Providence of God.

God wants our faith to grow continuously without halting. Therefore, He sometimes plans an event that will plow up our circumstances so that the field of our mind can be more receptive, like the case of the guide. Faith grows, and the faith that was praised yesterday is the faith of yesterday. Our faith should grow newly today, and God leads us to the way of growing it. There is no faith that grows by our endeavoring. God raises our faith all the way, as we have seen the above two cases.

What I want to point out through this testimony is that the miracle given through the shaman is also under the mighty hand of God. Even if some miracles may occur in Esoteric Buddhism in Tibet, all things are caused by the will of God, are allowed by Him, and are progressed by His plan. Therefore, it is an error for us to say that there is a God for the shaman and there is another God for the Buddhist. There is one God. All human beings are the creatures of God and are to know God only through Jesus.

According to the arrangement of the Scripture, when Malachi, the last book of the Old Testament, ends, Matthew, the first book of the New Testament, begins. When we who are under the law and have the faith of the Old Testament stage meet Jesus, then our faith will grow to the Matthew stage, the New Testament stage.

3

STAGE OF MATTHEW — REPENTANCE

When we meet Jesus in our individual life, the faith of the Old Testament period finishes, and we enter the faith of the New Testament period. However, we should undergo a step before going from the Old Testament to the New Testament in the faith-growing steps. It is the step of John the Baptist.

In Matthew, John the Baptist appears before Jesus comes. John preaches repentance in the wilderness, and he baptizes people with water for receiving the forgiveness of sin. It means that the repentance symbolized by John the Baptist should come first so that we may receive Jesus in our lives. By this repentance, each of us can meet Jesus in our individual lives, and our faith then enters the stage of the New Testament.

Imperative Mood of Present vs. Past of the Word *Repentance*

In the Greek grammar, the imperative mood of the verbs conveys either a meaning of repetition or a meaning of one time action, depending on the tense. The imperative mood of the present tense has the meaning of repetitive action and that of the past tense indicates the meaning of one time action.

I will describe this with an example. Matthew 4:17 reads, "...Repent: for the kingdom of heaven is at hand."

Here, the Greek for *repent* is *metanoeite* which is the present tense imperative and has the meaning of repetition. Therefore, repent in this context does not include the meaning of one time action, but it represents repentance in repetition.

In contrast, I will consider the case of using repent as the past tense imperative mood in the Greek. This is the case in Acts 2:38: "...Repent, and be baptized every one of you in the name of Jesus Christ for the remission of sins, and ye shall receive the gift of the Holy Ghost."

Here, the Greek used for *repent* is *metanoesate*, which is the past tense imperative and has a meaning of one time action. Therefore, repent in this case carries the meaning of repentance once.

A good example of showing the difference of usage between them appears in the Lord's Prayer. Refer to Matthew 6:11: "Give us this day our daily bread." In this sentence, *Give (*Greek:*dos)* is the past tense imperative mood. The sentence takes the proper imperative mood for *this day* which is the concept of 'only once.' However, the word used in the Lords' prayer in Luke is the present tense imperative mood. In "Give us day by day our daily bread," *Give (*Greek:*didou)* is the present tense imperative mood (Luke 11:3). The present tense imperative mood is used because of the repetitive concept of 'day by day.' Accordingly, in the Greek, the past tense imperative mood of a verb is used to indicate a single act, and the present tense imperative mood of the same verb is used to show a consecutive and repetitive act.

In Scripture, the commandment "Repent!" is used distinguishably as the past tense imperative mood and the present tense mood in Greek, from which we can understand also that repentance is distinguished as both repetitive repentance and repentance that is done once.

Frequently we sin and repent to God. Quite naturally, we must repeatedly repent and be forgiven our sins since we sin quite often. This type of repentance is repetitive. However, while doing such repetitive repentances more sincerely, we will be led to the true one-time repentance. This one-time repentance is that to which what Acts 2:38 refers.

What Is True Repentance?

'One-time repentance' will be referred to as 'true repentance' hereinafter because it is the true aspect of repentance that God wants from us. True repentance means finally turning from the world where we repeatedly sin and repent.

People under the law must repent each time when they sin. However, even though they repent a good number of times whenever they break the law, their nature is not changed at all. As a result, they sin again and repent again inevitably. The believer trapped in the vicious circle of sinning and repenting shows the typical pattern of those who are under the law.

Peter comments on this cycle as follows:

> But it is happened unto them according to the true proverb, The dog is turned to his own vomit again; and the sow that was washed to her wallowing in the mire. [2 Peter 2:22]

We cannot escape from this vicious cycle of sinning and repenting by ourselves. We feel the limit. Anyone running the race with every effort to live according to the will of the Lord will agree with this thought from the bottom of his heart.

While exerting all possible efforts for the purpose of keeping the law of God and living a life by the law, the time will come when believers under the law get exhausted and fall down. It is the time when they have reached the uppermost limit of their efforts, and then, if they seek God and repent, they will then meet Jesus. God sends Jesus to those who have fallen down by the law and repented. This is the true repentance of receiving Jesus.

We can find repentance many times in the Scripture, but all of it converges on the true repentance which represents the time when a person meets Jesus Christ and changes into a new man. Having experienced this repentance, the believer gets out of the world in which he used to sin; he repents and enters the new heavens and a new earth.

We should truly repent if we are to meet Jesus. Even if we may confess sincerely, "Jesus, please come to me," or "Jesus, I love you more than my life," we cannot receive Him without true repentance.

True Repentance of Disciples

How could the disciples receive Jesus and follow Him? Could it be possible without true repentance? Luke Chapter 5 details the meeting between Jesus and Peter. Peter forsakes all and follows Him after he met Him:

> And it came to pass, that, as the people pressed upon him to hear the word of God, he stood by the lake of Gennesaret, And saw two ships standing by the lake: but the fishermen were gone out of them, and were washing their nets. And he entered into one of the ships, which was Simon's, and prayed him that he would thrust out a little from the land. And he sat down, and taught the people out of the ship. Now when he had left speaking, he said unto Simon, Launch out into the deep, and let down your nets for a draught. And Simon answering said unto him, Master, we have toiled all the night, and have taken nothing: nevertheless at thy word I will let down the net. And when they had this done, they enclosed a great multitude of fishes: and their net brake. And they beckoned unto their partners, which were in the other ship, that they should come and help them. And they came, and filled both the ships, so that they began to sink. When Simon Peter saw it, he fell down at Jesus' knees, saying, Depart from me; for I am a sinful man, O Lord. For he was astonished, and all that were with him, at the draught of the fishes which they had

> taken: And so was also James, and John, the sons of Zebedee, which were partners with Simon. And Jesus said unto Simon, Fear not; from henceforth thou shalt catch men. And when they had brought their ships to land, they forsook all, and followed him. [Luke 5:1-11]

In summary, Peter was trying to catch fish in the lake of Gennesaret together with James and John. They toiled all the night through but took nothing; they were washing their nets to withdraw from the lake. At this very moment, Jesus came to Peter and said, "Launch out into the deep, and let down your nets for a draught." When Peter did so at His word, they caught a large number of fish and their net broke. Peter confessed that he was a sinful man, forsook all he had, and followed Him.

🗁 Time When Jesus Came to Disciples

Here, Jesus did not come to Peter when he caught many fish and was enjoying affluence to the full. He came to him when he caught nothing, gave up, and was about to go back home. This is shown from what Peter said:

> And Simon answering said unto him, Master, we have toiled all the night, and have taken nothing: nevertheless at thy word I will let down the net. [Luke 5:5]

Peter lived on fishing. He had to catch fish for a living, and he sometimes stayed up all through the night wandering here and there to catch fish. However, this day, he toiled all the night but failed to find any. We can easily guess that he was totally disappointed and frustrated when washing the net without a fish and preparing going home.

Jesus came to him at this moment. These passages are the record of when Peter literally met Him, but they also have spiritual meanings. We labor to lead our own life like Peter did. We toil for wealth, fame, and power all night long on the path of life as Peter did. However, the time will come when we realize that we cannot get what we want, and we will feel frustrated and abandoned like Peter, even though we poured out our souls and spared no pains.

At this very time, Jesus can come into our individual lives. Therefore, if we wish to meet Him, we should first pass through a life of disappointment and abandonment.

🗁 Why Did Jesus Come Only at This Time?

Why does Jesus seem to show up at the last moment of our strength? In reality, Jesus is always around us. However, we do not hear Him because we do not want to hear Him. He waits for us with patience, allowing us to have our own way as we please. Therefore, we go on the path of life at our pleasure. Only when we are exhausted and have given up will we stretch out our hands to God. Only at this time in our lives are we able to hear what Jesus says to us.

It was like this in the case of Peter. He grew up as a fisherman in the Lake of Galilee, and he knew better than anyone else that no one could catch fish in the deep water. However, he followed His unreasonable word: "Launch out into the deep, and let down your nets for a draught;" he had no other alternative. Peter had searched all the possible areas in the lake with skill and reasoning. He failed. If he went home with no fish in the nets, his family might skip a meal instantly. Further, he had no other counter plan, so he despaired.

At that time, Jesus spoke to him. If it were at ordinary times, Peter might have ignored His word by saying "None of your nonsense!" However, he could not do so in this situation. He had no solution other than listening to Him. This was the very instant when the word of Jesus meant something to Peter.

Not knowing Peter's inside story, some preachers say, "Peter had a great faith on the word of Jesus to obey Him. Now, why don't we follow after the faith of Peter and obey the words of

Jesus?"

However, Peter had no belief in His word, but he obeyed as a drowning man catching at a straw. Faith like a straw, thinking, "I shall be none the worse for it," was generated in him at that time. That kind of faith does not deserve praise.

I Am a Sinful Man

With no great hope, Peter threw nets into the deep at His word. However, differing from his expectation, he caught many fish so that the net was broken, and he beckoned unto his partners who were in the other ship that they should come and help him. At this moment, he fell down at Jesus' knees and confessed, "...Depart from me; for I am a sinful man, O Lord."

This confession is the true repentance of which Scripture speaks. Peter had been the lord of himself; not knowing God in his life in the past, he had acted as he wished and led his life as he wished. As a result, he became exhausted and fell down on the path of life. Jesus came to him at that very moment.

After this event, he depended on Jesus for everything: "And when they had brought their ships to land, they forsook all, and followed him" (Luk 5:11).

We can find a lot of people around us who think they believe in Jesus, love Him, and would lay down their lives to follow Him. However, if we are to follow Him truly, we must experience that we, each of us, is a sinful man. We must truly repent as Peter did. Then, we can follow Him. None of us are exceptions in this matter. The disciples, such as Peter, James, John, and Matthew, also passed through this step of repentance. Levi (Matthew) was called by Jesus as follows:

> And after these things he went forth, and saw a publican, named Levi, sitting at the receipt of custom: and he said unto him, Follow me. And he left all, rose up, and followed him. [Luke 5:27-28]

The publicans were equally treated as harlots and sinners (Mat 9:11; Mat 21:32). Therefore, we can imagine that the publican Matthew had been pointed at with scorn and left out in the cold. Consequently, he was exhausted and fell down on the path of life. When Jesus spoke to him in this condition, he instantly repented, forsook all, and followed Him.

Many people doubt saying, "How could the disciples leave all and follow Him at His one word?" The answer is that they despaired of their life, and as a result, they could hear Jesus. They truly repented and could follow Him. Therefore, we might conclude that the word of Jesus worked because the appropriate condition was prepared; they were then ready to follow Him at His one word.

We need to repeat repentance in daily life, but what matters most is true repentance. The man having truly repented receives Jesus in his life and enters Matthew stage, which is the New Testament period of the faith life.

One Lost Sheep

The parable of the lost sheep sufficiently explains what true repentance is. We will now correctly read a parable that is frequently misunderstood:

> Then drew near unto him all the publicans and sinners for to hear him. And the Pharisees and scribes murmured, saying, This man receiveth sinners, and eateth with them. And he spake this parable unto them, saying, What man of you, having an hundred sheep, if he lose one of them, doth not leave the ninety and nine in the wilderness, and go after that which is lost, until he find it? And when he hath found it, he layeth it on his shoulders, rejoicing. And when he cometh home, he calleth together his friends and neighbours, saying unto them, Rejoice with me; for I have found my sheep which was lost. I say unto you, that likewise joy shall be in heaven over one

> sinner that repenteth, more than over ninety and nine just persons, which need no repentance. [Luke 15:1-7]

🗁 The Pharisees' Murmur that Seems Reasonable Somehow

The Pharisees and the scribes murmur as Jesus gathers together with the tax collectors and sinners and eats with them. On hearing this, He answers them through the parable of the lost sheep to explain why He does so. All believers, as well as the Pharisees, want(ed) to be friends of God because being joined with Him is the actual purpose of believing in God. So, if someone says that he believes in God or Jesus, it means that he wants to be a friend of God. Through the parable of the lost sheep, Jesus explains the qualifications for men who wish to be friends of God.

The Pharisees were strongly against Jesus in each case, and Jesus had to rebuke them, calling them children of the devil (Jhn 8:44). They seemed to be Jesus' opponents. From this, we tend to think that the Pharisees were ugly, criminal-faced, and full of greed and wickedness. However, they were not like this. They were gentle looking and were devoted to God with all their hearts and souls. We cannot imagine how zealous they were in keeping the law of God. We will see their faith in this passage from Luke:

> The Pharisee stood and prayed thus with himself, God, I thank thee, that I am not as other men are, extortioners, unjust, adulterers, or even as this publican. I fast twice in the week, I give tithes of all that I possess. [Luke 18:11-12]

There are many believers who say, "I sometimes do evil things;" "I will give tithes when I have made sufficient money;" "I am not fond of fasting because of my physical constitution" and so forth. However, the Pharisees were different. They did not rob, did not do evil things, did not commit adultery, but they did fast and give tithes. If the believer in this age leads a Christian life as the Pharisees did, he will be spoken of very well by others.

It is quite natural for the Pharisees who were living such a devout life not to highly estimate Jesus who gathered together with the tax collectors and sinners. They instinctively questioned, "How can He mix with sinners or robbers instead of avoiding them?"

The Pharisees' murmur may seem to be natural. For instance, if a so-called devout Christian makes friends with harlots and sinners and hangs out with them, we would accuse him. If we have accusations toward such a man, then we have the same mind of Pharisees who murmured against Jesus having mixed with sinners. Therefore, their murmuring looks quite reasonable to our eyes.

However, we are different from the Pharisees in that we do not quarrel with Jesus who has associated with the sinners. We always take sides with Him in any case, right or wrong, thinking that unquestioning obedience is the right way to believe in and serve Jesus. But, the Scripture doesn't support these behaviors as right believing. If we continue to believe in Him in this manner, we will be for Him outwardly, but we will be like the Pharisees who murmur against His behavior inwardly.

🗁 Meaningless, If the True Understanding Is Missing

Upon hearing the Pharisees and the scribes, Jesus told them the parable of the lost sheep.

It will be of no use to read the parable if we cannot understand what it says rightly. For example, let us assume that Jesus wrote a letter to us: "I will see you at the watermill over the brook at 9:00 p.m." We will never see Him if, after reading the letter, we conclude that He wants to see us at the brook at 9:00 p.m. We must catch what He meant in the letter and come to the right place, the watermill, not the brook.

The Scripture says that Jesus will meet us and abide in us forever. We, of course, are to come to the right place at the right time as the Scripture indicates. If not, we cannot meet Him, even though we have read the Scripture a hundred times. If we understand the true meaning of the parable of the lost sheep, we will realize that we have been waiting for Him at the wrong place thus far.

This is a very well known parable, and we think we all know very well the meaning of this parable. The meaning of this parable that we traditionally have is as follows: The one lost sheep represents a person who once was a church member but became disappointed and went out of the church. So we must find him and persuade him to come back to the church. Our understanding is that being one lost sheep is not good but being amongst ninety-nine sheep is considered good. We are very much mistaken in this matter.

There are several points that cannot be explained by the traditional understanding.

Firstly, the shepherd, when he found the one lost sheep, brought it to his home, not to the place where the other sheep had been left, i.e. where ninety-nine sheep were.

Secondly, Jesus refers to the one lost sheep as the one sinner that repents and over whom heaven has joy. From this, we can understand that the sheep are a metaphor for sinners. Therefore, this is a parable about one sinner that is lost versus ninety-nine sinners that are not lost yet. Remember! No joy of heaven was expressed over the ninety-nine sheep.

Thirdly, Jesus poses this parable to explain why He mixes sinners with joy. Naturally, the parable is to explain why Jesus is the friend of sinners. Nevertheless, the traditional understanding says, "You! Go and find dismayed former church members, and bring them back!" This thought is totally out of context.

The true meaning of this parable is that one lost sheep refers to a believer whose faith is sound and the ninety-nine sheep are those who have misguided faith. Our traditional understanding is quite the opposite of the true meaning. This will be revealed as we go on.

🗁 The Wilderness: Where Jesus Feeds Sheep

The shepherd in the parable feeds a hundred sheep in the wilderness. The term *wilderness* is translated from the Greek *eremos*. The Greek *eremos* was translated as the wilderness in many other cases in the Scripture (e.g., Mat 3:1; 4:1; 11:7; Jhn 3:14; Rev 12:6). However, the *eremos* in this parable is translated into various English words such as wilderness, open country, open pasture, *et cetera*. *Eremos*, however, needs to be translated into the 'wilderness' to reflect the spiritual world correctly. It seems that some of the translations have digressed from the spiritual meaning because of the idea that sheep are fed in a pasture.

I will explain why it is appropriate to translate *eremos* into the 'wilderness.' The world we live in now is a world that produces thorns and thistles; it is hard to live here. The Scripture uses the wilderness as a metaphor for this hard world. The law dominates men in the wilderness.

🗁 Who Are the Lost Sheep?

We come to the church to believe in Jesus. In church, we do various many things such as attending every service, praying, donating, worshiping, sharing, teaching, studying the Bible, *et cetera*. However, even though we have spent a long time up until now in doing so, we still feel lack and futility deep inside of us. Further, we have never been able to love our neighbors as ourselves for one moment.

We keep on sinning, even though we believe that Jesus has forgiven our sins once for all. We have done many so-called spiritual things for many years, but there is no change in us at all. What is the reason for this emptiness? It is because we have been living in the wilderness under the law as one of the ninety-nine sheep.

You might query, "How come? We came to the church to believe in Jesus, not the law." I will reply, "No, sorry! We cannot meet Jesus unless we have spent a long time under the law. When we are exhausted and consequently fall down, being lost like one of the sheep here, then we can meet Jesus. Only at that moment will we repent and be able to follow Jesus from the bottom of our hearts." The sinners and tax collectors, the woman caught in adultery, and the prodigal son in the Bible represent such lost sheep. The lost sheep will be made spiritually perfect by Jesus by reaching the home of the shepherd.

We all are to start our faith life as one of ninety-nine sheep in the wilderness. Only when we fall down completely from such a life under the law, being one lost sheep, will Jesus find us and bring us to His home. At that time, our faith will change from a legalistic one to a true one. Then, we can love our neighbor as ourselves, and our sins will be forgiven once for all.

God permitted this hard world, the wilderness, through Divine Providence. When each one of the sheep is lost in the wilderness, not the green pasture, he is then brought to the home of Jesus. In a spiritual sense, it is quite evident that Jesus feeds sheep in the wilderness on purpose. For if the sheep become lost there, they have a chance to return home.

Being one lost sheep in the wilderness is 'true repentance.'

🗁 Friends of the Shepherd

We can find no text in the parable to indicate that, after having found the lost sheep, the shepherd returned to the place where the ninety-nine sheep had stayed. Instead, he put the sheep on his shoulders, went home, and rejoiced with his friends and neighbors.

In general, it might be easier for us to understand if the shepherd had brought the lost sheep to the original place where the other sheep stayed. However, the shepherd went home with the lost sheep and had a feast. From his behavior, it seems that he was eagerly waiting for sheep to be lost; relatively speaking, he does not seem as pleased with the ninety-nine sheep remaining in the wilderness. The shepherd is much more pleased with the one sheep that is lost.

The shepherd found the lost sheep, came home with it, and called together his friends and neighbors to rejoice together. The home of the shepherd corresponds to the kingdom of God where Jesus is living together with His believers. The believers are to enter this kingdom within their lifetime. Therefore, we can reckon that the shepherd has great joy over the one lost sheep, not only because he has found it but also because the sheep has finally returned to the home of the shepherd, the kingdom of God.

Who are those friends and neighbors that are invited to the feast of the shepherd? Of course, the shepherd indicates Jesus Christ. The friends and neighbors are the other lost sheep, each of which was lost and brought home earlier. Jesus says He Himself is the friend of the disciples:

> Henceforth I call you not servants; for the servant knoweth not what his lord doeth: but I have called you friends; for all things that I have heard of my Father I have made known unto you. [John 15:15]

Jesus said to his disciples that He would be their friend after the crucifixion. This means that the friends of Jesus are those disciples who are born again by the crucifixion of Jesus. Therefore, we can reckon that the lost sheep brought to the shepherd's home represents the born again man, like the disciples. In fact, the disciples were once lost and are now found by Jesus, and after the cross of Jesus, they got to the home of Jesus, the kingdom of God. When they come to the home of Jesus, they become friends and neighbors of Jesus.

In the parable, bringing the lost sheep home and allowing it to join the group of friends and neighbors means that if a man is saved, then he belongs to the existing group of saved men. Lost sheep gather together in the home of Jesus, and this gathering represents the church in this world. The true church is an organic gathering of the lost sheep, the kingdom of God in this world.

🗁 Ninety and Nine Sheep in the Wilderness

At the end of the parable, Jesus says, "Likewise joy shall be in heaven over one sinner that repents, more than over ninety and nine just persons, which need no repentance."

Jesus is metaphorically saying that one lost sheep is as one sinner that repents, and the other ninety-nine sheep are as ninety-nine righteous men that do not need to repent.

In the parable, the shepherd is Jesus Christ, of course, and the sheep are believers. One hundred sheep refers to all believers under the sun; one lost sheep is the true believer, being a rare breed as the number one out of one hundred implies, and the ninety-nine sheep are self-righteous believers with whom Jesus is not so much pleased.

At first look, the ninety-nine sheep seem to have good faith because Jesus is saying that they do not require repentance. However, it would be a big mistake if we think they are real righteous men. We should read between the lines to catch Jesus' real intention. He is somehow sarcastic here. Ninety-nine sheep refer to the believers who think that they are righteous by themselves. Jesus can do nothing for them as long as they hold fast to their thoughts of self-righteousness, and so, He calls them righteous sarcastically.

Let us have another case where Jesus refers to the Pharisees as the righteous even though they are not in reality:

> And it came to pass, as Jesus sat at meat in the house, behold, many publicans and sinners came and sat down with him and his disciples. And when the Pharisees saw it, they said unto his disciples, Why eateth your Master with publicans and sinners? But when Jesus heard that, he said unto them, They that be whole need not a physician, but they that are sick. But go ye

> and learn what that meaneth, I will have mercy, and not sacrifice: for I am not come to call the righteous, but sinners to repentance. [Matthew 9:10-13]

In the above scene, the Pharisees saw Jesus was with the tax collectors and sinners, and they criticized Him. On hearing this, Jesus referred to Himself as a physician and said that the healthy need no physician but the sick need one. In other words, the tax collectors and sinners are the sick who need Jesus, and the Pharisees are the healthy who do not need Jesus.

Here, Jesus calls Pharisees as healthy and righteous, but Pharisees are neither healthy nor righteous. Here is another verse about self-righteousness:

> And he said unto them, Ye are they which justify yourselves before men; but God knoweth your hearts: for that which is highly esteemed among men is abomination in the sight of God. [Luke 16:15]

The Pharisees, even though they are believers of God, cannot associate with Jesus. Why? Because they do not yet recognize that they themselves are sinners. Maybe they thought their sins were forgiven, as they were the chosen Jews, just as we, the believers, think our sins were forgiven as we came to church to believe. Unfortunately, that is not the true sin forgiveness of Jesus, which is mentioned in the Bible.

Earlier we saw Peter's case, whereby at the end of his tether, he recognized himself as a sinful man and repented. After that, he was able to associate with Jesus and follow Him. However, as for the Pharisees here, they do not reach Peter's status whereby they realize that they are sinners. Therefore, they cannot eventually realize that they are sinners who need repentance, and thus, they cannot repent. Jesus describes this kind of people when he said, "repentance is not needed," in the negative sense. The ninety-nine sheep in the wilderness are the believers who think they are righteous by themselves, so they do not repent. Therefore, they cannot follow Jesus. The Pharisees are ninety-nine such sheep.

One lost sheep taken home is the believer who is made really righteous by Jesus. He repents and follows Jesus to His home, the kingdom of God. He is saved and becomes a true believer.

🗁 Context Here...

Jesus gave the parable to explain why he mixed with sinners, not with Pharisees who seem righteous. Jesus was with sinners because they were ready to follow Him to the kingdom. But the Pharisees refused Jesus because they themselves thought righteousness came by keeping the laws. Naturally, Jesus could only be the friend of the sinners, the one lost sheep in the parable.

The righteousness of God is only given by Jesus Christ who comes to a man through true repentance. Other ways of righteousness, except Jesus, are self-righteousness that make doers arrogant and boastful. The ninety-nine righteous men are self-righteous men. All men who come to church and believe in Him belong to the multitude of the ninety-nine. They are in the wilderness and are under the law spiritually. The time will come during their individual faith lives when they will become exhausted and fall down, being the one lost sheep. Jesus will gladly meet each of them and lead him to His home, the kingdom of God.

Our faith starts with the ninety-nine sheep; we become the one lost sheep when we repent.

The Parable of the Lost Son

The parable of the lost son in Luke Chapter 15 dramatically shows a scene in which a person meets Jesus Christ through true repentance. This parable hides profounder meanings than we generally realize. Let's get started:

> And he said, A certain man had two sons: And the younger of them said to his father, Father, give me the portion of goods that falleth to me. And he divided unto them his living. And not many days after the younger son gathered all together, and took his journey into a far country, and there wasted his substance with riotous living. And when he had spent all, there arose a mighty famine in that land; and he began to be in want. And he went and joined himself to a citizen of that country; and he sent him into his fields to feed swine. And he would fain have filled his belly with the husks that the swine did eat: and no man gave unto him. And when he came to himself, he said, How many hired servants of my father's have bread enough and to spare, and I perish with hunger! I will arise and go to my father, and will say unto him, Father, I have sinned against heaven, and before thee, And am no more worthy to be called thy son: make me as one of thy hired servants. And he arose, and came to his father. But when he was yet a great way off, his father saw him, and had compassion, and ran, and fell on his neck, and kissed him. And the son said unto him, Father, I have sinned against heaven, and in thy sight, and am no more worthy to be called thy son. But the father said to his servants, Bring forth the best robe, and put it on him; and put a ring on his hand, and shoes on his feet: And bring hither the fatted calf, and kill it; and let us eat, and be merry: For this my son was dead, and is alive again; he was lost, and is found. And they began to be merry. Now his elder son was in the field: and as he came and drew nigh to the house, he heard musick and dancing. And he called one of the ser-

> vants, and asked what these things meant. And he said unto him, Thy brother is come; and thy father hath killed the fatted calf, because he hath received him safe and sound. And he was angry, and would not go in: therefore came his father out, and intreated him. And he answering said to his father, Lo, these many years do I serve thee, neither transgressed I at any time thy commandment: and yet thou never gavest me a kid, that I might make merry with my friends: But as soon as this thy son was come, which hath devoured thy living with harlots, thou hast killed for him the fatted calf. And he said unto him, Son, thou art ever with me, and all that I have is thine. It was meet that we should make merry, and be glad: for this thy brother was dead, and is alive again; and was lost, and is found. [Luke 15:11-32]

This parable is very common to most people, whether they are Christians or not. The famous painter Rembrandt painted a picture entitled "The Return of the Prodigal Son" in which the father receives the younger son graciously. Many preachers have illustrated many times, by quoting this text, the love of the father who gladly accepted the younger son. We generally come to be thankful for the father's forgiveness and everlasting love when we hear it, and some resolve to be obedient to their fathers.

However, this parable does not describe the father who welcomes the younger son with love, even though he came back after having squandered his money in dissolute living. This parable speaks to us the deep truth of life. That is, the younger son who returned to his father discloses what true repentance towards God is like, and the comparison of the younger son to the older son clearly uncovers the differences between law and grace. Also, the course in which the younger son left the house of his father reveals the reason why Adam had to eat the forbidden fruit, and the fundamental reason why all mankind, after Adam, had to live a hard life on this earth that produces thorns and thistles.

Every word and parable in the Bible is precious and valuable, and I assert that the parable of the lost son is the most precious and valuable one of them all. This ordinary parable has wonderful truths you could not find, even if you had spent your whole life looking. I will explain three major topics here.

Firstly, I will describe the fundamental reason why each person has to leave God and is born to be a sinner by explaining the course in which the younger son leaves the house of the father. Secondly, I will tell you what true repentance is by quoting the return of the younger son. Lastly, I will clarify the difference between law and grace, which is hard to understand, by comparing the older son who stayed home to the younger son.

Why Are Men Born As Sinners?

First of all, we will study this parable to see the reason why all men are born as sinners. Let's consider the following question: Why did the younger son want to leave home?

Why did the younger son want to leave home?

Characters in this parable include a father, an older son, and a younger son. In this instance, the father symbolizes God, the home symbolizes the kingdom of God where God abides, and the older and younger sons symbolize believers, i.e., Christians, who serve God as their Father. The believers can be divided into two groups: some believers belong to the older son group who did not leave home, and other believers belong to the younger son group who left home and came back again.

The head of the home where the younger son lives is the father. The father, as a head of the household, has the final say over all household affairs. The sons must accept the father's decisions, even though they may not agree with those decisions, because they are not the head of the household. One option available to them when they do not agree with him is to leave home.

The younger son in the parable made up his mind to leave. It was the younger son himself who decided to go, considering that the father did not ask him to do so. He came into conflict with the life of being obedient to the father's headship. He disliked it.

Of course, he was not in trouble with the father regarding trivial problems. Such problems are not addressed in the Bible, which is concerned with the important and fundamental issues of human life.

The conflict with the father that caused the younger son to leave home was fundamental. We can read one example of that conflict in the latter part of the parable. When the younger son had returned home, the father gladly received him, and they began to be merry. However, the older son who had been in the field got angry at what his father did. He thought that it was not right for his father to celebrate for the brother who had run through his father's money with harlots. But, it is natural for the father to have festivities in that situation. He can make room for the older son for anything else, except the present case. This conflict runs deep and will remain until it has been solved fundamentally.

The younger son wanted to be separated from his father and to live an independent life rather than enduring the conflict in his mind. He thought it would be better for him if could live his own individual life, and he then came to a determination. He would have pondered the decision many times until reaching that determination. He would have considered fears of facing the strange world after having left home, and he would have also thought about how, once he left, it would not be easy to return home again. However, all these considerations were not so serious compared to his current life under the dominion of his father. So he left.

The younger son was able to leave his father and be independent from his father by himself because of the wisdom he had. That is, he decided to leave home since he thought he had wisdom by which he could do better and lead a better life than under his father's control. He tried to have 'headship', being confident that his wisdom could compare to that of his father.

Even though wisdom made the younger son leave home, the wisdom of the younger son was ultimately given by nature. The wisdom of the younger son had the same quality as that of the father. Thus, they can be compared to each other. No housedog, for example, can rise in revolt against its lord and leave him because it has no such wisdom and no such power at all. We can conclude now that the younger son was able to leave home because he had wisdom.

🗁 The Process for Adam to Leave Eden

The process by which the younger son left home in Luke 15 matches the process for Adam's leaving the Garden of Eden in Genesis. The two processes are substantially the same in nature. Many of us will wonder how the lost son and Adam are connected and why I said that the parable of the lost son and the description of Adam contain the same message. We will find no connection between them if we read Scripture only to catch literal meanings. However, ponder the verses in detail and in depth, and you will get to know that the lost son is equal to Adam.

As the younger son left home because of wisdom, Adam also left God because of wisdom. Let me explain more of Adam's wisdom. God created Adam in His image, and Adam was a very wise creature after His likeness (Eze 28:12). Adam ate of the tree of the knowledge, which God forbade, and left Eden, God's dwelling place. And the fundamental reason why Adam ate the forbidden fruit was his wisdom.

As for the course that led to Adam eating of the tree of the knowledge, the serpent tempted the woman, she gave it to her husband, and he did eat. Because of the fundamental temptation by the serpent, Adam and the woman ate the fruit and walked on the way of disobedience after that. They would not have eaten if it had not been for the serpent. What was the real nature of the serpent that tempted them and led all mankind astray?

The serpent in the Scriptures represents wisdom spiritually. Let us look at the following verses:

> Now the serpent was more subtil than any beast of the field which the LORD God had made. And he said unto the woman, Yea, hath God said, Ye shall not eat of every tree of the garden? [Genesis 3:1]

Here, the term *subtil* is translated from the Hebrew word of *aruwm* which means wise or prudent. According to the context, this word is translated negatively like 'crafty' (Job 5:12; Job 15:5) and positively like 'prudent' (Pro 12:16, 23). The word *aruwm* here was naturally rendered in the negative since it was used to describe the serpent that is the common enemy of all human beings.

The Hebrew word *aruwm* in the Scripture can be rendered both in the positive and in the negative. Therefore, the word *aruwm* in this text could be translated into prudent if we could get rid of our existing negative opinion of the serpent. Have I gone too far? I do not think so. The serpent was not created as a negative creature. No creatures in the world are created absolutely negative, but they are viewed relatively as negative or positive by mankind. In contrast to our eyes, Jesus was not prejudiced against the serpent. He says it is the symbol of wisdom:

> Behold, I send you forth as sheep in the midst of wolves: be ye therefore wise as serpents, and harmless as doves. [Matthew 10:16]

The serpent symbolizes wisdom in the Scriptures. Accordingly, we should read Genesis 3:1 as follows; "Now the serpent was wiser than any of the wild animals the LORD God had made," which mostly matches the biblical context.

It was the woman who was tempted first by the serpent, but I will go on explaining with Adam's name as he is the prototype of all mankind. Spiritually, the woman and Adam are one anyway. The fact that Adam was tempted by the serpent symbolizing wisdom reveals that he had wisdom. He agreed to what the external serpent said and then opened his internal mind since he had the nature of the serpent in him. Hence, there is no need to blame the serpent as it tempted the man. Adam opened his mind because he was connected to the serpent, and therefore, it was Adam himself who is to be blamed.

Adam has the nature of the serpent since God created Adam to be wise. Wisdom is one of Adam's fundamental attributes, which is inseparable from him.

If we think that the serpent is a fundamentally wicked creature, it is required for us to explain how the serpent was in the Garden of Eden. However, there is no need to do so because the serpent is the wisdom Adam has in him. Thus, where there is Adam, there is the serpent also, such as in heaven, on earth, or in the Garden of Eden.

Because Adam has wisdom, he thinks of leaving the Garden of Eden when God seems unacceptable to him. That wisdom is the question. Adam has secret confidence in himself that he can do no less than God does and can live a better life. He thinks in the same way as the lost son did before leaving the house of the father.

In this situation, Adam's wisdom whispers to him as follows: "Do you know why God forbade you to eat the fruit from the tree of the knowledge of good and evil? It is because God was wary of your being like Himself, knowing both good and evil, when you eat it." This dialogue is written in Genesis:

> And the serpent said unto the woman, Ye shall not surely die: For God doth know that in the day ye eat thereof, then your eyes shall be opened, and ye shall be as gods, knowing good and evil. And when the woman saw that the tree was good for food, and that it was pleasant to the eyes, and a tree to be desired to make one wise, she took of the fruit thereof, and did

eat, and gave also unto her husband with her; and he did eat. [Genesis 3:4-6]

If Adam had thought that his wisdom would never reach the level of God, the serpent would have failed to tempt him. He would have refused the suggestion by the serpent outright by saying, "How could I? I can never be like God, even if I eat something better than the fruit of that tree."

However, Adam had wisdom, and he accordingly concluded it would be possible for him to struggle with God. He ate of the tree after long thought and left the Garden of Eden. He had to leave once he had eaten the forbidden fruit.

Why? Because disobedience meant that Adam knew more than God and was wiser than He is. Thus, Adam is separated from God because there cannot be two masters in a family. Adam was separated from God and had to live his own life out of Eden.

The course for Adam to leave Eden matches the course for the lost son to leave home.

The Father Who Let His Younger Son Leave

The father in the parable let his younger son leave home since the son was eager to do so. Since he knew that the son would have a very hard time, he would have dissuaded his younger son from leaving home with all his heart. However, it would be no longer sensible to persuade the son once he had made up his mind to be independent of his father. The father cannot catch the son's mind, even if he could have caught the son's body by force. The father let him go since he had no better way.

However, the father, in letting him go, has one hope. That is, he hopes that the younger son will come back home after having experienced the true bitterness of the far country. With this hope in his mind, he lets the younger son go.

God Who Let Adam Leave

We will now read the text in which Adam leaves the Garden of Eden, which is comparatively quoted with the parable of the lost son. Records for Adam in Genesis Chapter 3 are as follows:

> And unto Adam he said, Because thou hast hearkened unto the voice of thy wife, and hast eaten of the tree, of which I commanded thee, saying, Thou shalt not eat of it: cursed is the ground for thy sake; in sorrow shalt thou eat of it all the days of thy life; Thorns also and thistles shall it bring forth to thee; and thou shalt eat the herb of the field; In the sweat of thy face shalt thou eat bread, till thou return unto the ground; for out of it wast thou taken: for dust thou art, and unto dust shalt thou return. [Genesis 3:17-19]

We generally know that Adam was expelled from the Garden of Eden as a punishment because he disobeyed the commandment of God. But, it is not true.

There is another reason why Adam had to leave Eden. He was born in the Garden of Eden and longed for the unknown world he had never seen. The unknown world means the world where human beings are living without God and without obedience to the commandments of God. Adam, who never experienced that world, would be naturally lured by the world.

It may look good if Adam only stays in the Garden of Eden, but it has a fundamental problem. If he only lives in Eden, he cannot recognize Eden for what it really is. He has to undergo another world so as to be able to recognize Eden as Eden. For example, we cannot recognize light as light if there is only light in this world. Light will be light only when there is also darkness. If Adam lives only in Eden where he was created, he cannot recognize the joy of life in Eden, as he experienced no counterpart life, which is life outside of Eden.

God knows that Adam will be made perfect after he leaves

God. So God overlooked when Adam left the Garden of Eden. How can we say that God overlooked Adam's leaving?

First, God placed the tree of the knowledge of good and evil in the Garden of Eden, so He provided a fundamental cause for Adam to leave Eden.

Second, God kept silent while Adam was eating the forbidden fruit, and He appeared only when he finished eating. If God really wanted to prevent him from eating, He would not have put the tree of the knowledge in the center of the Garden of Eden, or He would have placed a sword whirling and flashing near the tree so that Adam would not hang around it. God did not do so.

In this context, God opened the way for Adam to eat of the tree, and He overlooked the eating, just as the Father in the parable let the younger son leave his house.

Some people say that all of these temptations were given to test the free will of Adam. He fell and was punished. Does God have any reason to test the free will of human beings and lead them into a life full of trials and troubles? God does not test us for the sake of testing, but He raises us with His power of life. Adam's eating of the tree of knowledge is the course of God's creation, which will make Adam perfect after all. It does not mean that Adam disobeyed for a little while.

If we understand God's plan properly, we will no longer make a meaningless resolution as follows: "I will never eat of the tree of knowledge of which Adam ate." As mentioned earlier, we were born in this world because we already had eaten the fruit. So, our determination not to eat it has no meaning at all. Sorry! We have already eaten the fruit that we firmly determine not to eat.

"I've Never Eaten of the Tree of the Knowledge"

In general, it is hard for us to admit that every one eats the fruit because we think we have never seen it nor eaten it. However, it is true that each of us have eaten it. We only cannot remember the fact. That's all. The Scriptures testify it through the story of Adam.

Let us look at Adam's life. His life has two parts: one is in Eden before eating fruit and the other is out of Eden after eating the fruit. So are our lives. We do not begin our existence when we are born in this world. Before we are born, we abided with God in Eden as spiritual beings. We can know this through the record of Adam, our prototype, in the Scripture. Thus, each of us who were once in Eden came to this world with human flesh. Therefore, our spirits/souls already existed before we had a body.

Further, once we ate of the tree of knowledge, then our entire life goes along based on the knowledge of good and evil. Don't we lead life like that now? From this, we can understand that we surely ate from the tree of knowledge.

Anyhow, if you, as one human being, say, "I've never eaten of the tree of the knowledge of good and evil," it means that you are not a man, which is absurd enough.

Far Country

Let's get back to the parable of the lost son. The younger son leaves the house of his father and goes to a far country. When he was in the house of the father, the relationship between the father and the son is life itself. However, when he is in the far country, the relationship between the ruler and the prodigal is the law. The relation of life is totally different from that of law. The former relationship is connected with love unconditionally; the latter relationship is connected by the give-and-take that shows another phase of the law.

The house of the father in the parable symbolizes the kingdom of God where we will abide with Him when saved: "Surely goodness and mercy shall follow me all the days of my life: and I will dwell in the house of the LORD for ever" (Psa 23:6).

On the contrary, the far country signifies the world where many younger sons, having left the house of the fathers, live their lives by maintaining the system of the world by the law. It means the present world where we now live. Scripture points out that the ruler of the world is the devil. Consider what the devil said while tempting Jesus:

> And the devil, taking him up into an high mountain, shewed unto him all the kingdoms of the world in a moment of time. And the devil said unto him, All this power will I give thee, and the glory of them: for that is delivered unto me; and to whomsoever I will I give it. [Luke 4:5-6]

As the above verses indicate, the devil says this world has been given to him and is under his control.

Indeed, within this world lies the evil one. John makes a similar statement in 1 John 5:19: "And we know that we are of God, and the whole world lieth in wickedness."

The world in this text does not represent the materialistic world we can see, but it indicates the world that is reflected in the mind of each human being, having left God. This world is controlled by those who have left God and made their own laws and rules for the purpose of realizing their ideal. Therefore, the real ones that rule this world are the human beings who have left God. Scripture reveals that the human beings who control this world system are the evil ones.

The persons living in this world are destined to be exploited, suppressed, and destroyed by the law. The law leads us to death. Both the woman caught in adultery and the younger son in the parable of the lost son represent those who lived in the world of the law, failed to survive, and finally faced death. The younger son longed for this world and came into it without proper awareness of all these things.

Adam left the Garden of Eden after eating the forbidden fruit, and he came to this world. We also came into this world following after Adam. In other words, we are born here as the younger sons who have left the house of the father.

Model of True Repentance

The return of the younger son shows us a prototype of true repentance. The parable demonstrates the dramatic state in which one man comes back to God, seeking Him. Shall we go?

The Younger Son's Riotous Living

The younger son was released from the father's control, and going to the far country, he enjoyed freedom to the fullest extent. He left his father's house for the very purpose of finding enjoyment, as a matter of fact. He did everything in obedience to his father's commandments while living in his father's house. After leaving, he had to plan everything about his life and decide things for himself. He expected this independence, actually. Therefore, we might think that he would have made every effort to be successful in his life.

However, contrary to our thoughts along this line, the Scriptures say that he actually wasted his substance with riotous living. It is not easy for us to understand why he lived a wild life instead of struggling hard to succeed as an independent man. I will now explain why.

🗁 The Younger Son Did Not Want Riotous Living

We find fault with the younger son because he left the house of his father and lived a wild life in the far country. Therefore, we call him a prodigal son without hesitation. However, it will be very inappropriate if we look down on him and conclude that he is a man who has nothing in common with us. If we stand in such self-righteousness, we will then fail to catch what Jesus says to us through this parable. Hence, we need to have a deeper understanding of the parable so as to uncover or reveal its true meaning.

In contrast to our judgmental assumptions, the younger son attempted to live a noble life in the far country because he had to make it at all costs. However, the life given to him in the far country ended in failure, in spite of his every effort; he never wanted his life to be that way. I can say that he was lost against his will based on the fact that he eventually longed to eat the livestock's pods and was very miserable with regret. If he had aimed at wasting his substance and losing his life in the far country, he would have killed himself in his miserable condition instead of trying to survive on the pods. But, he desired to live. He longed to survive and succeed in his life. Therefore, he did not choose the riotous living, but his life and noble aims deteriorated into riotous living.

In Scripture, tax collectors, sinners, harlots, and the woman caught in the act of adultery represent those who were eager to live an earnest life. However, they produced shameful results in life against their intention. They are to be blamed if they have chosen such lives according to their will. But they are not to be blamed because they have produced such life against their will. They deserve pity only.

🗁 If the Younger Son Had Not Lived a Riotous Life

We will read this parable from a different point of view. We generally understand riotous living as squandering material wealth. We accordingly blame the younger son as a prodigal son on the basis that he squandered his father's wealth in riotous living. Then, what will he be if he had greatly succeeded in the far country and had gained great wealth, enough to make a living even in a severe famine? Would he then be considered a good son as he did not live riotously but made his fortune? No. In such a case, we would have to think that he would have had no opportunity to return to his father for reconciliation.

He made up his mind to return home when he came to the end of his rope after having lost everything in the far country. Only at that moment did he finally begin to think about coming to his father's house. He would have never returned to his father if he had earned a large sum of money, i.e., if he did not squander his living.

Consider now which one is more important: the younger son's coming to his father, or the wealth he lost? Absolutely, the former. The father was not sorry at all for the wealth his younger son spent in riotous living; you will notice that he asks his son nothing about it. He was only thankful since the younger son returned home as a result of the riotous living.

Therefore, if anyone of us blames the younger son's riotous living, he reveals that he prefers wealth to the younger son's returning home. There is one man in the parable who is interested only in the wealth the younger son wasted. He is the older son who had stayed home. He rebukes his father:

> But as soon as this thy son was come, which hath devoured thy living with harlots, thou hast killed for him the fatted calf. [Luke 15:30]

This verse shows what matter the older son is interested in. He cares nothing for his brother's safe return. He is only interested in the property his brother wasted, and he thus hates him without knowing the Father's mind.

We have considered the younger son in the light of the lexical meaning of riotous living. We will now think through the spiritual meaning of riotous living and examine the fundamental problem of the younger son living in the far country.

🗁 Greek Word for Riotous Living

The word for riotous living used by Jesus is not the literal meaning that we can find in the dictionary. 'Riotous living' is translation of the Greek *zon astos*.

This Greek word can be analyzed as follows:

zon	*asotos*		
	a	+	*sotos*
	negative prefix	+	variant of *sozo*
life	not	+	save or make safe

Here, *zon* indicates *life* and *asotos* means *riotous*. *Asotos* is the compound of *a*, a negative prefix, and *sotos* of variant of *sozo* or *save* or *make safe*. Accordingly, *zon asotos* means the 'life without salvation.' Thus, the younger son's riotous living represents the life without salvation.

What does the younger son's life without salvation mean? The far country in the parable indicates the place without salvation and security, and the younger son accordingly had a hard time living there. On the contrary, the house of the father represents the place of salvation and security. Thus, the younger son's living without salvation means that he left his father and lived alone in the far country. Jesus points out that his life was riotous because he left the father's house.

Therefore, the younger son's riotous living does not mean that he was wasteful and prodigal during his life in the far country. His riotous living already started when he left the house of his father. Thus, in the far country, no matter what he does is riotous living. Even if he practices sharing, peace-making, loving, non-riotous living, and even goes to church, all of his actions must constitute riotous living without any exception. If he had wished not to live riotously, then he must not have left the house of his father from the beginning. It is the only way.

Younger Son in the Far Country Represents Us

We have been comparing the younger son to Adam. The younger son who left Father's house is Adam who left the Eden, God's house. The younger son and Adam are us. We are them, and they are us.

The younger son reflects us who left God and came to this

world. Like the younger son, we struggle to succeed in this world, that is, the far country. For example, we are anxious for gathering wealth, winning power, or achieving fame, during which all of us become frustrated and lost. None of us is lost after intentionally having lived a wild life. Nonetheless, this world brings riotous living to all its inhabitants by nature. When we breathe our last, we are to leave everything that we have acquired behind in this world. Do we agree that we are living riotously, trying to achieve the above-described things?

In this world, we are leading our lives alone after having left God. The life given after having left God is the life without salvation, defined by riotous living. Thus, we are already destined to live riotous living in the far country, no matter how hard we may try. Jesus enlightens us from this parable that we left God, and we are now experiencing riotous living. This parable is not about the prodigal son; it is about us all.

Return of the Younger Son

The younger son wasted his substance, even though he had tried every effort to live an earnest life. Nobody gave him husks that the swine ate since there was a mighty famine in the far country at the time that he had wasted his substance. Now, the younger son speaks to himself,

"How many hired servants of my father's have bread enough and to spare, and I perish with hunger. I will arise and go to my father, and say to him, Father, I have sinned against heaven and before you, and am no more worthy to be called your son; make me as one of your hired servants" (Luk 15:17-19).

This confession that he has sinned against heaven and his father does not mean that he is repenting for one or more mistaken deeds. Rather, he is repenting his whole life during which he has left his father and lived his own life in a far country. His sinful life already began when he left his father. He realized his sinful life when he faced death. The confession that he has sinned against heaven and his father is the true confession that comes from the bottom of his heart before death. He has become one lost sheep, which is to be carried to the home of shepherd. This is true repentance by a man.

If we desire to know that we ourselves are sinners, we need to undergo the life of the younger son. If we confess by word of mouth that we are sinners without having led such a life, it is not a true confession. We are told in church that each human being is born as a sinner and is to repent in order to believe in Jesus, and as a result be blessed. However, frankly speaking, we have no idea how we have sinned and why we are sinners. Nevertheless, we just simply agree that we are sinners since we want to be blessed by believing in Jesus. Those who make a confession as sinners without undergoing the life of a sinner are not sinners. They are so-called 'fake sinners.' Only true sinners would repent and be saved by Jesus.

Anyway, in the course of life, each of us will come to a time when we are driven into a corner as the younger son was. When we truthfully pant for God and repent our sin at that time, it is true repentance.

🗁 Merry Father

The younger son returns home after facing death, that is, the limit of his self-centered life.

While the younger son is still a long way off, his father sees him, runs to him, flings his arms round him, and kisses him. The father first sees his son coming in the distance. This detail means that the father was watching the horizon day by day, looking forward to his son's returning home. We can gather from this passage the earnest passion of the father waiting for the younger son.

Each of us is the younger son before God, the Father. We will repent and seek for God when we have encountered the limit of life after having left the house of God and having lived by ourselves. Even today, God finds any of us who truly repents:

> The fool hath said in his heart, There is no God. They are corrupt, they have done abominable works, there is none that doeth good. The LORD looked down from heaven upon the children of men, to see if there were any that did understand, and seek God. They are all gone aside, they are all together become filthy: there is none that doeth good, no, not one. [Psalms 14:1-3]

Some may think, “Why doesn’t the father aggressively send a guy to him or directly go to find him?”

If the father could have solved the problems by doing so, he would not have let his younger son depart in the very beginning. He would have tried to take his son under his control by force. Even if his father had brought him home before his ‘ripe time’, the younger son would have continuously thought of leaving home. That is why his father did not intervene by force. The parable spoken by Jesus is the word of truth to shed light on the essence of all issues in our lives.

The father begins to celebrate when his younger son returns. He asks his younger son nothing about ‘how much money he had left’ or ‘what kind of business he had done,’ because the father’s purpose in letting his son go to the far country was not about increasing his wealth. The father only wanted his son to realize himself and come home. As a matter of fact, the father was worried about his son when he first decided to let him go because his son might not return. But, the father is very glad indeed to see his son return alive. The return of the younger son fulfilled the intention of the father who had let him go.

The father and the younger son are reunited through the above-mentioned series of events, which represents repentance by a sinner in the Scriptures. Hence, there is joy in heaven:

> I say unto you, that likewise joy shall be in heaven over one sinner that repenteth, more than over ninety and nine just persons, which need no repentance. [Luke 15:7]

God will be glad for each of us who repents. He does not care about how much money we earned or how godly we were by not mingling with the prostitutes. He considers nothing about what we did in this world in terms of the world's standard of success. He is only glad when each of us repents and comes back to Him while we are still alive.

🗁 Far Country from the Father's Viewpoint

The far country gave the younger son a hard life, squeezed him, and destroyed him, but it performed a job the father wanted done. That is, after such tribulation, the far country returned the younger son as a true son to the father. The far country must always give its inhabitants a hard life and troubles, which is the mission God has given to the far country. We select the hard life in the far country for ourselves when we leave God, the Father, as an Adam.

The hard life given in the far country, therefore, suits God's purpose: first, the hard life makes each of us know that it is painful to leave God, and second, the pain leads us to return to God again.

Some people try to deceive us by saying that the kingdom of heaven will come to the world where we are, the far country in the parable. However, no such attempt has ever achieved its purpose during the history of human beings. It is fundamentally impossible to let the kingdom of heaven come to this world. God himself is the kingdom of heaven, so the world formed by those who have left God can never be the kingdom of heaven. The one and only way of letting the kingdom of heaven come on this earth is to let Jesus Christ come into the minds and hearts of each of us. We can then see the world as the kingdom of heaven/God.

Jesus Christ Comes to the Younger Son Who Repents

The father orders a fatted calf killed and then has a feast for the younger son. He gives the younger son the best robe, ring, and shoes to put on in order for him to stay at the house. The spiritual meaning of this scene is that Jesus Christ comes to the one who truly repents, in order to lead him to the kingdom of God, i.e., salvation.

All items that are given to him symbolize Jesus Christ. The Greek *protos* is translated here as the 'best.' *Protos* is also translated as the first in the saying of Jesus, "I am Alpha and Omega, the beginning and the end, the first and the last" (Rev 22:13). Therefore, the best represents Jesus Christ. Also, the robe indicates righteousness. In detail, the robe symbolizes righteousness since it covers our shame in front of God. Adam and the woman ate of the tree of the knowledge of good and evil, and their eyes were opened to know the feeling of shame. At that time, they made clothes for themselves by sewing fig leaves, but God made garments of skin and clothed them:

> And the eyes of them both were opened, and they knew that they were naked; and they sewed fig leaves together, and made themselves aprons. [Genesis 3:7]

> Unto Adam also and to his wife did the LORD God make coats of skins, and clothed them. [Genesis 3:21]

In this instance, the clothes they made with fig leaves symbolize the self-righteousness achieved by men. Self-righteousness comes from deeds of keeping the law. Those who have kept the law of God are proud and self-confident because they think God cannot treat them unkindly as they have done God's will. They will say to God in their heart at the judgment, "I have done many good things. I have done works eligible for entering the kingdom of heaven. So, I am not ashamed."

🗁 The Meaning of God Replacing the Coverings of Fig Leaves

Self-righteousness is figuratively expressed as clothes (coverings) sewed with fig leaves together in Scripture. God takes off the clothes, which means that God does not accept the righteousness man makes.

Some people may wonder why He does not accept the righteousness of man. This kind of question occurs to us when we think there is little difference between the righteousness of man and the righteousness of God. This may seem to be the case when we take only a superficial view.

But, there is righteousness that is accepted by God and another that is not accepted by God, even though the righteousness may look the same. For example, we consider gifts to the poor, tithes, and church service to be righteous things, but those righteous deeds done by Pharisees were rejected by God. The righteousness that is not accepted by God is called self-righteousness, which, in fact, is not really righteousness at all. We are to give up the righteousness of man, i.e., self-righteousness, and accept the righteousness of God when we wish to enter the kingdom of God. We need to follow the law of God in the kingdom of God.

Let us look at Chapter 20 of Matthew, which contains the parable of the vineyard workers. Here, the marketplace symbolizes human society in which the give-and-take rule is applicable, and the vineyard indicates the kingdom of God which operates by the rule of life. When the workers, who have the marketplace mindset, wish to find fault with the principle of the vineyard, the landowner says, "Is it not lawful for me to do what I will with my own?" (Mat 20:15).

The vineyard works by the rule of life according to the will of the landowner. We are mistaken if we think the vineyard works by the righteousness of the marketplace. We will be able to abide in the vineyard when we have the righteousness of the vineyard.

Anyway, our attempts to hang onto self-righteousness reveal that we are sinners, have left the Garden of Eden where God dwells, and have come to this world. The righteousness of man is not righteousness in the kingdom of God as mentioned in Isaiah 64:6: "But we are all as an unclean thing, and all our righteousnesses are as filthy rags; and we all do fade as a leaf; and our iniquities, like the wind, have taken us away."

It's a fake. If we are expecting God to accept our self-righteousness, we are making an absurd demand on God. He will not accept the fake as true. The righteousness of God is the one and only righteousness (Mat 19:17).

I described for ease of our understanding that God accepts no righteousness of man. However, it is natural law, which is not the question about whether God accepts the righteousness of man or not. In fact, we are free to do whatever we want. However, not everything is good for us, even though He allows it. If we live in self-righteousness, we will be distant from God.

For example, it is not a bad thing for us to carry a gallon of gas with us. However, we will be burned to death if we are standing before a fire while carrying the gas with us. Accordingly, those who know this will try to force the people carrying the gas to put it down. Self-righteousness is figuratively identical with the gas. No one who has armed himself with self-righteousness can enter the kingdom of God because of that very self-righteousness.

We will be able to understand this statement if we consider the case of the older son in the parable of the lost son. He was armed with self-righteousness. We can see it when he says, "Lo, these many years do I serve thee, neither transgressed I at any time thy commandment:"(Luk 15:29). Because of his self-righteousness, he could not enter the house of his father.

Hence, God shows us now through Scripture that we should not bring self-righteousness to the judgment seat in the afterlife. This is the reason God replaces the coverings of fig leaves made by Adam and the woman.

🗁 What Do the Garments of Skin Mean?

God takes the coverings made of fig leaves from them and clothes them with the garments of skin, and in this instance, the garments of skin correspond to the best robe in the prodigal son parable. The younger son did not himself produce the best robe and put it on. He received it, as a free gift; the father prepared it for him. Likewise, believers are clothed in Christ:

> For as many of you as have been baptized into Christ have put on Christ. [Galatians 3:27]

Paul says those who died with Christ and are born again have put on Christ. That is, they have become those whose sins are forgiven, and they can stand rightly in front of God. Self-righteousness is a makeshift attempt at covering sin, much like the coverings of fig leaves were a feeble attempt to hide nakedness; however, the perfect garments Jesus Christ gives set people completely free from sin.

In addition to the best robe, the younger son receives a ring. It also symbolizes Jesus Christ who is entrusted with all authority.

Read Matthew 28:18:

"And Jesus came and spake unto them, saying, All power is given unto me in heaven and in earth."

and John 5:22:

"For the Father judgeth no man, but hath committed all judgment unto the Son."

Jesus came to this world, entrusted with all authority from God. Therefore, being entrusted with all authority from God represents Jesus Christ, and it is symbolized as the ring in the parable. In Genesis, Joseph gained the confidence of Pharaoh and was entrusted with all authority. Here, he received the same two items as those the younger son received, that is, the robe of fine linen and the ring:

> Thou shalt be over my house, and according unto thy word shall all my people be ruled: only in the throne will I be greater than thou. And Pharaoh said unto Joseph, See, I have set thee over all the land of Egypt. And Pharaoh took off his ring from his hand, and put it upon Joseph's hand, and arrayed him in vestures of fine linen, and put a gold chain about his neck; And he made him to ride in the second chariot which he had; and they cried before him, Bow the knee: and he made him ruler over all the land of Egypt. [Genesis 41:40-43]

Indeed, the ring represents being entrusted with all authority, and it indicates Christ. As a result, the younger son's receiving a ring from his father indicates that he received Jesus Christ.

Further, the younger son received the shoes and ate the fattened calf, which describes life given by Christ. The shoes symbolize the life of preaching Jesus Christ (Eph 6:15), and his eating of the fattened calf indicates that the son will now live his life with Jesus Christ as the bread of life.

The younger son lived a hard life in the far country after having left his father. Having reached total exhaustion, he fell down and realized deep in his heart that the house of his father was the kingdom of heaven. When he repented and came back to the house of his father, his father prepared the best robe, ring, shoes, and fattened calf for his son. All of these items symbolize Jesus Christ.

In the same manner, we will meet Jesus Christ in our lives when we truly repent as the younger son. When the younger son came back home after repentance, his Old Testament faith step was finished, and the step of the New Testament began in his faith journey.

Difference Between the Law and the Grace

Now let us understand the difference between the law and grace by comparing the younger son to the older.

Who is the Older Son?

Let's read the verses about the older son in Luke Chapter 15:

> Now his elder son was in the field: and as he came and drew nigh to the house, he heard musick and dancing. And he called one of the servants, and asked what these things meant. And he said unto him, Thy brother is come; and thy father hath killed the fatted calf, because he hath received him safe and sound. And he was angry, and would not go in: therefore came his father out, and intreated him. And he answering said to his father, Lo, these many years do I serve thee, neither transgressed I at any time thy commandment: and yet thou never gavest me a kid, that I might make merry with my friends: But as soon as this thy son was come, which hath devoured thy living with harlots, thou hast killed for him the fatted calf. And he said unto him, Son, thou art ever with me, and all that I have is thine. It was meet that we should make merry, and be glad: for this thy brother was dead, and is alive again; and was lost, and is found. [Luke 15:25-32]

We may easily think that the older son is not a troublemaker as he never left home and followed his father's orders well. Therefore, we simply guess that the older son gave vent to his anger this one time when he saw his father making a feast for the younger son. If we understand the older son in this way, we may only take the following lesson from this passage: we should not be like the older son, but we should forgive our brothers generously.

However, the parable does not aim at giving such a simple moral lesson. The older son belongs to the genealogy of Cain, who is the first murderer in the Bible, and likewise, he is related to the Pharisees and scribes who have Jesus crucified. If we cannot understand this, we are missing the point of the parable. Because we often believe in God in the same pattern as the older son, we may fail to find the serious problem the older son has.

Jesus compares the younger son who is justified through grace with the older son who tries to justify himself by obeying the law. He clarifies the difference between the righteousness of God and the self-righteousness of man by comparing the two sons. Paul the apostle describes the Pharisees and scribes, who were keen on their own self-righteousness like the older son was, as follows:

> For I bear them record that they have a zeal of God, but not according to knowledge. For they being ignorant of God's righteousness, and going about to establish their own righteousness, have not submitted themselves unto the righteousness of God. [Romans 10:2-3]

The older son did not leave home and obeyed his father's orders for many years. This is what is written in Romans: "they are zealous for God." Nevertheless, he was ignorant of his father's righteousness. As a result, the older son produced miserable results because he stuck to self-righteousness. The miserable results include his failure to join the father's celebration, which will now be described.

Anger of the Older Son

The older son, on his way back after working hard in the field, heard music and dancing and then became angry. He was indignant that his father would celebrate with a feast when his younger brother, who had wasted his substance, turned up. In contrast, the father had not given him so much as a young goat, even though he had worked faithfully at home.

We are inclined to consider getting angry as evil. Here in this passage, therefore, we tend to focus on the anger of the older son. We would say that he should have controlled and suppressed his anger. Yes, he should have done so. In line with this, many preachers of Christianity and seekers of other religions have written best-selling books about how to control anger. However, we will never meet the man who can tell us that he has truly mastered his anger.

Why? Suppression is not the proper approach to anger. The natural emotions God gave us include anger, and hence, we cannot say that getting angry in itself is an evil thing. We should be able to be angry at whatever we have to be angry about. Therefore, if we somehow succeed in getting rid of anger by suppression and self-control, then we have become malfunctioning people who cannot be angry.

Of course, we must control our anger to a healthy extent. But that is not the fundamental solution. In the parable, the main point concerning the older son's anger is not whether he should be angry. Instead, one must consider why he was angry. That is the point.

As we can read and find in the Scriptures, Jesus expressed anger when he called the Pharisees and scribes a 'generation of vipers,' and when he said, "Ye are of your father the devil" (Jhn 8:44). Paul the apostle similarly said, "their throat is an open sepulcher" by quoting from the Scripture (Rom 3:13). These expressions are uttered by angry men. We cannot say that Jesus or Paul is evil, as they got angry because they were certainly righteous men. They are angry at the right things with the right reasons. Thus, anger can be esteemed as either good or evil depending on the man who gets angry and the reason for his anger.

As such, the anger of the older son is not the main issue here. Rather, the main issue is that he does not understand his father's decision; he immediately gets angry at it. He should not be angry at the decision of his father. If he does get angry, he cannot stay together with his father in the house. Here we can see that because he got angry at his father's decision, he had to stand outside the house on his own, in spite of his father's plea.

All the problems occurred because he had a different view towards his brother than his father did. In other words, he should have had the same mind as his father, and then he would have been happy about what made his father happy and angry over what made his father angry. In this case, he could have shared the same view with his father towards the younger brother. And he could have gladly joined the feast instead of staying outside of the house.

The older brother needed to have one mind with his father to stay together with his father in the house. So controlling or suppressing his anger is not the fundamental solution for him in this case. Ultimately, he must have the mind of the father. Otherwise, he may tolerate the father's decision in this particular case, but he could not do so repeatedly.

The Older Son, the Pharisees, and Us

Readers of this parable do not often think deeply about the older son. As to our understanding of him, we generally think the only message is that we should control our temper as Christians, even if we get angry. We think controlling our anger is the deed required by faith and obedience, saying, "As I am the older son, I will try to understand my father celebrating when my younger brother is back. Of course, I will."

We think we will be rewarded in heaven or blessed in some way here for controlling our temper. This, controlling of the temper is, however, the self-righteousness that the Bible warns us about so seriously; it is the useless attempt to become righteous through controlling our temper, which is the work of law.

Please do not misunderstand. I am not saying that we should be out of control with anger, but whilst we are controlling our anger, we should realize that in that manner we could not control the anger at all. Not knowing and not even trying to know that truth, we focus on trying to do something to please Jesus by pledging loyalty through our actions in order to have blessings. We imagine that we will finally be able to say boastfully to God as follows:

"I controlled and suppressed my temper." Or, "I attended every church service according to the Lord's commandments." Or,

"I gave a tenth offering to God. I worked for Him. I fasted, and I donated to poor people."

Do these statements sound familiar? Yes, because the older son said similar statements: "Lo, these many years do I serve thee, neither transgressed I at any time thy commandment:" Also, the Pharisees, having the same nature as the older son, confess as follows:

> The Pharisee stood and prayed thus with himself, God, I thank thee, that I am not as other men are, extortioners, unjust, adulterers, or even as this publican. I fast twice in the week, I give tithes of all that I possess. [Luke 18:11-12]

The reason people continue making these attempts to please God through self-effort is that they have never lived the life of the lost son or the one lost sheep.

In summary, the older son and the Pharisees come to God while in self-righteousness, claiming, "I did something for God." This is faith according to the law.

🗁 To Do Or Not to Do

Often times, a certain man will doubt and ask, "What does it mean if I don't give a tenth and an offering, if I don't donate and fast, and if I don't attend morning service? What if I even rob other men, do something bad, or commit adultery?"

These kinds of questions prove that he has the same faith as the older son and the Pharisees. Since he stays in the same mindset of the older son, focusing on deeds, the above-noted works become a question to him, his focus. Therefore, if he gives a tenth, it becomes self-righteousness to him. If he does not give a tenth, he thinks he is no longer a Christian and his basis that he is a Christian disappears. Hence, he cannot avoid giving a tenth. Consequently, he is always in trouble regarding whether he gives a tenth or not.

Blessed is he who understands that in reality he has the same faith as the older son. Then, he will be eager to grow out of his current position through Jesus. He will be eager to get his eyes off of deeds and onto true repentance.

When he comes out of the older son's position and becomes the younger son, then whether to give a tenth, offerings, donations, and services no longer troubles him. He will do it if he wants to do it, and he will not do it if he does not want to. However, the older son cannot pretend to be in the younger son's position by doing the younger son's deeds. He must become the younger son himself.

🗁 Who is the Pharisee?

Some believers have a faith in which they strive to do something that God can reward them for. Not some, as a matter of fact, but most Christians have that kind of faith. This kind of faith is the faith of the Pharisee. The Pharisee in the Bible is not just a proper noun that indicates a group of Jews who lived in the time of Jesus. This proper noun in the Bible also functions as a common noun that indicates all persons who substantially do the same deeds. Therefore, any persons who believe in Jesus now as the Pharisees did then are, in fact, Pharisees.

The older son in the parable of the lost son represents those who have the faith of the Pharisees. All the works the older son does were troublesome and heavy burdens since he did not go through the younger son's experience, which is true repentance.

Anyhow, it was natural for the older son to long for the reward for the hard work that he had done so far according to the commandments. He was living day by day, eagerly waiting for the judgment day to come so he could receive the reward for his works done.

Finally the day has come; it was when the younger son came home. On that day, totally contrary to his expectation, the younger son was rewarded while he was left to walk back and forth outside the house. Amos 5:18 says to the older son here, "Woe unto you that desire the day of the LORD! to what end is it for you? The day of the LORD is darkness, and not light."

He was driven out of the house because of the self-righteousness he was so eager to earn. This is the principle of God's judgment. We will eventually follow the older son's way if we continue to believe in Jesus without true repentance.

However, most of us do not realize that we believe in God in the fashion of the older son because we think we have already confessed Jesus as our Lord when we first came to the church. We believe that we were born again at that time and will definitely go to the kingdom of heaven when we die. The pastors have said so and many fellow Christians have agreed to it. So we do our best and show our loyalty to Jesus by keeping His commandments. In this way, we think, quite naturally, that we deserve to be at Jesus' side and all that is left before us is to get a reward in the kingdom of heaven.

Unfortunately, reward is what the older son thought about. Jesus spoke this parable to us so that we may see ourselves as we are: those who believe in God as the older son does. We should read and understand the parable accurately.

The Older Son Who Refuses to Go into the House

In general, we think that God leads those who did 'good' for God to the kingdom of heaven and that He punishes with unquenchable fire those who did 'evil.' However, God does not restrict the number and qualification of those who will enter the kingdom of heaven, nor does He push by force a specific man into the hell fire. God will let each person go to the place where he wishes to go.

For example, I like the songs that I used to listen to when I was young. I feel comfortable with those songs, but I do not like today's popular singers that much. Therefore, I go to the concerts of the singers of my age, not to those of young singers, because the young singers are not my style. In the same way, the fans who like the old songs will go to the old singers' concerts, and those who like the new songs will go to the new singers' concerts. The kingdom of heaven and hell are divided according to this principle.

Now, the father asks with all his heart that the older son join the feast. However, the son refuses to enter the house. He cannot stand to see his father cherishing the younger son. It's hard work for him to be in the house. So, he cannot go into the house because it's comfortable for him to stay outside.

As we all know, the father symbolizes God. In the kingdom of heaven, God abides, and we are to stay together with Him. The kingdom of heaven is open to anyone of us so that each of us may enter if we wish. In fact, God invites all of us, be it sinners or righteous men, to enter the kingdom of heaven, eat, drink, and be happy together. However, sinners dislike God. They prefer staying outside the kingdom of heaven in the darkness as the older son, even if God pleads with them many times.

We must think profound thoughts at this stage. If the kingdom of heaven suits a man's nature, he will enter it, and if hell agrees with a man's nature, he will go there. When anyone who dislikes God is forced to enter the kingdom of heaven, it could be hell to him because his nature is against the kingdom of heaven. Here, in the parable, if the older son repressed his anger to go in and join the feast, it would have been a torment for him to be there.

Older Son Is to Be Born Again as Younger Son

What, then, is the solution? The fundamental problem the older son has is that he has never left the house. In this state, even though he follows and keeps his father's commandments, he does not understand the father's mind and gets angry at His decisions. If he truly wants to stay with his father forever, he must set off for a far country, live his own life, repent, and come back as the younger son. This is the only way. He would then understand his father who has accepted the younger son. In that case, he would not necessarily be angry; rather, he would be very much pleased with his younger brother. He would no longer be against his father in his house.

The older son represents those who believe in Jesus according to the law. The meaning that the older son should set off for a far country represents that we should realize that our Christian life has been the life in the far country, far from God. In other words, we should understand that we were misguided in our beliefs, even though we thought our Christian life had been brilliant in the past. With this recognition of our true status, God can then heal us.

Also, each of us is the younger son, having left God and living in a far country. When we truly repent, we will see Jesus and stay in the house of the father, that is, the kingdom of heaven forever. Therefore, anyone who desires to come into the kingdom of heaven must repent now.

In the parable of the lost son, the older son symbolizes the believer who is under the law, and the younger son symbolizes the believer who is under grace. The two sons clearly show the difference between living under the law and living under grace.

Our faith in the church will start like the older son, but we become akin to the younger son when we are born again through Jesus.

Jesus That I Met

Now, I shall complete the contents on true repentance with the testimony of God whom I met in my life.

I am not saying this with the dogmatic mindset that Jesus is the only God around, but it is true that God through Jesus is the only God for all mankind. If I met God according to the sutra, Buddha would be God of all, and if I met God according to the Koran, Allah would be God. Of course, if I met God as is written in the Scripture, then that God is God of all. And yes, truly enough, I met God of the Scripture, and He is God for all mankind.

🗁 How Did Our Family First Go to Church?

I was born in a small town in the middle part of Korea. My family had no idea of Jesus, but they started to believe in Jesus because of me. According to what my family seniors have told me, my life was threatened because of severely loose bowels when I was two years old. My grandmother offered Buddhist masses with much effort and also took me to a famous hospital in order to make me live, but I did not get well at all.

One day, her acquaintance living in the same village suggested going to church and praying to God for my healing. My family had no faith that I could be restored from illness if they went to church. However, they had no further choice because they had been to many Buddhist temples and hospitals; hence, they went to church according to the neighbor's advice as a drowning man would catch at a straw.

They were attending church and praying without great expectation, so they were greatly surprised when I gradually became better and finally got over my illness. This miracle led our family to the church. My aunt sometimes tells me when seeing me, "You led our family to church." But sorry, I have no memory of it. That is only what I have heard from the elders of my family.

Since all my family attended church services, I also naturally went to church. After having moved to Seoul, I was going to church; however, it was always a burden to me. When I heard the sermons, I felt very sleepy and the sermons did not move me at all. My wife also happened to be a Christian, and I attended church with her. I had no confidence that I would go to the kingdom of heaven if I went to church, but I did so habitually.

At that time, I was working for a company and the company repeatedly asked me to transfer overseas apart from my family. I finally decided to tender resignation, but I had no plans as to what to do after my resignation. However, I had a vague thought in my mind that I could do anything.

🗁 Private Small Business

After quitting that job, I rented a shop in the downtown area in Seoul to start selling clothes. Before opening the shop, my wife suggested a shop-opening service led by the pastor. At that time, I was not very well acquainted with the pastor because I was not so eager for the church life; in fact, I sat in the rear row of the pews. So, it was a bit awkward for me to call him. However, I invited him to my shop, and he offered a service with the hope of successful business. The pastor kindly came and prayed for me and for the prosperity of the shop.

Notwithstanding my sincere wish and the prayer of the pastor, the business did not go well, and I had to close the shop before one year had passed. The causes of my failure can be analyzed in many ways, but the only reason was that I was not in good relationship with God, which I realized much later.

I failed in clothes sales, but I could not sit still because I had a family to support. I had to think of other things to do, so I met with friends, looking for possible business opportunities. I was ashamed of myself as a jobless man when I would meet any friends whom I had not met for a long time. I would pretend that we were close friends in order to network for job prospects.

Whilst wandering around, I happened to get in touch with a high school friend living in the United States. He gave me a very good business idea. He advised that I should import baby oils from the U.S. and sell them in Korea. Further, he told me to attach my private label to the baby oils when importing them. In this case, I would give credit that the products were 'made in USA,' but I could secure the trademark rights with the sole selling rights in Korea.

This business intrigued me so much. It could give me the opportunity to visit other countries on business and counsel foreigners about transactions in good manners with formal suits on. How could it be compared to my past during which I wore plain clothes and wandered in the market with bundles of clothes over my shoulder early in the morning? Further, if my private label became known to many customers and sold well, I could be honored to manage big manufacturers in the U.S. as my subcontractor. I thought, "Now my life will get underway."

I was so excited that I had a restless night. I made up my mind and started this business. However, differing from my dream and the throb of joy in my heart, it progressed very slowly. Since the U.S. manufacturer had no experience in exporting their products, they did not react promptly to my requests. After many problems that spanned more than a year, I received one container of baby oils.

However, contrary to my expectations, these oils did not sell well. The baby oils had a big market because women used them for oil massage in bathhouses. When I first ordered them, similar products were selling at good prices in the market, but when they arrived in Korea, the market price had been reduced to be near to the import cost. The price went down because other importers also imported other brands of baby oils at the same time, and the country was then oversupplied. I missed the opportune time of selling them because the goods came in far later than I expected.

Even though the baby oils did not sell well, I could not give up the idea of this private label business. I kept on trying to find other products. I gathered some samples of lipsticks and nail polishes and listened to the opinions of potential customers before importing more.

I was totally giving myself up to the work, looking for businesses to make money. My sister-in-law also heard of my move, and she prayed to God. She told me of God's reply to her prayers: "The Lord says you are called to be a missionary, so you are not to do such business. You'll suffer a greater loss than the case of baby oils if you import other products."

I felt very uneasy when I heard this. I thought, "Even the missionary needs money. What do I do while I have nothing to eat now?" I got angry at her and said, "Hey, why do you step in my way instead of blessing me as you see I'm planning a new business to make money?" Because of this, I was uncomfortable with her for a long time.

I knew it later that God called me through what she said to me. However, I was spiritually deaf and could not hear it as the message of God.

🗁 Getting a Job at a Foreign Company

When the baby oils were just imported, I saw a job opportunity advertisement in the newspaper about a foreign company. I briefly thought to apply for that company, but I soon threw the paper down because the job was far from my career path. However, the company came to mind again a few days later. Since the baby oils would arrive in Korea late, I thought I had better submit an application because their marketability was uncertain.

So, I filled out the application form and submitted it. I found out later that a few hundred applications were submitted. Fifteen persons were selected and were given an interview at a hotel. Strangely, I was the first interviewee, and I felt it in my bones that the interviewer gave me a good score during the interview. As a result, I was finally singled out from among the applicants. I used to think it was very peculiar that I was chosen as I was following a totally different career.

As a matter of fact, I did not apply for the work with a big dream. I, who quit the previous job because I hated the office worker's life, was not greatly attracted by the new start as an office worker, and I had no great expectation because it did not pay much. I applied for it as a temporary shelter from the passing rain. However, I worked for the company for the longest time in my office worker's life.

I still longed for the baby oils to sell well, even after having entered the company. However that business did not go as I wished. I was finally beaten.

🗁 Trouble in My Body

I was entirely frustrated after having sequentially failed in the office worker's life, fashion store, and the sale of imports. I could find no satisfactory way to live and wondered how to feed my family. If I were young, I would have a dream, but I was forty years old and felt miserable and hopeless, having nothing to try. The foreign company was only makeshift and gave me no comfort.

One day in the summer when I was disappointedly working for the company without any earnest desire, I was resting on the sofa at home without a jacket. My wife looked at my back and told me, "Ah, you have spots on your back."

I was shocked to hear her say that. The AIDS epidemic had appeared as the serious social problem, and all the people were scared of it. I worried about that disease, wondering if I was affected with it. Therefore, her comment really surprised me. After that time, I became indisposed. I felt itchy on my arms, and I felt like a log in my whole body. I knew it by intuition that my illness was serious.

However, since I could not talk about it in public, I was in great trouble all alone. In the summer of the year, I traveled to an island on the western shore together with my brothers-in-law and sisters-in-law. They were all having fun playing cards and swimming, but I was in trouble all by myself and feeling lonesome, far from them.

In the autumn, my health became worse. I traveled to Busan on business. I tried to carry a shopping bag with some books in it to be distributed to the agents at the hotel, but I could not lift it. How could I be so powerless that I could not even lift a shopping bag with some books in it? In despair, I burst out crying on the bed.

After weeping for a long time, I telephoned my sister-in-law in Seoul, wanting her to tell me the will of God. Even if she knew God's will very well, I did not respect her so much because she was actually living a very hard life. However, in those days, it did not matter. I only wanted God to save me from this desperate situation, so I called her. She, however, did not answer to me clearly. All she said was, "I want you to come to Seoul. I will talk with you then." Even after I met her when I came back, I could not get satisfactory answer.

At that time, the fear of AIDS was the major social issue, and the press and broadcasting stations reported it in competition. Naturally, fear and attention about the disease were reaching the climax. A man in his sixties was infected with it during a heart operation. In despair, he tried to commit suicide with his wife by cutting his artery, but they failed, and she was also infected with it. She appealed to her husband to kill her, and he finally choked her to death. It was very shocking news. Whenever reading such news, I was seized with the fear of death. I wondered, "Do I have the same disease?"

My fear was reaching its peak. If I was really affected, I thought everything would be over. I reasoned that my kids could not go to school and my family would be completely ousted from society. This kind of thought made me feel heavy in the chest and at a loss.

I went to a Chinese herb medicine shop. I knew that if I went to a general hospital, doctors would examine my body in many aspects to identify the disease. In contrast, the doctor at the Chinese herb shop would only examine my pulse for diagnosis; hence, I did not need to be afraid of feeling the unrest that would be caused by the identification of such a socially unacceptable disease. I trusted the Chinese herb shop because I got well after taking the herb medicine prescribed by the doctor when I once had a cough in the past. He examined my pulse and told me that my liver, kidney, and stomach were bad; he prescribed herb medicine to take for twenty days. I took it wholeheartedly, wishing complete recovery from my illness.

However, I gained no improvement in my illness. I gained further confidence that I had my back to the wall because even the famous herb doctor could not heal me.

One day I went to the bookstore to search for writing about AIDS, but I could not find any hope of remedy except one that I guessed wouldn't be developed until I was already dead. I was afraid someone would tell me to get examined as I frequented the bookshelves packed with the books on AIDS.

I went to the public health center to learn more, and I also called the National Institutes of Health and asked some questions at a public pay phone in the street: "What are the symptoms of the AIDS?" A man replied to me that it was not an easy question to answer over the phone. After hanging up the phone, I was nervous about whether a caller tracking system might be in place.

However, I could not give myself up to despair, so I took great courage to go to the Hospital. It was the greatest courage I had ever summoned. I went to the internal department and waited for my turn. I was full of all fears while I was waiting. I kept thinking, "What if I am diagnosed to have the disease I am afraid of?"

On this thought, I just wanted to rush out of the room without any medical examination. While I was in a great conflict in my mind, my turn came before I could leave. The nurse called my name and then said something very unexpected to me, "You should come again tomorrow because the doctor in charge of you is off today." I had been to the same hospital to see the doctor when I had bronchitis, and now she said that he must examine me. I did not ask her, "Why should I see the same doctor?" But, I returned home saying to myself, "Well done."

When I prepared myself to go to the hospital again the next day, my mind changed abruptly. I lost the courage to have myself examined because I dreaded that I could be diagnosed with AIDS, the last period of liver cancer, or other incurable diseases.

This feeling must be similar to that of the person in the news who jumped down from a building to kill himself (without having had a medical examination) because he was afraid he was infected with AIDS. The autopsy determined that he was not infected with it. However, he thought within himself that he must have been infected with it, and he finally committed suicide. People easily say, "He would have been fine if he had himself examined once." However, I now saw that it is not easy to submit to a medical examination, especially if one is confident of having such infection.

Anyway, I could not go to the hospital because of fear, and I got worse during that time. My acquaintances asked me why I looked so pale, so I was thought that I was the man who had incurable disease.

🗁 Thinking of Dying

When this condition lasted for two to three months, I had to think of my death. There was no other way. I regularly attended church services, but I did not believe in the existence of heaven and hell. Rather, I believed that when people die, that is the end of everything.

I believed that if I died, my being would be extinguished for good. Considering that the cows or pigs consumed by us have a life, but we have no trouble killing them, I thought my guess was right. Also, even if we do not kill them, the animals in nature devour one another according to the law of the jungle. Presuming these things, I thought that God established this kind of law because everything was over when the creature is dead. If not, God will have to judge the tiger having eaten the hare. Because of this reason, I thought that human beings become extinct completely when they die. After having concluded death happens in this way, I feared death no longer.

However, I had one thing left to do before I died; it was to make arrangements for my family. I have a son and a daughter, who were elementary school students at that time, and I was about to send my son to the family of my older brother and my daughter to the family of my younger brother so that they could be raised. I thought my wife could manage by herself somehow because she was an adult.

I felt uneasy as yet, even though I arranged my family in my mind in this manner. If I had made sufficient money, I could have left it for my family and could have breathed my last in peace. Alternatively, if there had been a trustworthy guardian who could take care of the bereaved, I would have left all for him and then have died peacefully.

However, I had no fortune because I failed in the life of an office worker and also in the business world. Also, I had no reliable guardian whom I might ask to help in the support of my family. I felt an agony of mind when I had to think of dissolving my family. But, what else? That's all that I could do.

I proposed a final trip to please my wife because I knew I would die soon. I liked to stay at home, but she, having an outgoing personality, liked traveling. She was very happy to hear about my plans to travel, not knowing what I was thinking about. We drove the car to the eastern seashore and stayed at an inn there. When I woke up to turn on the TV in the morning, I watched a program showing the hopeless death of those who are infected with AIDS. She watched the program in a serene state of mind, but I could not put up with it because I thought I would be like them sooner or later. I rushed into the bathroom and washed my hands and face and waited in there until the program was finished.

When we returned home from the trip, I told her all about

my fears for the first time, to prepare her for my death. She would not believe that I had a fatal disease. Anyway, I became light-hearted after unburdening myself of the troubles by speaking out. Death seemed less frightening because I told everything to her.

However, as I thought more about it as time went by, I felt pain when I thought about my son and daughter. I worried, "Will they be ridiculed at school as those having no dad? Will they get along well with their cousins?" All these thoughts troubled me, and I could not stand the stress of the troubles. I thought of every scenario and reached the conclusion that I should die as the final escape from these problems. However, when I thought about my children, I found that even death could not be a solution. I could not leave them, so I had to spend each day with affliction and severe torment.

When these thoughts came to mind while driving, tears would stream down over my cheeks. I frequently thought of driving the car and falling from the cliff. My wife comforted me in many ways, which encouraged me, but I was in pain and trouble again after a couple of days had passed. It was because her consolation could not be a root solution.

One day, I was coming home with my wife. She stared at me, troubled in the car, saying, "Why don't you go to a prayer house and pray to God? He will cure all the diseases." I instantly said to her, thinking she was ridiculous, "Hey, if I could be healed in the prayer house, who would ever die of any disease in the world? Everyone would go to the prayer house to pray and be healed, and nobody would die of diseases." I flatly refused her offer.

Really, it was so to me. I could not believe I would be healed if I prayed to God in the prayer house. Never!

🗁 Seeking God

One day in September in the days of inevitable despair, I laid by myself alone in my room, thinking one thing and another. I really could find no way out of my desperate situation, not even through death. My situation at that time was inexpressibly dismal; I was in total despair.

While I was pillowing my head on my arm and lying on my side on the floor, hot tears ran down over my cheeks, and I then wept bitterly. Bending like a hunchback, I was crying, full of sorrow. Many thoughts flashed through my mind. I could say a lot of excuses about myself, but eventually, I was a loser in my life. It was very sorry and sad for me to finish my life in this miserable way. I wept and wept for a long time, and thereafter, I sought God, not knowing myself.

I prayed in mind, "God, I am wrong. If it is true that I was affected with this disease because I was not eager for church services, I'll go to church seriously from now on. It is not a big problem to die, but I must live further in this world until my kids have grown up to stand on their feet. This is not the right time for me to die."

I sought God very eagerly from the bottom of my heart. At that time, I guessed that He got angry with me and consequently allowed this thing to happen to me because I was not a sincere believer.

I knew it later that my confession at that time was true repentance towards God for all of my life. I worked for a company, managed my own shop, and imported some items so that I might live somehow in this world. However, I folded up. Now, I was too sick to encounter the miserable situation in which I could not die even if I tried to do so. Therefore, I sought God at last.

I was a prodigal son of Luke 15 who came to the end of his tether and confessed, "I perish with hunger here!"

🗁 Jesus Came to Me

After having wept and sought God from deep in my heart, something was changed in my mind. When my wife suggested going to the prayer house a few days ago, I scolded her saying,

"It's nonsense," but now the following thought came across my mind:

"What have I got to lose if I go to the prayer house?"

On Thanksgiving Day, I changed my schedule and went to the prayer house instead of going to my hometown. When we arrived there, the entire service schedule had been finished with the early morning service of the day, and all the people there packed their belongings and left for home. There was nothing much I could do. I prayed in the service hall, bought a couple of sermon cassette tapes, and got home.

After the fruitless visit, it repeatedly occurred to me that I was to find another church service. So, for a long time, I went to a church located south of the river to attend the Friday night service. My home was located north of the river that time, and I ran to the church every Friday without hesitation in spite of the long distance. No one forced me to do so, nor did I reach the conclusion that I should go there through reasoning. I did so because I was moved in the heart.

When I had been attending for about twenty days, I found out that I gained strength again and the itch on my skin disappeared. It was early October. I have never felt any greater joy in my life than this. I cannot express with words the sense of freedom I had from the desperate condition in which I could neither live nor die.

🗁 Who Healed Me?

While enjoying my sense of freedom from the disease, a thought occurred to me: "Who on earth healed me?"

If a doctor had healed me through an operation, I could say the doctor healed me. If I had gotten well when a pastor laid his hands on me, I could say the pastor healed me, but I could not say who healed me. I had a vague impression that my healing was connected with the church, but there was nothing manifest about my healing, and my question grew.

I wondered if I was healed because my blocked bloodlines were accidentally opened when I woke up in the morning and stretched myself, or if I was made whole by the food I ate by chance. Or, did Buddha heal me, having pity on me? If Buddha was God, he could have compassion over his creature and heal the same, even when the creature believed in Jesus and got ill.

Anyway, in November, one Sunday, while having this question, I attended service at the church. I had never heard any sermon seriously until then.

🗁 Where Are the Nine?

However, the sermon of that day was something out of the ordinary. That week was Thanksgiving Week in the Korean Churches. The title of the sermon was "Where Are the Nine?"

The corresponding passage was Luke 17:11-19. In summary, when Jesus entered a certain village between Samaria and Galilee, ten lepers came to Him, begging him to have mercy on them and heal them. He did not lay His hands on them, and He also did not make clay of the spittle and anoint the eyes of the lepers with the clay as He did to the blind man. He just said, "Go show yourselves to the priests." As they heard Him and went to the village, their bodies were cleansed. One of them who was healed turned back to Jesus and gave Him thanks, glorifying God. Jesus said to him: "Were there not ten cleansed? But where are the nine?" Jesus sought the nine, and said to him who turned back to Him, "Thy faith hath made thee whole."

I began to shed tears unceasingly not long after the pastor began to give the sermon. I felt my heart break when I thought I was like one of the nine who were healed but did not turn back to Him.

The pastor continued, "Many people say, 'Jesus, heal me first, and I'll obey You. Bless me, and I'll be loyal to You. Show me signs and wonders, and I'll trust You.' However, these words run counter to the principle of faith. Jesus wants us to obey in advance."

Especially, when he repeated, "If you do me something in advance, I will be obedient and loyal to you" for the third time, my heart almost froze. I talked to myself, "I understand what you mean. Why are you saying it again and again?" and "Please stop it." He stopped fortunately after repeating three times. If he had repeated it once more, I would have fallen to the ground from the pew. I felt that a man could possibly kill another with words only.

As a matter of fact, at that time I was thinking I would believe in Jesus ardently, only if I could see a believer around me blessed greatly.

Anyway, when the pastor finished preaching and the congregants sang the hymn "Amazing Grace," the service of that day seemed to be prepared only for me. I felt shy when having found that I was the only person who wept while the others did not, but I was unable to control the shedding of my tears. I wept on and on and on, feeling like my heart was torn. I met Jesus Christ on November in my life in this way, who came to this world two thousand years ago.

After these events, the Lord always stays with me. While walking with the Lord, He has shown me various truths many people could not imagine.

🗁 True God

After having heard my testimony, some people ask what the name of my disease was, but I have no idea because I was scared of any medical examinations. I knew it later that my disease was not incurable. However, God allowed me to think that my disease was incurable so that I would surrender to Him. When I went to the hospital for an examination, He did not allow me to have myself examined. If I had myself examined at that time, the doctor would have said I had no big problems. Then God's plan to make me repent would have failed. And when I went to east shore, He made me watch the AIDS program on TV to press me for repentance.

Other people, having heard about my story, think that I was healed, not by the works of God, but by misunderstanding. That is, they say it would have been a miracle and a work by God if incurable AIDS or the cancer had been healed. But my disease was that which would be healed automatically, and as such, my case is no marvel at all.

When some people heard my testimony and responded in this way, I felt sorry for myself, saying, "Good Heavens! I could testify more impressively if He had healed me after the doctor had diagnosed my case as a cancer in the terminal stage or as AIDS."

Quite recently, I found that my confession is more valuable than the testimonies of those who had been healed of cancer or AIDS. It is because God, whom I experienced, is the very God found in the Scripture. Referring to 2 Kings, Chapters 6 and 7, in the time of Elisha, Samaria was besieged by the army of Ben-hadad, king of Aram, and many people hungered to death in Samaria. God made the army of Aram to hear the noise of chariots, horses, and a great army. On hearing, they thought that the king of Israel has hired the Hittites and the Egyptians to come on them. They arose and fled in the twilight, leaving their tents, horses, asses, and even the camp (2Ki 7:6-7).

However, in fact, the Israelites were suffering from a famine and trembling with fear in the city, and they had not hired the kings of the Hittites or the Egyptians. God made the Arameans hear the false noise of an army in order to make them withdraw in fear. They misheard it as the sound of a real army and immediately withdrew from there. They did so out of misunderstanding, which God had developed.

Of course, God could have made fire fall from heaven in order to make then withdraw. However, He did not do so. Instead, he deceived them with the noise of the army to make them withdraw by themselves. Isn't this God much more God-like?

God deceived me by using the same method that was applied

to the army of the Arameans. He threatened me that I was really incurable, and I was accordingly deceived like the case of the army of the Arameans. I surrendered to Him. God who took care of me is the very God who took care of Israel against the army of the Arameans some three thousand years ago.

We hear of many cases in which God actually healed people. However, it is not usual for God to deceive a man and fulfill His purpose like in my case. In this sense, my experience is more valuable and my testimony is more precious than the actual healing. Therefore, I further appreciate God who has worked this way. I do not feel sorry at all and do not say, "If only He had healed me from a real disease."

After reading my testimony, some people ask what made me think that I had AIDS. I would answer that God made me think this way. Nevertheless, that is not the point of this testimony. The point is to share how God appeared to me, worked in me, and healed me. I hope all of us get this point.

Epilogue

I left God for a far country, this world, as a prodigal son. I tried every effort to manage to live in this hard-to-live far country, but all my plans ended up in smoke. I was taken ill, and I was finally left behind as a straggler in the society. Only at that time, I realized that I was the sinful man who left God all long. Then, I could not help stretching my hand to God, and He held it tight by allowing me Jesus. Since then, I have been following Jesus, leaving all other things in the world behind.

Thus, the New Testament period of my faith began.

Up to here, I have described true repentance, which corresponds to the stage of Matthew in the faith-growing steps.

4

STAGE OF THE SYNOPTIC GOSPELS — FOLLOWING JESUS

The person who has passed the stage of John the Baptist will meet Jesus Christ in his life. When we meet Jesus, we will follow Him, leaving everything behind. This period represents the Synoptic stage (Matthew, Mark, and Luke) of faith, and it can be called "Following Jesus."

In a sense, an individual's entire Jesus-believing process could be called the period of following Jesus. However, the period from the time when we meet Jesus to the time of crucifixion is specifically mentioned here as "Following Jesus," because that is the only period when Jesus appeared in the flesh to be followed by disciples.

Jesus sequentially appeared to His disciples first as 'Jesus in the flesh' (from the first meeting to the Crucifixion), second as 'Jesus of resurrection' (from the Resurrection to the Ascension), and third as 'Jesus of the Holy Spirit' (after Pentecost). In this instance, the period referred to as "Following Jesus" indicates the time when Jesus appeared to the disciples as 'Jesus in the flesh.'

When reaching the Synoptic stage, we forsake all and follow Jesus. During this period, we met Jesus in our life and truly experience that God is alive. So, we follow Him above anything else in the world. No one urges us, but we attend church ardently, give tithes and offerings, and join church activities unsparingly. Also, we pick up the Bible that laid aside in the room, brush away dust from it, and start reading it, or we might buy a well-decorated Bible. The reason why our lives come to be changed is that we start listening to the voice of the Lord Almighty.

We hear the Lord and obey Him. He trains us and disciplines us in earnest. This period is the best time for the Lord to discipline us. Since we were dead towards God before we met Him, we did not know whether we were chastened by God or not, even when we were, indeed, chastened by God. Of course, we have no idea of the will of God hidden in the chastening. Therefore, chastening cannot work perfectly. However, when we start to hear the Lord, the situation will change. The Lord exposes and heals the parts to be corrected in us through intensive discipline. It can be a very hard time for us who are His disciples.

If we go through this stage with Jesus completely, then we will be born again, saved, have our sin forgiven forever, have the life of Jesus, have the faith of Jesus, and enter the kingdom of God.

Those Who Cannot Follow Jesus

The period of following Jesus will be given only to those who have repented truly in their lives like the prodigal son. Many people try to follow Him according to their will, without true repentance, but they cannot follow Him. It is because they will surely change their minds and return to the world anytime they meet a struggle while following Him. Therefore, only those who failed in the world totally can follow Jesus.

Consider this passage:

> And a certain scribe came, and said unto him, Master, I will follow thee whithersoever thou goest. And Jesus saith unto him, The foxes have holes, and the birds of the air have nests; but the Son of man hath not where to lay his head. And an-

other of his disciples said unto him, Lord, suffer me first to go and bury my father. But Jesus said unto him, Follow me; and let the dead bury their dead. [Matthew 8:19-22]

When a scribe says he will follow Him, He says he cannot do so because He has no place to lay His head. We may easily understand this dialogue by thinking that He refused him because Jesus had no house and no room to accommodate him. However, it is not so. That is clear when we read the next verse in which He says to another disciple to follow Him by letting the dead bury their dead.

If He had a room to give to the disciple, the latecomer, He would also have room to give to the scribe, the first-comer. So, His yardstick to allow people to follow Him does not depend on whether He has enough room for them or not.

Then, why did He refuse the man who was ready to follow, and why did He say, "Follow!" to the man who actually was not ready because he had to bury his father first? In order to meet Jesus and to follow, we have to repent truly first. True repentance is the only prerequisite to following Jesus. So we can assume here that the scribe did not repent truly, so he could not follow, even though he said he would. But the disciple did repent, so he could follow Jesus, leaving everything, including the burial of his father, in obedience to Jesus.

Then what would be the true meaning of the words Jesus said to the scribe? When we truly repent, Jesus will have a place in our heart and mind, playing the most important role in our lives. That is why we follow Him, leaving everything. On the contrary, the mind of the man who did not truly repent is filled with various worldly lusts and desires that control his life. This man can follow Jesus, but he does so to achieve his worldly desire.

Jesus said that there is no place for Him to lay His head. The head is the control tower of our body. If we truly repent, Jesus is laying His head inside of us. Then we will be able to follow Jesus, our Head, leaving all behind.

But in the scribe's case, there is no place for Jesus to dwell in his mind because foxes and birds of the air work as his head. In this state, even if he tries to follow Him, Jesus will only be used as a tool for achieving the goals of the foxes and birds of the air. We will know later that the foxes and birds of the air signify things of the world, and Jesus did not come to give such things to us. He came to give us a new world, which is the kingdom of God. To achieve it, Jesus, not foxes nor birds, should work as our head.

Foxes

What are the foxes and the birds of the air in the Scripture?

> The same day there came certain of the Pharisees, saying unto him, Get thee out, and depart hence: for Herod will kill thee. And he said unto them, Go ye, and tell that fox, Behold, I cast out devils, and I do cures to day and to morrow, and the third day I shall be perfected. [Luke 13:31-32]

King Herod symbolizes the power of the world and the desire to rule and be exalted. Jesus says that Herod, wanting to kill Him, is the fox. When mentioning that foxes have holes, He points out that the scribe has Herod, the fox, in his heart, and he follows Him only in order to fulfill his dream. Jesus rejected his request because the scribe cannot hear Him and follow Him as long as his heart is full of pursuing the power of the world.

This story is not for the scribe only. It is also our story. We long to receive spiritual gifts and great power for the purpose of doing the works of the Lord or for the growth of the church. However, we should watch ourselves carefully to check whether internally we seek to exalt ourselves with these gifts and power when our wishes have come true.

Most of us will not think this could be true of us. However, if we think in depth, we will know that such prayer aims at our own personal desire. Accordingly, if we pray to God, not knowing the personal desire in our hearts, we would be same as the scribe here who wished to follow Jesus with the hole of the fox in him.

🗁 Prayer of Pastor's Wife

Not long before starting ministry at my current church, I used to frequent a church located near my home to do daybreak prayer. At that time, I was still registered with the church in Seoul because I had only recently moved to this area. So I was attending the church nearby for daybreak prayer for convenience.

That church had recently opened; seven to eight persons attended the morning service and prayed. I was really happy to attend the services of this church close to my house. I was not late for the daybreak prayer, even if I woke up fifteen minutes before the prayer time. I used to quickly wash my hands and face and leave for the church. And I felt at ease, even if I went with disheveled hair, since I met no acquaintances.

In those days, a woman, looking like the wife of the pastor, always sat in the very last seat, praying to God by saying, "Let this church be big in local areas;" "Send many people to this church;" "Allow great power to the pastor."

Hearing her prayer, I guessed that she was the pastor's wife. She seemed mainly to pray for the growth of the church.

One morning, she was praying for great growth in the church as usual, and she cried and prayed very sincerely to God. I, hearing it, was moved by her sincerity. And I prayed to God in my heart: "Lord, let this church grow rapidly, and let many people come!" The Lord said to me in my heart as soon as I prayed, "She is praying with avarice!"

On receiving this word, I had to think for a while. I was dazed at His unexpected, instant response, and I did not know what to do with it. Wondering if it might be originating from my own thoughts, I returned home and prayed again about it. The Lord convinced me that it was coming from Him. At that time, I understood the message as a warning that I must beware because I could also pray with greed for the rapid growth of our church.

However, this situation was not to be resolved as I wanted it to be. The next day, I told this story to one of my brothers in Christ. He said to me that I must tell her about the response of God. He added, "She will understand you because she is the pastor's wife."

Upon hearing this, I thought that it would be impertinent of me to convey such a message to her while I was not a member of that church. Furthermore, if I spoke to her, she might get angry with me and she might say, "How dare you say it to me? You will not be welcomed here any longer." In that case, I would have to look for another church for daybreak prayer, leaving a most suitable church.

I accused my brother in my heart, and I thought he told me to approach her because he did not fully understand the whole situation. Therefore, I concluded it was not a message to her, but I took it to be for me as a warning. So, I ignored his advice speak to her.

The next day at daybreak prayer she was, as usual, praying eagerly for the church to grow. Looking at her, I felt troubled in my mind. While clearly knowing that her prayer was not being welcomed by God, I felt that it was not right to watch her quietly like that. However, I returned home without saying a word since I did not have the courage to speak to a woman who was a stranger to me.

I attended daybreak prayer the next morning, too. It was the end of the year. During the sermon, the pastor said that he would be going to the prayer house with his wife at the beginning of the New Year, so the daybreak prayer service would stop for a while and start again in three days. Having heard that, I felt I should tell her about the message of God immediately; otherwise, it would be too late. So, I firmly decided to tell her.

When the pastor finished the sermon, individual members began to pray to God. I prayed to the Lord to allow me a good opportunity to tell her and to let her receive the message without anger. As the time approached 6:00 a.m., most people finished their prayers and went home. Only some were left still praying. The pastor was praying at the pulpit, and his wife was praying in the rear row. I was sitting in the pew just before her. I girded myself and encouraged myself. I told her, looking back,

"Well, you prayed for the rapid growth of the church for a few days, didn't you?"

She was speechless for a while, not knowing what was going on, and then she agreed by saying,

"Yes."

Maybe she thought that undeniably it had been her usual prayer. I continued to say,

"Upon hearing your prayer, I was moved, so I also prayed for the growth of this church. However, the Lord responded to me that you were praying to fulfill your greediness. The Lord wants you to pray for the glory of God." I could not bring myself to tell her just as He expressed, "You are praying with avarice." I changed the message to "You are praying with greediness."

She answered, bewildered,

"Oh really? Please pray for our church."

Fortunately, she did not get angry with me. This was different from my expectation. She, however, may have thought inwardly, "What a stupid guy talking nonsense!"

I prayed a little further after the dialogue with her, and as soon as I stood up from the pew to go home, the pastor likewise finished his prayer, saw me, and smiled at me, saying,

"Hallelujah! Welcome."

I had never had a chance of talking with him during the past daybreak prayer services. Having seen him welcoming and smiling at me, I instantly sensed God's smile in his smile. I could see the gladness of God there. God was happy with my obedience to talk to her.

Anyway, that day passed in such a difficult way, and some more days passed. The pastor and his wife returned to the church from the prayer house. After that conversation, I felt awkward with her each time I saw her at daybreak prayer.

One day, to my consternation, she called me. She said,

"You're a deacon, right?" She continued saying,

"When you told me that message, I had no idea what the Lord intended to tell me, but now I have found out. Thank you for telling me. Please let me know if He tells you something for me from now on."

I was very pleased to hear this. I felt as though a heavy and big burden was lifted. It was the Lord who initiated all these series of happenings to convey His message to her, and He finally fulfilled His will.

Even if we pray for the growth of churches and missionary works, we can pray with our own avarice. This avarice is the Herod, i.e., the fox, symbolizing the power of the world in the mind of those who decide to follow Jesus. It is very difficult for us to see this in our mind by ourselves because everything is wrapped up with the name of God. Our avarice is wrapped up with church growth, missionary works, preaching, and aid to others. Therefore, it is not easy to detect such hidden avarice.

Some days passed until she found the fox in her by the leading of the Lord. The foxes existing in our minds must be disclosed. If not, we will be one of those who cannot follow Jesus, even if we may try very hard, like the wife of the pastor. The Lord let her know her hidden faults since He loves her. She also was of a mind to welcome the Lord. Therefore, she could receive the word of a stranger, whom she could easily ignore, as the word of God, and then she could repent and obey.

Birds of the Air

We are now back to the Scripture. The scribe has the birds of the air in his mind, so Jesus cannot work in him. Here, we need to know what the birds of the air mean. The birds of the air also appear in the parable of the sower:

And he spake many things unto them in parables, saying, Behold, a sower went forth to sow; And when he sowed, some seeds fell by the way side, and the fowls came and devoured them up: Some fell upon stony places, where they had not much earth: and forthwith they sprung up, because they had no deepness of earth: And when the sun was up, they were scorched; and because they had no root, they withered away. And some fell among thorns; and the thorns sprung up, and choked them: But other fell into good ground, and brought forth fruit, some an hundredfold, some sixtyfold, some thirtyfold. [Matthew 13:3-8]

The parable of the sower is also recorded in Mark Chapter 4 and Luke Chapter 8 in addition to Matthew Chapter 13.

When the seed/word falls on those whose mind are the 'wayside', there appears a 'being' that takes the seed/word away from their mind so that the seed may not grow and bear fruit. The 'being' is expressed as the 'wicked one' in Matthew, as 'Satan' in Mark, and the 'devil' in Luke.

I may need another chance if I am to explain the wicked one, Satan/the devil, in detail. In short, this is not a monster with ugly and dreadful looks as we traditionally think. They represent thoughts that arise in our mind which are against God's will.

For example, when someone receives a true word of God with gladness and tries to act on it, he may consider the word to be out of line with traditional theological interpretation or doctrine and therefore reject it. This is the example for the birds of the air that eats up the seed/word that was sown on the field of his mind.

The birds of the air, the wicked one, always provoke us to seek the well-fed, well-clothed, well-being life in this world. So, the delusion is strong and sweet. When Jesus said the scribe has bird's nests in his mind, it means that his mind is full of thoughts of worldly welfare. The scribe cannot follow Him, even if he tries hard, because he is not ready yet to receive Jesus' word, which would speak against his worldly desires.

Then, how can the scribe ever follow Jesus?

He should become exhausted and collapse and realize that his life is filled with nothing more than vanity and futility; then he may wish to abandon such a life. Only then will the holes of the foxes and the nests of the birds of the air lose their power in his mind. This is the true state of the heart of a man who has truly repented.

Nevertheless, in a spiritual sense, at this stage, he is actually employing Jesus as his 'head' in order to achieve worldly goals. But Jesus will lead him to the kingdom of God, which he will realize only when he really gets there.

In the quoted Scripture passage, Jesus tells 'another of his disciples' to follow Him, even though the man has an urgent need to bury his father in this world. Jesus called this other disciple because he truly repented and was ready to follow Jesus rather than the foxes and birds in his mind.

Jesus told him, "Follow me, and let the dead bury their dead." Who can follow Jesus' word, unless he is the one who has truly repented? In this instance, the first 'dead' represents the spiritual dead, those who are not concerned about the truth but are engrossed in the life of the world, and the second 'dead' indicates the physical dead, those who have breathed their last and left the world.

🗁 The Place Where Jesus Goes

Where does Jesus go by the way? The final destination of Jesus is the bodies of the disciples. Jesus brings the kingdom of God to His disciples when He has come into the bodies of the disciples as the Holy Spirit after the cross.

Therefore, the place where Jesus goes is not a place with a good view in this world, nor is it in the heavens. It is inside the disciples, each one of them. This is what Jesus meant when he said he allows his disciples to stay where He is.

John 14:23 says, "Jesus answered and said unto him, If a man love me, he will keep my words: and my Father will love him, and we will come unto him, and make our abode with him."

Jesus wants to make His home within us. He can achieve this when he functions as our 'head'. However, it will take a long time for Jesus to work as our true head. In the disciples' case, it took three and a half years. After this period when Jesus manifests in the disciples' minds as the Holy Spirit, then Jesus is working in the disciples' minds.

Jesus came to this world in order to live inside of every believer; when we believe right.

Requirements for Following Jesus: Self-denial

> Then said Jesus unto his disciples, If any man will come after me, let him deny himself, and take up his cross, and follow me. [Matthew 16:24]

What is required for us when following Jesus is to deny ourselves and take up our own cross. Jesus does not do it for us. Each of us following Him should do it on our own.

Salvation represents the entire process in which our old man is cast out of us and Jesus Christ comes on us to stay forever. The old man controls us before Jesus comes on us, i.e. before we are saved. The life controlled by the old man surely reaches a time when we finally fail, and we are exhausted and fall down. It is the time of true repentance as already explained in the previous chapter.

However, the old man has not been perfectly destroyed at this point. (More on this issue later.) Those having passed through such an experience are able to hear the voice of Jesus Christ and can follow Jesus. Jesus now will finish our old selves. In the case of His disciples, this process took three and a half years. This is the period of following Jesus and the time of self-denial.

In this passage, the word *our* in the phrases 'our old selves' and 'meet Jesus in our life' indicate each one of the readers individually.

🗁 What is Self-Denial?

Many people decide to follow and believe in Jesus. They attend church and confess that they believe in Him and will follow Him wherever He may go. Jesus says to them, "If anyone would come after me, he must deny himself and take up his cross and follow me" (Mat 16:24).

What does it mean for one to deny oneself? What is his cross? If we wish to follow Jesus, we should deny ourselves. In other words, following Jesus is self-denial. Therefore, if a man has no idea of what denying himself means, he has not followed Him up to this point. To him, following Jesus makes no practical sense; he doesn't see how to live it out.

However, self-denial and taking up the cross are the essence of following Jesus.

When the will of the Lord is different from one's own plans, denial represents giving up your own will and following the will of the Lord. It is real! Denial doesn't just happen in the mind; we must live it out. Here, the will of the Lord does not mean the law written with letters in the Scripture; it means the guidance given by the Lord in real life.

Among those who decide to follow Him, there will be few, if any, who intentionally fight against the will of the Lord. The main reason why we do not deny ourselves and fight against His will is that we do not know His will in our lives. To those who have no idea of His will, denial has no meaning at all. That is, if we are to deny ourselves, we must suffer the case in which our will is against His will, but while we do not know His will, we get no opportunity of denying ourselves. Therefore, the denial of oneself is only applicable to those who met Jesus in their lives and hear Him.

Accordingly, the current section you are reading will be hard to understand if you have no experience of hearing the Lord. However, if you read this article seriously, it will lead you in this direction.

God Speaks to Everyone

A blind man cannot see, not because there is nothing that exists, but because he has a problem with his eyes. Let's compare this example to God's leading. God reveals His will through any and every means. For example, He is revealed through sermons preached from the pulpit, Scriptures, experiences, newspapers, movement given in the heart, and other available methods. However, many people do not know what God says in these ways. So they lead their lives not knowing His will, even though God speaks to them continuously during their lifetime.

If we are to follow God, we should first seek the will of God. However, it is not so easy to catch God's voice and sense it because our old selves reign over us. So, if we are to know the will of God, we need a long-time under the law. When this time is up and we meet Jesus, we will gradually see and hear the will of God through Jesus. Only at this time will the opportunity of self-denial be given to us.

Denial of oneself is to take up one's own cross and follow the Lord. Jesus took up his own cross and was crucified on the same cross. When we take up the cross of self-denial, our old selves will die on that same cross. In other words, when we have lived lives of self- denial, our old selves die as a result.

Now, I should like to share one of my testimonies when I denied myself and took up my own cross in this stage.

Daybreak Prayer

I am a 'sleep late in the morning' type of person. I had never attended daybreak prayer, even after I started to regularly attend church, and I never dreamed of beginning to do so. Further, it was my thought that it would look miserable and defeated for a man to go to the daybreak prayer service. Even after I met the Lord, this opinion of mine about the daybreak prayer did not change. The daybreak prayer, a unique service, is not found in the Scripture, and it is not usually performed in other countries. I felt confident that daybreak prayer as performed by Korean Christians was a man-made system initiated by some over-zealous Christians.

Further, considering that the churches in Korea developed and institutionalized the overnight service and the midnight service in addition to daybreak prayer, I judged these services to be foolish and stupid because the participants chose a difficult worship time in order to torment themselves whilst the Lord did not ask them do so.

Also, when we think about the case of the famous foreign pastors who are blessed by God, apparently they do not perform daybreak prayer, the overnight service, or the midnight service. No need to discuss this further, it was quite obvious to me that it was not necessary to perform these difficult services in order to please God.

After I met the Lord, He never told me about daybreak prayer. It was the last thing I expected. However, one day, about one year after I met Him, I woke up and was brushing my teeth in the bathroom. He told me suddenly, "Attend daybreak prayer!" This word did not come to me when I was thinking about the availability or uselessness of daybreak prayer. It came into my heart unexpectedly.

At first, I thought long and hard about where this particular thought came from. I wondered if it was given by Satan. But he would not take the initiative in suggesting daybreak prayer. Consequently, I admitted that the message was given by the Lord. So, even though daybreak prayer did not suit me well, I started it at a church close to my home the next day, full of joy about the fact that He directly told me to go. The service started at 5:00 a.m., so I got up at 4:20 a.m., washed my face quickly, and went out to the church.

🗁 Daybreak Prayer Was Not Easy

However, it was not so simple and easy to attend daybreak prayer regularly. When I attended it, the rhythm of my day went to pot, so I worked in a state of exhaustion all day, and the people whom I met asked me why I looked so tired. I was attending the prayer session under tremendously difficult conditions. As days went by, it became a heavy burden to me, and it was a sort of torture to me. I would have soon stopped it if it had been the pastor or someone else who had persuaded me to do it. However, it was a commandment from the living Lord, so I could not easily stop.

While dragging myself to it for some months, I happened to read some books. The author of the books criticized the hypocritical faith of Christians who base salvation on works. In short, he stated that works, such as tithing or doing church activities, are not what brings true faith to us. His writings impressed me for a long time. Then I started to wonder whether the Lord would really want the daybreak prayer from me.

One day, I returned home from a difficult daybreak prayer session and was sitting on the sofa. At that time, the following passages of Scripture flashed across my mind:

"For my yoke is easy, and my burden is light" (Mat 11:30),

"For they bind heavy burdens and grievous to be borne, and lay them on men's shoulders; but they themselves will not move them with one of their fingers" (Mat 23:4),

"The thing that hath been, it is that which shall be; and that which is done is that which shall be done: and there is no new thing under the sun" (Ecc 1:9).

These three verses were combined together in my mind, and the Christianity of today seemed to be imposing heavy loads on me as that of the Pharisees and the scribes of the old times. I was very happy to realize this, and I slapped my hand on my knee, thinking, "Yes, right! The Lord does not want me to labor under daybreak prayer!" I thought that the keeping of the Lord's Day, collections, fasting, and daybreak prayer were man-made things that made believers carry heavy burdens on their shoulders.

After that day, I did not attend it any longer, and I became free from the pressure of daybreak prayer. A friend of mine, watching me enjoying the freedom to the full extent, was also troubled, wondering if he was attending daybreak prayer in vain.

However, since I could not be completely disconnected from the burden of attending it, I woke up one hour earlier than usual and prayed at home for about forty minutes to one hour before leaving for office. However, since I dozed over the prayer at home, my prayer time gradually decreased as days passed. I immediately slept when I felt tired. I found at that time that praying thirty minutes in church was better than praying an hour home.

Anyway, I quit attending the daybreak prayer service in that way. After that, I found an acquaintance who had met the Lord later than me but had grown faster spiritually than me in many aspects. For example, he had received the spiritual gift of speaking in tongues. I got uneasy and nervous. I knew then that I had something wrong with the Lord.

One day, I asked my sister-in-law, who used to help me spiritually, for advice. Having prayed to God, she told me, "When I prayed to God, 'Lord, shall I suggest daybreak prayer to him?' The Lord said, 'The guy will not listen to me!'" Her word pierced me and I found that I was spiritually blocked because I had stopped attending daybreak prayer.

🗁 Starting Daybreak Prayer Again

Getting back home, I repented and prayed to the Lord that I

would start to attend daybreak prayer again. When I was just finishing the repentance, my sister telephoned me. She just happened to call me, but she also began to talk about daybreak prayer. She said, "I know a man and a wife in my church. The man went to the daybreak prayer with his wife for a couple of days, and then he said it would be terrible to attend it for good."

Thinking about it after hanging up the phone, I found the will of the Lord from what my sister said to me. That is, He was saying to me, "If you will go to daybreak prayer, do it all your life." I felt terrible, but unavoidably, I said I would. I begged the Lord to lead me to the good way. After the vow, I felt very bitter against my sister who had phoned me and talked about daybreak prayer. I felt like telephoning back and shouting at her, "Why did you telephone me uselessly?" However, it is manifest that all these things are not coincidental but the Lord's program.

When I got up from the bed next morning to go to prayer, the Lord told me two Scriptures verses:

> But I keep under my body, and bring it into subjection: lest that by any means, when I have preached to others, I myself should be a castaway. [1 Corinthians 9:27]

> And one of you say unto them, Depart in peace, be ye warmed and filled; notwithstanding ye give them not those things which are needful to the body; what doth it profit? [James 2:16]

The Lord let me realize through James that even if I confessed that I believed in the Lord but I did not actually follow His commandments, I was not acting fully in His will. Through 1 Corinthians, I saw that I should be more determined in believing in Jesus than before.

Recollecting it, I had first received the commandment of the Lord, "Do daybreak prayer," with gladness, but my mind had been changing little by little because it was a heavy burden to actually attend the prayer. Not realizing the fact that it was my own reluctance, I tried to find an excuse to stop it. At that very time, I encountered the message through reading books that attendance to the daybreak prayer had no great importance. That was the message and the logic I wanted to hear, so it sounded to me like a word of grace.

Anyway, I restarted daybreak prayer and I fasted three days from that morning to show God my humbleness.

🗁 Grumbling Against God

Even if I started with a brand new mind, it was still difficult for me to attend always. Had He given me a spiritual gift, I would have attended the prayer times more easily, but I was not sure if I had received any gift from Him. I got the feeling that I had been driven into a corner.

One day, returning home from daybreak prayer in the morning, I thought my circumstances were very miserable. Tears streamed down my cheeks, thinking that I had to do this painful work for the rest of my life. I thought, "There are a lot of people who do not do daybreak prayer, so why does God give this hardship only to me?"

"Why me? I am so unfortunate to be trapped by an evil god." I deplored my circumstances. And I hated those, over-devoted to Him, who created daybreak prayer, and I called them names. I had no idea how long I had to do this and why He allowed me these difficulties. I thought He was cruel in making me suffer the agony. Instantly, I talked to myself. Calming myself, I said, "Not this way." I tried to drive this blasphemy out, resisting it. I wanted to think that He intended to give me good things in life.

When I got back home, I had a nap before going to work, and God gave a message to me through a dream. In the dream, I was driving a car and was about to make a U-turn on a crossroad where a signpost saying "No left turn" was posted. There was no signpost of "No U-turn," but I was not sure whether a U-turn was allowed at this point, so I made a U-turn hesitatingly. While making the U-turn, the cars coming rapidly from the opposite direction dodged my car with difficulty.

A traffic police officer, watching me from a distance stopped me. I defended myself and won him over by saying, “If you excuse me now, I will also do you a favor when you ask me a favor.” Graciously, he told me to be more watchful henceforth, and he let me go. However, his leniency was not a result of my persuasion. When he was approaching my car, he was already wearing a smile and did not mean to ticket me. Then, I came out of the dream.

It was a warning from God concerning the blasphemy that I had in my mind in the morning. The police officer in the dream represented God. Again, He told me through Hebrews:

> Lest there be any fornicator, or profane person, as Esau, who for one morsel of meat sold his birthright. For ye know how that afterward, when he would have inherited the blessing, he was rejected: for he found no place of repentance, though he sought it carefully with tears. [Hebrews 12:16-17]

Since the Lord gave me a promise that He would use me as a very rare servant all over the world, I thought I could not give up daybreak prayer with which God was pleased. I decided firmly that such blasphemous ideas should not control me any longer.

After that, if I happened to sleep late and failed to attend the daybreak prayer, I was afraid of being scolded by Him. If I sometimes missed something He told me to do, I was scared of His fierce hand. I went to daybreak prayer with severity and hardship.

Here, the reason why I provided this portion of my testimony is not to advise you to do daybreak prayer or not to do it. I am telling you that the Lord, whom I met, disciplined me and trained me through daybreak prayer, which was one of the hardest things for me to do. If anyone reading this book is currently going through this kind of process with the Lord, please be comforted that you are not the only one.

In meeting the Lord and following Him, we will encounter a lot of tough discipline, and this is the essential course of self-denial.

Let us look at the self-denial case of Peter.

Peter Rebuked Severely

For him who hears the voice and the will of the Lord, the New Testament period begins. Now, the process of perfect self-denial will be opened to him. The Lord can scold us as when he told Peter, "Get behind me, Satan!" (Mat 16:23). If scolded in this way, we may be shocked and experience great pain. The pains in the heart that we feel are unspeakable. Only those who have suffered them will understand it. However, it is ultimately a blessing to be rebuked by the Lord because His rebuke manifests that the individual already met Jesus and has the faith of the New Testament period.

Therefore, even though we are rebuked, we should not leave Him or feel deeply discouraged. If we do, our faith-growth will naturally be delayed. Nevertheless, when rebuked, many believers do not receive His rebuke as a blessing and therefore leave Him. It means that they still desire to seek something in the world, like Lot's wife. However, they will eventually come back again someday when they have filled up on the vain experiences of the world. Then, they will not leave Him, even if rebuked by Him severely.

🗁 Get Behind Me, Satan!

Let's think about the process by which Jesus made Peter, the typical follower, clean by washing him with words and destroying his old man. Read the following verses:

> Then Peter took him, and began to rebuke him, saying, Be it far from thee, Lord: this shall not be unto thee. But he turned, and said unto Peter, Get thee behind me, Satan: thou art an

offence unto me: for thou savourest not the things that be of God, but those that be of men. [Matthew 16:22-23]

Peter forsook all to follow Jesus. On the coast of Caesara Phillippi, Jesus asks him, "Whom do men say that I the Son of man am?" Peter here made the very famous confession: "You are the Christ, the Son of the living God" (Mat 16:16).

The Lord says to him that He will build His church upon this rock, and He promises him the keys of the kingdom of heaven. Peter becomes encouraged by this praise. Jesus then explains to His disciples that He must go to Jerusalem, suffer many things, and be killed.

Peter became over excited and rebuked Him: "Be it far from you, Lord; this shall not be unto you." Jesus then severely scolds him: "Get behind me, Satan; you do not have the things that are of God but those that are of men."

We do not feel serious about Jesus' words because we read it as it applies to Peter, and we do not think of how it applies to ourselves. If we are scolded by Him this severely, we would almost faint. Only he who has suffered this sort of rebuke can understand how painful it would be.

In general, we cannot easily understand why the Lord scolded Peter. It seems very natural for Peter to stop Him after hearing Him say He will be killed. If we were in Peter's shoes, we would have said the same thing. Why did Jesus scold Peter so severely? To understand this, we first think about why Peter was dissuading Him from being killed. Judging from the scolding, Peter's dissuasion was not of God but of man. Peter's motivation to stop Him from being killed was based on the things that are of men.

Here, the things that are of men represent Peter's carnal profits. From Peter's point of view, Jesus' death would be a disaster. Peter thought that he would be rewarded for forsaking all and following Him when Jesus became a king in this world. If He died on the way, all Peter's efforts would end in smoke. So Peter tried to stop Him. Jesus wanted to disclose this mindset of Peter and scolded him to correct him.

Since the old man of Peter concealed itself most of the time, Peter could not realize this. Jesus wanted to show Peter the hidden old man. He thus prepared this happening on purpose. He praised him greatly to make him walk on air, and then He immediately says He will be crucified to induce the next interaction. When Peter tried to dissuade Him from death, He scolded him seriously in a sharp tone of voice as if He had been waiting for this protest. Peter must have been hurt, but he surely began to examine himself on this occasion. And, he realized that he plotted the things that are of men, not knowing what he was doing.

Through this interaction, the old man in Peter, of which he had no idea, was exposed, scolded, and corrected. Many people will not agree with this viewpoint immediately. Furthermore, it will be very difficult to accept that Jesus induced Peter's fault. However, it is true.

This interaction is not only limited to Peter. If we think a little further, we will know that all of us believe in Jesus with the same mind of Peter. Jesus points out that such faith is not the right faith through the case of Peter.

Therefore, the key point of this dialogue on the coast of Caesarea Philippi does not lie in the famous confession, "You are the Christ, the Son of the living God." In light of the severe scolding of Peter after this confession, we can know it does not have a great meaning as we traditionally think. At the time of this confession by Peter, he was not yet changed to be a man worthy of that confession. Therefore, his confession proceeded out of his mouth, irrespective of his state of faith.

For example, if a man who has lived a long and sufficient life comments on life, his word will be a true confession. However, if a very young man argues a point about life, his word cannot be a true confession. The inward man and the spoken confession do not match in the case of the young man. Peter's confession was something of that kind.

🗁 Why Did Jesus Praise Peter?

If you have followed me up to here, you may have a question rising in your mind. That is, why did Jesus praise Peter so much if he confessed only with his lips?

Hearing confession from Peter, Jesus said to him as follows:

> And Jesus answered and said unto him, Blessed art thou, Simon Barjona: for flesh and blood hath not revealed it unto thee, but my Father which is in heaven. And I say also unto thee, That thou art Peter, and upon this rock I will build my church; and the gates of hell shall not prevail against it. And I will give unto thee the keys of the kingdom of heaven: and whatsoever thou shalt bind on earth shall be bound in heaven: and whatsoever thou shalt loose on earth shall be loosed in heaven. [Matthew 16:17-19]

All Christians would hope to hear such praise from Him. When praising Peter, He praised the very word he said. In other words, although Peter had not yet grown to be a man who could confess the Lord as Christ, his word was the truth. So, He praised him based on the truth.

The Pharisees and the scribes are examples of those who preach the word of truth, but they themselves are not men worthy of it. Under such circumstances, they preach and confess only with their lips. However, the words they spoke are still the truth. Therefore, Jesus said in Matthew 23:3, "All therefore whatsoever they bid you observe, that observe and do; but do not ye after their works: for they say, and do not."

We can find many cases in the Scripture in which God takes the words of man and infuses them with another meaning. For example, the Jews wrote the superscription of His accusation over Jesus: "The King of the Jews." They said it to mock Him, but God accepted it with a greater meaning: "The King of everyone who believes."

Also, the word of the high priest Caiaphas who was at the head of crucifying Jesus is another example. When the Pharisees and chief priest plotted to crucify Jesus, Caiaphas receives a revelation of God:

> Nor consider that it is expedient for us, that one man should die for the people, and that the whole nation perish not. And this spake he not of himself: but being high priest that year, he prophesied that Jesus should die for that nation; And not for that nation only, but that also he should gather together in one the children of God that were scattered abroad. [John 11:50-52]

Caiaphas said the intention of having Jesus killed was to make the people keep quiet, but God used his word as proclamation that Jesus would be as a ransom for the sin of many people. Here, Caiaphas spoke the word He gave to him, but it was not a confession reflecting his true motives. Nevertheless, since he was the high priest, God had the profound intention of having him proclaim that Jesus was a ransom.

Jesus listened to Peter's confession and praised him according to this logical connection. At that time, he was not yet changed to be a man who could make a confession such as, "You are the Christ, the Son of the living God," based on his spiritual growth. However, He accepted and praised Peter's confession on the right side on purpose. Therefore, strictly speaking, Jesus did not praise Peter. The praise was intended for everyone who confesses out of his or her spiritual growth, "You are the Christ, the Son of the living God." Jesus proclaimed the blessings such a man would receive.

🗁 The Nature of Faith of Peter at That Time

Peter met Jesus when he felt the limitations of his fisherman's life. He was attracted to Him who had fishing abilities far greater than he. Further, since Jesus had great power to walk on water and heal the sick, Peter determined to follow Him. He tried to get, through Jesus' hand, what he could not get through his own power. However, at this vital point, he misunderstood Him. Jesus did not come to give Peter many fish, great power, or a high position. What He wanted to give was the Spirit of Christ.

As described, since the party to give and the party to receive had different minds with each other, Jesus conflicted with Peter frequently. All kinds of discord originated from these different mindsets. While Jesus leads him and corrects him according to His will, Peter's heart frequently gets hurt. So, he sometimes gets angry and has a mind to quit following Jesus.

Anyway, Jesus intended to expose the thoughts of Peter's old man through this incident and rebuked him in order to purify him. This is the spiritual purification process of sinners who are following Jesus. He employed this same process with the disciples who were following Him during the three and half years before the crucifixion.

Where Is Your Faith?

The following scene was also planned by Jesus to reveal and purify the wrong thoughts of the disciples. The faith of Jesus and the faith we understand are different. Because of this difference, those having started to follow Him are frequently scolded. There are those in the Bible who were models, playing the difficult roles of being scolded and corrected by Jesus; they were Peter and the other disciples. What they learned then is what we are to learn now. He wants us to grow in faith as the disciples did:

> Now it came to pass on a certain day, that he went into a ship with his disciples: and he said unto them, Let us go over unto the other side of the lake. And they launched forth. But as they sailed he fell asleep: and there came down a storm of wind on the lake; and they were filled with water, and were in

> jeopardy. And they came to him, and awoke him, saying, Master, master, we perish. Then he arose, and rebuked the wind and the raging of the water: and they ceased, and there was a calm. And he said unto them, Where is your faith? And they being afraid wondered, saying one to another, What manner of man is this! For he commandeth even the winds and water, and they obey him. [Luke 8:22-25]

One day, Jesus, together with His disciples, set sailed for the other side of the Lake of Galilee. As they sailed, He fell asleep, and at that very time, there came a storm of wind on the lake. It appeared that they were about to sink. After making their own vain efforts, they awoke Him out of sleep, and He arose and rebuked the wind and the raging of the water, and they ceased. There was calm. He scolded the disciples, "Where is your faith?" Heedless of His scolding, they were struck with wonder, saying one to another, "What manner of man is this! For He commands even the winds and water, and they obey Him."

After reading this story, we conclude, "Yes, Jesus is the man of power who can control the winds and raging water as He pleases. It's very good to believe in Him." We also think that He scolded them because they were afraid of death in the winds and waves while Jesus Almighty was with them. We learn that we must be strong in faith so that we will not wake Him when the winds and water come in our lives. However, this story is not given to afford such lesson to us. Shall we go further?

🗁 Faith the Disciples Had

Fundamentally, the faith the disciples had at that time was generated within themselves when they saw His power, and they intensified their will to believe in response to it. Considering them who acclaimed the power of Jesus after He had calmed the wind and the waves, we can easily guess that their faith originated from themselves. This means that by watching the miracles of Jesus the disciples are determined to have faith in Him. This kind of faith is of men. Faith that comes by through self-discipline is not the true faith Scripture calls for. It will be changed anytime their mind changes.

However, we often accept this kind of faith without giving it serious thought. According to this understanding of faith, we analyze the behavior of the disciples and reach the conclusion that they were scolded by Him because their minds wavered with the winds and raging water. It is a natural consequence. However, such faith is not true faith of Scripture. It is the faith that is of men. True faith comes from God: "For by grace are ye saved through faith; and that not of yourselves: it is the gift of God" (Eph 2:8).

Faith, the Scripture says, is not of men, but it is given by God. The gift of God represents the Holy Spirit. When the Holy Spirit has come on us, we will have faith from God. The Holy Spirit was given to us when Jesus was crucified. The faith that the disciples had at that time was not the gift of God, but it was made in them.

However, even if their faith was not of God, it was stronger than the faith we have now. It is because our faith is generated when we know and believe in Jesus through the Scripture, two thousand years after the events recorded there occurred. In contrast, the disciples' faith was made when they directly saw His power. Therefore, we dare not judge them or think that we have stronger faith.

It would be a big mistake if we think they cried, "Master, master, we perish," because they had no faith. They had greater faith than we.

🗁 Natural to Wake Him

Since the winds and waves were high and the ship was about to sink, they were compelled to wake Him. Think about it. If they did not wake Him while they were dying, their reluctance could not be seen as an act of faith. In fact, it would actually be an expression of their unbelief, meaning that they thought it would be of no use to wake Him up.

For example, even though I had attended church for a long time, I did not pray to Jesus when I was experiencing difficult conditions. It was because I thought I would gain nothing from Him through prayer. If I believed I could receive something through prayer, I would have sought Jesus and prayed to Him ardently. So, the fact that they awoke Him when they were in danger proves that they had great faith because they trusted that the problem would be solved once He woke up. Such behavior should not be criticized.

🗁 Faith of Jesus

If their faith was, in fact, strong, why did Jesus rebuke them saying, "Where is your faith?" The faith that Jesus refers to here differs from the faith that the disciples understood him to mean. He wanted to show them the faith He wished to give through this boat trip, which is also applicable to us. However, His intention was veiled to their eyes, as it is also veiled to our eyes now.

He talks about faith that is totally different from the faith the disciples had at that time. This faith represents the faith the disciples would have after He was crucified and had come on them as the Holy Spirit. In a way, the Holy Spirit that comes on believers is the true faith the Bible speaks of. It is faith that is not of man; rather, it is the faith of Jesus given by Jesus.

🗁 Location of Faith

The faith of Jesus did not come on the disciples when they followed Him. It came on them when He was crucified and came as the Holy Spirit. Hence, He spoke of the faith they would have in due time after His crucifixion. When He comes again with faith as the Holy Spirit, His coming is inside of their bodies.

Therefore, His word, "Where is your faith?" could possibly have a double meaning.

First, it is a rebuke meaning, "I can't find any true faith in you. Where is it?"

Second, it could be that Jesus is asking them to check whether the location of their faith is inside the disciples or outside of them. Of course, at that time, the location of their faith was outside of them because the location of Jesus, the author of faith, was outside of them. However, when He comes on them as the Holy Spirit after the crucifixion, the location of faith becomes inside them, which is the right and true faith of a man.

True faith is Jesus Christ Himself who is to come into us. We cannot speak of faith before He has come into us. By saying, "Where is your faith?" He wanted to reveal what the true faith is to disciples and us. Where is your faith now? Is it outside of you, or inside of you?

Even though Jesus revealed what true faith is, the disciples did not understand what His words meant at all. That was because they had not matured sufficiently at that stage. Nevertheless, He speaks about the way in which they should go, and He leads them in that way. They would understand what He had said after all the things that happened to them.

Before they had grown or matured to that stage, they were still concerned about worldly things. When He calmed the winds and water, they were attracted to His great power, saying one to another, "What manner of man is this! For he commands even the winds and water, and they obey him." As I previously said, faith that is developed in this way is not true faith.

During the 'following Jesus period,' the disciples were destined to deny themselves and to take up their own crosses. In this way the disciples were purified and healed spiritually by Jesus.

We too are to go through the same process as the disciples to be purified from our sins once and for all.

All these things are happening during the course of "Following Jesus," the stage of the Synoptic Gospels in the faith-growing steps.

Now, I will proceed to the stage of John according to the faith-growing steps.

5

STAGE OF JOHN — BORN AGAIN

In the faith-growing steps, the stage of John represents the time when a man is spiritually born again. This spiritual rebirth can be called the perfection of faith.

Take for example a tree; this spiritual rebirth corresponds to the state in which the tree bears fruit. Being born again means that the old man dies and is born again to be a new man; the man who was a sinner is changed into a righteous man by Jesus.

Being born again has the same meaning as salvation. However, salvation in this case does not mean going to heaven rather than hell after death. The salvation the Scripture speaks of indicates that a man, while living in the world, enters the kingdom of God.

Meaning of Being Born Again

Now, we shall start with 'being born again,' a familiar expression to us. Being born again corresponds to the stage of John in the faith-growing steps following the order of the Bible's books. So, being born again is mentioned in the Gospel of John, Chapter 3.

Being born again is generally accepted as the change in which a man who was caught up in the world changes his mind, comes to the church, joins church activities, and regularly attends services. However, the phrase being born again in the Scripture indicates a completely different meaning from such general opinions. It shows the state of a man full of grace and truth since the Word was made flesh and dwelled among us (Jhn 1:14).

Shall we read what Jesus said about being born again? Regarding being born again, we always think of the dialogue between Jesus and Nicodemus:

> There was a man of the Pharisees, named Nicodemus, a ruler of the Jews: The same came to Jesus by night, and said unto him, Rabbi, we know that thou art a teacher come from God: for no man can do these miracles that thou doest, except God be with him. Jesus answered and said unto him, Verily, verily, I say unto thee, Except a man be born again, he cannot see the kingdom of God. Nicodemus saith unto him, How can a man be born when he is old? can he enter the second time into his mother's womb, and be born? Jesus answered, Verily, verily, I say unto thee, Except a man be born of water and of the Spirit, he cannot enter into the kingdom of God. That which is born of the flesh is flesh; and that which is born of the Spirit is spirit. Marvel not that I said unto thee, Ye must be born again. [John 3:1-7]

🗁 Did Nicodemus Ask Jesus a Question?

Nicodemus, coming to Jesus by night, basically says, "I have been watching what You have done, and I have seen the signs and wonders You have performed. I know from these signs that God sent You and He is with You." Jesus answered and said to him, "Except a man be born again, he cannot see the kingdom of God."

Regarding this dialogue, the Scripture says Jesus 'answered' and said to him (Jhn 3:3). If we read it carefully, Nicodemus never asked Him a question. He only accepted that God was with Him. However, Jesus, whether knowing it or not, answered him and described how a man can enter the kingdom of God. This was not Nicodemus' question.

Did Jesus mistakenly understand what Nicodemus had said and answer to him as such? Maybe not. In the literal sense, Nicodemus did not ask Him any question. However, his words were a question, even without the traditional questioning style. Jesus, knowing all, read his mind and gave him an answer to the question in his mind. Before explaining the answer by Jesus, I will first describe what question was hidden in Nicodemus' words.

🗁 Conflicts in the Mind

Up to the time when Nicodemus visited Jesus at night and confessed to Him, "God is with You," he had his own background story. He was a typical figure who served God with all his heart and efforts. He behaved himself according to the Scripture and led an exemplary believer's life.

He did not kill, did not commit adultery, and did not steal. He fasted, prayed, gave alms, and gave tithes. He was naturally admired and praised by people. Many tried to take him as a role model of faith and tried to imitate him. However, differing from what people thought, he felt unceasing doubt, conflict, and futility in his faith life. The Scriptures imply this by saying that Nicodemus came to Jesus by night which symbolizes non-truth.

This kind of conflict is natural and common to those who believe in Jesus without meeting the true Jesus, i.e., the living God. Under these circumstances, no matter how hard they may try to believe in Him, their faith will always be based on the law. This kind of faith will not resolve the conflict in any way because it is incomplete faith. This kind of faith is legalistic faith.

Nicodemus had legalistic faith. Jesus and Nicodemus read and talked about the same Scripture, but the interpretation by Jesus was different from his, and above all, He showed miracles and signs that would only be possible with God in Him. Nicodemus was sure that he believed in the same God as Jesus, but he could not do as He did. Quite naturally, Nicodemus was seriously wondering what was wrong with his faith. Therefore, he came to Jesus and confessed to Him that "God is with You" (Jhn 3:2).

The inner meaning of his statement was really a question, "How can I have such faith that God is with me, just like You have?" It was not framed as a question but Jesus, knowing the heart of Nicodemus, responded to his question and gave him the answer. Therefore, the Scripture says, "Jesus answered and said unto him."

Such zeal toward true faith gradually changes Nicodemus. He later defends Jesus, and after His crucifixion, he came with a mixture of myrrh and aloes to use in preserving His body (Jhn 7:50-51; 19:39). These passages hint at the changes in Nicodemus because of Jesus.

Like Nicodemus, there are a lot of people in churches who believe in Jesus without meeting the true Jesus, the living God. Naturally, God cannot be with them and is not with them. Faith, without meeting the living God, raises conflicts and questions in our minds about whether we currently believe in Him rightly or whether God is really alive. He who has such conflicts and questions in his mind will seek Jesus as Nicodemus did and will ask Him, "How can I have the faith of God with me?"

The conflicts within Nicodemus are natural and desirable because they drive him to seek God, the true Jesus. However, we tend to avoid such good opportunities to seek the true Jesus. For instance, when these troubling thoughts occur to us, we consider that we must have fallen into temptation, or we console ourselves by saying, "All other Christians believe in Jesus with these conflicts in their mind and all those people can't be wrong." However, we should know that these conflicts can lead us to the true Jesus, and we should seek the living God at this excellent opportunity.

Do not be troubled by this question: "Nicodemus could meet Jesus, but where can we go now to meet Him?" We can now meet Jesus at the very place where the word of the living God is preached. Here and now!

Kingdom of God

We have already found that Nicodemus' confession was really a question asking, "How do I become a man with whom God abides, and how can I be one with God?" Jesus answered him by saying, "Except a man be born again, he cannot see the kingdom of God." It means if a man wants to be one with God, he should enter the kingdom of God, and if he wants to enter there, he should be born again.

To understand this word, we should first have the correct knowledge of the kingdom of God. This word will not make sense as long as we think the kingdom of God is a place we enter when we die. If this were true, the dialogue between Jesus and Nicodemus would be ridiculous. Nicodemus might ask, "How can I be one with God and walk with Him?" The answer would then be, "You can do it when you are dead and go to heaven."

Nicodemus wanted the life of being one with God here on earth, like Jesus. In other words, he asked Him about the way of walking with God while he was alive, not about heaven, which he would enter when he died.

In explaining the kingdom of God on a theological basis, scholars often say the kingdom began some two thousand years ago when Jesus came to this earth, and it will be completed at His visible Advent. However, He states here that being born again is entering the kingdom of God. It does not make sense that a man should wait for His visible glorious second coming to be born again.

🗁 **The Kingdom Comes When I Am Changed**

We generally think that when this world has changed to be a good place to live in, it will be the kingdom of God. So many people take pains to change the world to make it the kingdom of

God. However, the true kingdom of God is the world that we see with a changed viewpoint after we have welcomed the Holy Spirit. That is, when we have been changed to be one with God, we then see a different world, which is the kingdom of God.

It is as if we are born with red-colored glasses on, and we see the world and all things under the sun and judge them through these spectacles. Because we look through them, everything we see always looks red, even if we try hard to see things as they are.

Therefore, if we want to change the world, we should correct our eyes through which we see the world. We should take off the colored glasses covering our eyes. Then, the previous world disappears and the new heavens and new earth open up. This is the principle for the kingdom of God to come on a man. The kingdom of God should come inside us so that we may perceive it. When it comes outside us, we have no way to recognize it.

In the movie *The Gods Must Be Crazy*, an airplane flying over African Bushman territory drops a Coke bottle. Sho picks it up and returns to his people with it, and they make a fuss about it. We know it is a Coke bottle, but he has no idea of it. What is the difference? We already know what a Coke bottle is, so we instantly know it when we see one. However, he is not familiar with it, so he could not recognize it when he sees it.

If we have no recognition of the kingdom of God in us, we cannot perceive it, even if it is provided to us. Therefore, in order to recognize it, it should come first inside us. Then, we can see it.

In fact, it exists here and now. However, we cannot see it because we have no kingdom of God inside us. Jesus makes us see the kingdom of God that exists here through our rebirth and the changes that take place within each one of us. This is how the kingdom of God comes on us.

So, now we know that the kingdom of God is not a certain kind of Utopia that is located here or there. It does not come outside of us, but it comes inside us. The one into whom the kingdom of God has come is he who has entered the kingdom of God. We should enter it while we are living.

It is within believers:

> And when he was demanded of the Pharisees, when the kingdom of God should come, he answered them and said, The kingdom of God cometh not with observation: Neither shall they say, Lo here! or, lo there! for, behold, the kingdom of God is within you. [Luke 17:20-21]

The Pharisees expected the kingdom of God would come in front of their naked eyes, but Jesus said it would come inside the man. Therefore, the kingdom of God does not come on all men at the same time. It individually comes on the person who takes off his colored glasses through Jesus Christ. With this right understanding, many difficult passages in the Scriptures are solved spontaneously.

Consider Mark 9:1: "And he said unto them, Verily I say unto you, That there be some of them that stand here, which shall not taste of death, till they have seen the kingdom of God come with power."

Some two thousand years have passed since Jesus said this word, but the kingdom of God has not yet appeared before us. Did he lie to us? No. He came on earth, fulfilled all, and returned.

Do not take it the wrong way that Jesus will bring the kingdom of God some day in the indefinite future. The kingdom of God has already come on this earth and was completely established right after He was crucified. Nothing remains but for each of us to enter the said kingdom of God. We will enter it when we are born again individually.

In this passage, Jesus does not mean a judgment day. He says some of His disciples with Him will see the kingdom of God. This word was actually achieved through the crucifixion and Pentecost, the descent of the Holy Spirit.

Thus, Jesus says,

> Verily I say unto you, There be some standing here, which

> shall not taste of death, till they see the Son of man coming in his kingdom. [Matthew 16:28]

Here, 'the Son of man coming in His kingdom' represents the coming of the kingdom of God. However, many people expound on this verse, saying it predicts the transfiguration on the high mountain in the next Chapter, Matthew 17. However, you will be mistaken in your understanding of the Scripture if you say that this word simply predicts the transfiguration that occurred six days later. The fallacy in such thinking is that this explanation applies the words of Jesus, which were to be for us all, only to Peter, James, and John alone.

Further, when the three disciples saw Jesus transfigured before them on the high mountain, they came down from there with nothing having changed in them. Did the Son of man come in His kingdom and then return to heaven again?

The reason why many people feel this passage is difficult is because their existing understanding on the kingdom of God is not the true meaning of the Scripture. Since they try to interpret the words of God with such a distorted understanding, their interpretation generates many inconsistencies. So they must interpret them by compulsion. When the compulsive interpretation does not work, they call it a difficult verse.

Jesus came in His kingdom for those whose time had come. He did so in the days of Pentecost. His word is not only applicable to the three disciples who went up to the mountain, but it is also applicable to all human beings in the same way.

🗁 Definition of Kingdom of God by Jesus

Well, now I need to summarize the dialogue between Jesus and Nicodemus. Nicodemus visited Jesus and asked, "How can I be a man with whom God abides?" Jesus answered him, "If a man is not born again, he cannot see the kingdom of God," and he talked about the kingdom of God. We can surmise from Jesus' answer that what Nicodemus wanted to know about was the kingdom of God. It does not matter whether he knew it or not.

However, what matters is that Jesus defined the kingdom of God with the words He used. Jesus has defined the kingdom of God as the state in which a man is with God. God with us represents the time when the Holy Spirit has come on us. When the Holy Spirit comes on Nicodemus, in the same manner that Jesus has the Holy Spirit inside Him, he can do the same things as He did. Nicodemus' wish to have the true faith will come true at this time. Jesus answered to Nicodemus in truth.

Our goal of faith, like Nicodemus', is to be a man with whom God abides. In other words, when Immanuel (i.e., God is with us) has been fulfilled in each of us, we will then have the same faith as Jesus had.

Conclusion: Meaning of Being Born Again

In conclusion, 'being born again' can be summarized as follows: to meet the living Jesus after repentance in the legalistic faith life and to follow Him in doing self-denial for spiritual purification. And after this process, Jesus will come upon us individually as the Holy Spirit and stay with us forever. Jesus calls this stage being born again and/or entering into the kingdom of God. Please bear in mind that the final born again stage cannot stand alone. It should come as a consequence of meeting Jesus and practicing spiritual purification.

Born Again of Water

I will continue with being born again of water and the Holy Spirit. Jesus says in John 3:5,

"Except a man be born of water and of the Spirit, he cannot enter into the kingdom of God."

What does water mean, and what does it mean to be born of the Holy Spirit? We can find various opinions among theologians, but the water here represents the word of the living Lord.

Consider Amos:

> Behold, the days come, saith the Lord GOD, that I will send a famine in the land, not a famine of bread, nor a thirst for water, but of hearing the words of the LORD. [Amos 8:11]

A man feels thirsty if he drinks no water. In the same way, if a man does not hear the Word of God, he will have no idea of the meaning of life and will feel futility and vanity. Hence, the Scripture likens the Word to water.

The next passage also shows that water signifies the Word. Read 1 Corinthians 3:6: "I have planted, Apollos watered; but God gave the increase."

The apostle Paul says to the Corinthians that he planted and Apollos watered, which does not mean they engaged in farming such as sowing and watering at the church in Corinth. It means that they preached the words of God to the church members, and thus, they sowed the seeds of Jesus Christ in their hearts. Paul and Apollos proclaimed the Word to water the seed to make them grow. Therefore, the Word is compared concurrently to the seed of life and the water for raising the seed.

Water is essential for us to live. Likewise, the Word is essential for our spirits to live. This is why the Word of God is compared to water.

Also, the Word is compared to another characteristic of water in that it cleanses:

> Husbands, love your wives, even as Christ also loved the church, and gave himself for it; That he might sanctify and cleanse it with the washing of water by the word, That he might present it to himself a glorious church, not having spot, or wrinkle, or any such thing; but that it should be holy and without blemish. [Ephesians 5:25-27]

Here, the word means the living and working word other than the law written in the Scripture. The living and working word indicates the word that a man hears when meeting Jesus in his life. The disciples were much scolded while following Him during His public life. This period represents the process in which they were cleansed with the living word.

We will read some passages that will substantiate the fact that the living word cleanses men:

> Jesus knowing that the Father had given all things into his hands, and that he was come from God, and went to God; He riseth from supper, and laid aside his garments; and took a towel, and girded himself. After that he poureth water into a bason, and began to wash the disciples' feet, and to wipe them with the towel wherewith he was girded. Then cometh he to Simon Peter: and Peter saith unto him, Lord, dost thou wash my feet? Jesus answered and said unto him, What I do thou knowest not now; but thou shalt know hereafter. Peter saith unto him, Thou shalt never wash my feet. Jesus answered him, If I wash thee not, thou hast no part with me. Simon Peter saith unto him, Lord, not my feet only, but also my hands and my head. Jesus saith to him, He that is washed needeth not save to wash his feet, but is clean every whit: and ye are clean, but not all. [John 13:3-10]

In John 13, Jesus gathers with the disciples and begins to wash the disciples' feet before he dies on the cross; this process is well known as foot washing. When it is Peter's turn, he rejects the thought saying, "How could I have my feet washed by You?" However, when He says, "If I don't wash you, you have no part with me," Peter then tells Jesus, "Wash my hands and head as well as my feet." He says, "He who is washed needs only to wash his feet."

Judging from this dialogue, Peter already had a bath before the foot washing. But, when did this cleansing happen to him?

Peter's whole life can be divided into three parts as follows: First, the days when he was catching fish as an ordinary fisherman before meeting with Jesus. Second, the days when he was following Jesus, forsaking all, for three and half years. Third, the days when he was perfectly being changed forever by the cross and Pentecost.

On the day of Pentecost, Peter was perfectly changed to be a man desired by God. That is, he was born again to be a new man on the day of Pentecost. Considering that a man will be a new man when he is born again of water and the Spirit, we can understand that Peter had gone through the born again process of water and the Holy Spirit before the day of Pentecost.

It is obvious that Peter underwent the born again process of water during the time when he was following Jesus because he never knew of Him before that time. He became changed after having met Jesus and his changes were completed at the coming of the Holy Spirit on the day of Pentecost.

At foot washing, Jesus said to His disciples that they already had a bath because they were cleansed by the Word while He was with them. Accordingly, the Word is likened to the water which washes away our blemishes, and the man having passed through this process of washing has been born again of water. This is what is referred to as being born again of water.

Therefore, the disciples only need to wash their feet. We normally and traditionally have been taught that washing feet means the repentance/forgiveness of the sins committed in everyday life, whilst the bath is the forgiveness of inherent sin given when we believed and confessed our sins at church. In this way, we are to continue to sin all life long, repenting and sinning repetitively. However, forgiveness of sin by Jesus is once and for all, if given correctly. This is biblical forgiveness.

Born Again of the Holy Spirit

First, I will explain the meaning of Jesus' washing of the disciples' feet. His foot washing is not meant to show an example of 'servant-ship' as is traditionally known. His act of washing their feet is given to reveal a spiritual truth, and it means, "Jesus receives His disciples." Spiritually, foot washing signifies 'welcoming' and/or 'being one.' In the Scripture, when a host receives a person, he prepares water for the feet and washes them (Gen 18:4, 19:2, 24:32, 43:24; Luk 7:38, 7:44).

Thus, Jesus' behavior in preparing water and to wash the disciples' feet symbolizes receiving the disciples in His house in order to be one with them forever. Here, His house refers to the disciples' bodies. When Jesus comes on them as the Holy Spirit, the co-master of their bodies would be Jesus. Therefore, He says His coming on the disciples as the Holy Spirit is His receiving of the disciples.

The disciples receive Jesus coming into their bodies as the Holy Spirit and Jesus' receiving of the disciples are revealed by the washing of feet by Jesus.

This is achieved when Jesus has come as the Holy Spirit on the respective bodies of the disciples. This is being born again of the Holy Spirit. Being born again of water and the Holy Spirit is for a man to meet Jesus, to undergo trails and purifications by Jesus, and to receive Jesus coming in as the Holy Spirit.

In other words, we are one with Jesus and are born again when we have had a bath and have had our feet washed by Him.

🗁 Breathing the Holy Spirit

I should like to add one more thing about being born again of the Holy Spirit. In John Chapter 20, Jesus, after the resurrection, breathes on them so that they receive the Holy Spirit:

> Then said Jesus to them again, Peace be unto you: as my Father hath sent me, even so send I you. And when he had said this, he breathed on them, and saith unto them, Receive ye the Holy Ghost: Whose soever sins ye remit, they are remitted

unto them; and whose soever sins ye retain, they are retained. [John 20:21-23]

In Genesis, in the creation of Adam, God formed him from the dust of the ground and breathed into his nostrils the breath of life to make him a living being. Spiritually, being born again includes two steps. First, He purifies His disciples for three and a half years. Second, He breathes on them with the Holy Spirit to give a new life to the born again body.

Being born again of water and the Holy Spirit is completed through His breathing the Holy Spirit. The disciples actually received the Holy Spirit on the day of Pentecost, the fiftieth day after Jesus' Ascension, as written in Acts. The Holy Spirit the disciples received here represents the prototype of the Holy Spirit who would come on the day of Pentecost. The time when the disciples receive a new life by being born again is the day of Pentecost.

Peter was born again through this process, as well as Abraham and David. We, living in contemporary times, can only be born again according to the same principle. The process of being born again has no exception throughout all the time.

Only a born again man can enter the kingdom of God, and the kingdom of God has come on him.

Pregnancy and Delivery by the Word

The process of pregnancy and delivery is required so that a new life may be born. Now I will explain how a new life is conceived and delivered spiritually.

Pregnancy by the Word

When we are born in this world, we are born with Adam's life, that is, a depraved life. We sin because of the depraved life. Our sinning is not a one time or on and off matter, but it is a matter of our basic nature, i.e., life itself. That's why we cannot get out of sinning, no matter how hard we may try. In order for us not to sin, the depraved life should end within us; we must have a new life. The new life is Jesus' life. When we have Jesus' life, we will be able to live as Jesus lived. This is being born again. So, being born again means that we have Jesus' life.

A person must first be conceived to give birth to a new life physically. Likewise, we should be conceived in order to give birth to Jesus' life within us. This pregnancy is achieved not by physical contact but through the preached word of Jesus, i.e., by spiritual contact. This is what we call pregnancy by the word.

We must meet the person who has the word of Jesus in him so that we may be conceived by the word. Then who is the person who has the word of Jesus? He is the man who met Jesus and followed Him for some years and on whom Jesus has come as the Holy Spirit, like the apostles of Jesus. He alone can plant the seed of the word. He alone can preach the living gospel that makes the dead arise. He is the man who is doing what Jesus had been doing.

🗁 Instructors and Fathers

Paul says, though we have ten thousand instructors in Christ, yet we do not have many fathers. Read this passage:

> For though ye have ten thousand instructors in Christ, yet have ye not many fathers: for in Christ Jesus I have begotten you through the gospel. [1 Corinthians 4:15]

The instructors are connected with their students by man-made relation, but fathers and sons are connected by life. Between the instructors and students, knowledge will be transmitted, but between the fathers and sons, life will be transmitted. That is, if a father begets a son, then the life of the father is transmitted to his son. So, it is crucial for us to meet fathers, not instructors, to receive the life of Jesus.

We can find ten thousand instructors teaching Jesus around us.

They are preaching Jesus from knowledge and learning gained through academic study. Surely, they can transmit knowledge of Jesus in a most efficient way to the hearers, but they cannot transmit the life of Jesus. It is because they have not received the life of Jesus in the first place. So it is natural for them that they cannot convey such life. They are instructors in Christ, but regrettably, they cannot convey the life of Jesus.

However, there are fathers, even though rare in number, who can convey the life of Jesus to others. They are the ones who have met Jesus in their life personally, were healed, and then received the Holy Spirit, as the life of Jesus. In this way, the fathers got to know Jesus, not by studying Him like instructors. Fathers have the seed, the word of Jesus in them. They are the life-giving spirits and can make neighbors conceived the word (1Co 15:45). This is what Jesus was doing during His public ministry, and the same is being done by fathers who have His life.

The apostle Paul compares the instructors having no seed of the word to the fathers having the same. There are many instructors in Christ, but fathers are few. It is so in the present age as well.

Delivery

The person who is conceived by the word of God will bring forth a man-child when the proper time has come (Rev 12:5). The man-child represents Jesus and at the same time represents himself who has begotten Him. The man-child has the life of Jesus Christ. That is quite natural because the word that made him that begot man-child pregnant is Jesus Christ Himself.

The pregnancy and delivery is the process in which the Christ is being formed in us. That is, by meeting Jesus in our life, we are conceived with His life, and by becoming one with Him at the cross, we deliver His life. Thus, the life of Jesus becomes our lives individually. Consider the following verse:

> Notwithstanding she shall be saved in childbearing, if they continue in faith and charity and holiness with sobriety. [1 Timothy 2:15]

This verse is called the most difficult among the difficult verses of the Scriptures. It is because this verse does not mean that a woman will be saved if she is delivered of a baby in the hospital of obstetrics and gynecology. Rather, the verse should be understood based on the explanation I have offered above.

All people are born in the flesh, and those born in the flesh are of Adam. Those who are born in the flesh are 'women' who are supposed to receive the seed of God in the spiritual aspect. Therefore, the word *woman* indicates the person who is not yet born again. The woman is under the law and is to receive the seed of Jesus Christ. On the other hand, the 'man' represents the person who is born again. Man has the seed of Jesus and is under grace.

Therefore, the passage "Let your women keep silence in the churches" means that the person who will be in charge of the church should be the man who is born, not the woman (1Co 14:34). Yes. What benefit is there for those who are under the law to talk about God of whom they have no sufficient idea? They will have to keep silent to hear and learn of God from the born again men.

Women will become conceived while hearing and learning the word of God from men, and each of them will bring forth a man-child who is the born again self. When a woman is born again as a man, then Scripture says it is salvation. She will be saved at the time when she delivers a man-child, so she is said to be saved in childbearing.

Please refer to Revelation regarding the delivery of the conceived woman:

> And there appeared a great wonder in heaven; a woman clothed with the sun, and the moon under her feet, and

upon her head a crown of twelve stars: And she being with child cried, travailing in birth, and pained to be delivered. [Revelation 12:1-2]

And she brought forth a man child, who was to rule all nations with a rod of iron: and her child was caught up unto God, and to his throne. [Revelation 12:5]

These passages also speak about our being born again. The child she brings forth is a man who will rule all nations with a rod of iron. As stated, the woman is a person who is not born again, and the man is a person who is born again. Here, when the woman delivers a man-child, it represents a person (the woman) who was not born again becoming born again. Therefore, when the man brings forth a man-child, a man-child is himself, and he will have the life of Jesus to have authority to rule all nations with a rod of iron.

This happened to the disciples of Jesus on the day of Pentecost. When reading the records in Acts, we can know that the men (the disciples) spiritually lived a life of ruling all the nations with the power and words of Christ.

Jesus expressed entering the kingdom of God as being born again. When a person is born again, he will be a man of spirit. The man of spirit is a man who is created in the image of God. This born again man is he who is shown in Genesis 1:27, and God rested after the creation of the man. The man in whom God rests is he who is perfectly changed into the image of God, so he is no longer to be processed. He is the person who is born of water and the Spirit.

Peter's Born Again Example

Now, we will consider the example of Peter as we think about being born again form two points of view. The first perspective is based on a change in behavior, and the second perspective is based on pregnancy and delivery.

🗁 Born Again in Terms of a Change in Behavior

Peter, while catching fish, met Jesus, forsook all (including his fishing net, which was his means of living), and followed Jesus. At a glance, it looks like a tremendous change for him. Yes, it was a great change. However, it was not the complete change that Jesus wanted him to go through. While Peter was following Jesus for about three years, he was not able to meet the expectations of Jesus.

For instance, Peter and the disciples disputed among themselves as to who was the greatest; one of them desired to sit on His right hand and the other on the left to take power over the world. Jesus had to say, "Get behind me, Satan!" when Peter rebuked Him about the death Jesus was to face (Mar 8:32).

Even before the cross, Peter was changed little. Observe this dialogue between Jesus and His disciples:

> Now are we sure that thou knowest all things, and needest not that any man should ask thee: by this we believe that thou camest forth from God. Jesus answered them, Do ye now believe? Behold, the hour cometh, yea, is now come, that ye shall be scattered, every man to his own, and shall leave me alone: and yet I am not alone, because the Father is with me. [John 16:30-32]

When they say they believe He came from God, He says it is far beyond their faith, saying, "You are saying you believe it now? No way. You will be scattered, leaving me alone." The disciples could confess with their lips that they believed in Jesus before the cross, but they did not have the faith Jesus hoped they would have. Of course, our belief in Jesus would be shabby compared to Peter and the disciples because we believe in Jesus without seeing Him personally, as they could.

Anyhow, one thing is interesting here. Some people understand John 16:31 as an exclamatory sentence, which is possible: "You believe at last!" This understanding has the nuance of "Wow, now you have understood it. OK, thanks for believing in me!" However, it does not go well with the meaning of the next sentence: "You will leave me alone and go your own ways."

Therefore, this word is only natural when it is understood as follows: "You are now saying you can believe me? No way. You will leave me and go on your own." In fact, Peter, having said, "I shall die with You," denied Him three times before the cock crowed, and he even cursed as Jesus foretold (Mat 26:33-35, 74-75).

Not only are these instances true; there are many other cases whereby Jesus rebuked Peter and the disciples during that period. Frankly speaking, the only change observable in them is a shift in their seeking of power. They tried to fulfill their dream of power on their own before meeting Jesus, but then they attempted to achieve it through His power and mighty works. It is apparent that Peter, as well as the other disciples, was not born again as righteous men until Pentecost.

Peter's behaviors were completely changed as worthy of God after the baptism with the Holy Spirit on the day of Pentecost. Before the baptism with the Holy Spirit, Peter denied Jesus, cursed Him, and ran away at the word of a maid. But, after Pentecost, he boldly preached before the Jews who sought to kill him. He was not able to cast out devils but was only groaning while following Him (Mat 17:16), but he did wonders and miracles (e.g., he lifted up a certain lame man) after having received the Holy Spirit. This is the change that Jesus wanted to give to Peter when He called him to follow Him. The same goes for us, of course.

So, the time when Peter is born again in terms of change in behavior is at the baptism with the Holy Spirit on the day of Pentecost.

🗁 Born Again in Terms of Pregnancy and Delivery

We will now think about being born again from the viewpoint of birth that is, childbearing or delivery. Before a life is born, the pregnancy and delivery process is essential. When we are born again with the word of God, we undergo the process of pregnancy and delivery. We will think about the time of pregnancy and delivery in the case of Peter and the disciples. Consider the basic truths of birth:

> A woman when she is in travail hath sorrow, because her hour is come: but as soon as she is delivered of the child, she remembereth no more the anguish, for joy that a man is born into the world. [John 16:21]

As His crucifixion approaches, Jesus says the time when the disciples will bear a child is near. It means that the disciples who are not yet born again will be born again by bringing forth a man-child. As we can see from this, before the crucifixion of Jesus, the disciples have not yet brought forth a child, signifying that they are not yet born again.

They are perfectly born again on the day of Pentecost and are then used as soldiers of the Lord, preaching the gospel to every nation. Being born again means receiving a new life from the Lord, and He can only give us this life by laying down His life on the cross. Therefore, without His cross, we cannot receive a new life and be born again.

If the cross signifies the delivery, then when was Peter's pregnancy time? It was the time when Peter truly repented, met Jesus, and followed Him, forsaking all. As a woman puts forth every effort to foster the new life in her once she conceives, Peter, being conceived spiritually, forsook all and followed Him. From that time on, Peter had the life of Jesus growing in him. Birth came after the cross when Jesus was resurrected from the dead and breathed on Peter to give him the Holy Spirit.

Here we might wonder whether Peter's delivery point was when Jesus breathed the Holy Spirit after the resurrection or at Pentecost. In fact, the two time points are the same. The breath of the Holy Spirit by Jesus is the figure of the Holy Spirit of Pentecost. So the delivery point of Peter is the time of the resurrection of Jesus or the coming of the Holy Spirit at Pentecost. This is Peter's moment of being born again, from the perspective of delivery.

Born Again: Our Traditional Understanding

Many among us will think that we are born again. It is because Jesus said no one could enter the kingdom of God if we were not born again. So we want to secure the born again status to possess heaven by fair means or foul. We have our own evidence and reasoning of being born again.

However, the evidence we have of being born again is not of God, but it is of the words of men. Therefore, we are offended when someone says to us that we are not yet born again. But we will be pleased when someone accepts us as being born again men. Although we defend our born again status by ourselves, we still feel futility in our hearts since it is not of God.

Under such circumstances, if we counsel about it with brothers and sisters in the church, they will comfort us with such words as: "You will be sanctified day by day;" "Everybody believes in Jesus like this. The multitude cannot be wrong. So don't worry." Time passes by as such, and we feel the emptiness and conflict in our hearts again, but again we take comfort with the same words and bear and forbear. Then, the time will come when we have to stand before God with nothing having been changed.

We should think long about the conflict and futility in our mind instead of suppressing it. This conflict leads us to Jesus (as in the case of Nicodemus). In addition, being born again is not so easily fulfilled in us as we might think. The Lord will confirm us when we are born again really. Please do think twice about the born again state.

Up to here, we have finished the stage of John in the process of growing in faith. The stage of John can also be called the stage of being born again. Now, I will testify about how I have experienced being born again personally in my life.

My Experience of Being Born Again

I will testify about my born again experience by referring to the journals that I wrote at that time. The story begins after the time of true repentance when I met Jesus in my life. He told me I would be born again only if the crucifixion was fulfilled in me personally. So, I waited for that time with great expectation and throbbing. When I used to ask Him when I would be born again to be a new man, He would answer me, "You have to wait for a little more time," and "Not so late, and not so fast." This message was spoken to me through the radio program *Focus on the Family*.

I was very much curious about how I would experience being born again, and I eagerly awaited it. The reason for my curiosity might be that I had yet to hear of any experience of being born again from the elders of faith. I will now make a testimony on my experience of being born again so that it may help to satisfy your curiosity.

🗁 Salvation Drawing Near

One day in April, when I was impatiently waiting for the experience of being born again, I woke up and was about to have breakfast before going to work. When I was about to eat my toast, the thought, "Fasting!" came across my mind. I made an effort to ignore it and thought that it was not from the Lord, knowing that fasting is really difficult. So, I neglected the message and carried on eating the toast. Having eaten a bite of it, I felt at ease because I was no longer troubled as to whether I should fast or not.

I went to my office, and around noon, I had lunch. After

lunch, I came back to the office and was working. Wondering if I was having an attack of indigestion after lunch, I felt like throwing up and had great pain in the back of my head on the right side as the afternoon wore on. The pain was growing worse and I felt as though I would fall out of my chair; I looked forward to going home. At that moment, I vaguely thought the idea of fasting this morning might have been the voice of the Lord. However, I hated to admit it. Because once I admitted it, I would have to begin painful fasting on the next day.

The morning of the next day came, and I had even greater conflict about whether to fast than I had had the previous morning. Because I thought the Lord was angry with me since I had eaten bread and neglected the message of fasting, I thought that He had given me indigestion. It became clearer than it was the previous day that fasting was the will of the Lord for me, so I could not easily ignore the idea of fasting that morning.

When I thought of beginning to fast, I could foresee many problems. Once I started, it would be at least three days long. Further, I had an appointment to go to another city on a business trip with the staff member of another organization on the following day. It seemed practically impossible for me to avoid lunch with him. Also, as I was not in good physical condition at that time, I had no confidence in three-day fasting at all.

However, in spite of all these negative thoughts, I also knew that there would be no problem as long as the Lord empowered me to fast. Anyway, there was a fierce battle in my heart in front of the toast for a while.

According to past experience, I usually started fasting when the Lord allowed me to do so. However, He did not answer me in this case, even when I prayed to Him. I guess that He was watching what I would determine to do by myself, without any answer from Him.

Anyway, two decisive thoughts occurred in my mind through that long conflict. The first one was that the idea of fasting came to me yesterday; the second one was that I felt sick when I ignored the idea of fasting. Consequently, I concluded this idea of fasting was of the Lord for sure. So, I left the baked bread and the coffee on the table and made up my mind to fast for three days.

Although I had made up my mind, when I got to the office, another idea hit me. If I misunderstood the will of the Lord, I would needlessly have a hard time while traveling to the other city on the next day. While thinking of many alternatives, I almost changed my mind again, but I withstood well, as I judged it afterwards, and carried on the fasting.

In fact, many people might give up at this stage, thinking within themselves that they inaccurately knew the will of the Lord. So they might then eat in disobedience to the Lord, not knowing their disobedience. Those who are seeking to obey His will should be really careful at this stage.

It was the night of that same day that the Lord praised me about my obedience to fast. I finished that day, being extremely hungry with fasting at the office, and returned home. My wife told me that the preacher visited our house that day, and he said, "God gave this message to your husband." She opened Psalm verses of the Bible and kindly put it on my lap.

It reads as follows:

> I will hear what God the LORD will speak: for he will speak peace unto his people, and to his saints: but let them not turn again to folly. Surely his salvation is nigh them that fear him; that glory may dwell in our land. Mercy and truth are met together; righteousness and peace have kissed each other. Truth shall spring out of the earth; and righteousness shall look down from heaven. Yea, the LORD shall give that which is good; and our land shall yield her increase. Righteousness shall go before him; and shall set us in the way of his steps. [Psalm 85:8-13]

Having read it, I knew that God really gave this message to me. God was telling me that my born again experience was near at hand, which I was eagerly looking forward to. As told in the Bible, the time of being born again is the time of salvation in which we will yield the fruit that God wants. Also, the glory of the Lord will dwell in us. We and the Lord will meet together and righteousness and peace will be fulfilled. It is the day when the prophecy of all the prophets of the Old Testament will be fulfilled, and it is the place to which the Lord had been leading me.

🗁 I Who Am Born Again

Several days later after I had received the words of Psalm 85, I went down to a restaurant near the office alone late in the afternoon. While waiting for the cooked rice with mixed vegetables (Bibimbab) that I had ordered, many thoughts about myself suddenly passed through my mind.

Having observed other Christians after I met the Lord, I found they had no idea of Jesus in the least. I shouted and cried out, but nobody caught what I said and would not listen to me. I felt they were living in real darkness. I felt heavy about them, and I was grieved when thinking of those who knew nothing but were zealous in their ways.

Gradually, I realized that the Lord was calling me to preach the right Jesus in this world. I realized that He had opened my spiritual eyes because of this calling.

I wondered if I was capable of carrying out this precious mission, but I was really grateful beyond expression, thinking of Him who entrusted me with this important task. Tears of thanks, coming from deep down in my heart, ran down my cheeks. I had to continuously dry my tears with tissues, avoiding the eyes of the waitress who brought the food to me. I shed uncontrolled tears for about five or six minutes, swearing that I would devote myself to the Lord to the last since He had chosen me for this precious mission.

As I did not know what this experience would mean to me, I did not remember the exact date. The Lord surely told me my being born again was near at hand, so I waited, but I had no other unusual experience except this. When I prayed to Him regarding this matter, He said what I experienced in the restaurant was the experience of born again. In fact, being born again is a gradual process, so its timing cannot be one single point in time.

This is my born again experience. The experience of being born again will vary for each individual. At any rate, I hope all of us will be able to testify of our actual time of being born again.

As explained Being Born Again is the stage of John in the faith-growing steps.

Meaning of the Forty Days' Stay after Resurrection

After his resurrection, Jesus breathed on the disciples with the Holy Spirit so that they were born again with a new life (Jhn 20:22). He showed Himself to His disciples for forty days after resurrection, ascended into heaven, and came back again as the Holy Spirit on the day of Pentecost:

> To whom also he shewed himself alive after his passion by many infallible proofs, being seen of them forty days, and speaking of the things pertaining to the kingdom of God. [Acts 1:3]

According to Scripture, the disciples were not changed much during this period. They did not even think of proclaiming Jesus, but they gathered together and locked the door for fear of the Jews (Jhn 20:19), and they, with Peter as their head, went fishing as they used to do in the past (Jhn 21:3). Jesus breathed on them with the Holy Spirit after resurrection, but their behaviors were not changed much.

Why so? It has a spiritual meaning.

The time when Jesus breathed on the disciples with the Holy Spirit after resurrection is when the disciples were born again as new men. But such new men could not do the work of adults because they were newly born babies. They needed to grow, and fifty days later at Pentecost, with the coming of the Holy Spirit, they were able to do what Jesus was doing. They became adult believers at that moment. Therefore, forty days is the growing period of a newly born life to become an adult.

In summary, when the disciples met Jesus, they were conceived with the life of Jesus. When they were breathed on with Holy Spirit after the resurrection of Jesus, they delivered the life of Jesus. They were born again. When they reached Pentecost, the life of Jesus had matured within each of them. Now they could experience real change in their faith and do what Jesus had done.

In the Old Testament, the soldiers of Israel are twenty years and older. Men under the age of twenty years are not qualified to fight. Spiritually, this means that even if one is born again, he cannot instantly be selected as a soldier of God to fight the enemy. He has to grow up.

As such, the disciples were born again when Jesus breathed the Holy Spirit into them, but they were not yet grown up to fight against the adversary. Forty days represents the period during which a young life grows to be twenty years old with the power and ability to fight against the enemy.

In the faith-growing process, Acts follows John. John indicates the time when a person is born again. Acts depicts the time when he is baptized with the Holy Spirit and starts to fight a spiritual battle as a soldier of God, as an adult.

As for the meaning of forty days, the number four represents the period for God to treat the man. For example, the forty years of life in the wilderness and the four hundred years of life in Egypt are growing seasons. Pentecost means the number fifty. After the forty days of growth, the fiftieth day of the grown-up man will come. We can know that fifty means maturity when we see the disciples worked as grown-ups at Pentecost.

It is no coincidence that the works of Jesus during the forty days is provided between the two stages, that is, between the end of John and the beginning of Acts. When the day of Pentecost comes after the forty days required for a child to grow up is over, the disciples are baptized with the Holy Spirit.

We will think about faith in the stage of Acts in the next chapter.

6

STAGE OF ACTS — BAPTISM WITH HOLY SPIRIT

Now we are considering the stage of Acts in the faith-growing process, following the order of the Bible's books. The stage of Acts is the stage of the Holy Spirit, which corresponds to the state in which a tree bears good fruit. The man in the stage of Acts is he whose faith is perfectly mature, who can do the works of God as His soldier. He has the power of loving his neighbor as himself. All the Scriptures ultimately say that man is to be baptized with the Holy Spirit through Jesus although this is expressed in many different ways.

In this chapter, I will explain baptism with the Holy Spirit as well as the second coming, the end time, the coming of the Lord, the end of the world, seventy sevens, and the dwelling of God and its glory. These terms all refer to the same event.

What Is Baptism with the Holy Spirit?

We frequently have questions in our mind while reading the Scriptures: "When was I baptized with the Holy Spirit?" Or, "Wasn't I baptized with the Holy Spirit because I already spoke in tongues?" And, "Can I be baptized with the Holy Spirit if I pray earnestly with fasting?" These questions arise because baptism with the Holy Spirit has not yet been accurately defined in Christian society.

In fact, this baptism with the Holy Spirit is really confusing whether it is the same or different from phrases such as; the work of the Holy Spirit, leading by the Holy Spirit, being full of the Holy Spirit, the gifts of the Holy Spirit, and the presence of the Holy Spirit.

All these things are a shadow of things to come, but in essence deal with baptism with the Holy Spirit. From the shadow, what we need is to get certain descriptions and images of the body to come. However, shadow is shadow. It cannot become the body or the main issue. So we should not stick to the shadow for long; therefore, we should know and understand the 'body.'

Likewise, if we only fixate on such spiritual gifts, such as speaking in tongues, healing by prayer, *et cetera*, we cannot see the baptism with the Holy Spirit. We should know the body to come:

> Then Peter said unto them, Repent, and be baptized every one of you in the name of Jesus Christ for the remission of sins, and ye shall receive the gift of the Holy Ghost. For the promise is unto you, and to your children, and to all that are afar off, even as many as the LORD our God shall call. [Acts 2:38-39]

In these verses, the meaning of receiving the gift of the Holy Spirit is that a person meets Jesus through true repentance. He is changed, and Jesus comes on him again as the Holy Spirit. It is the overall change process of the disciples, and the change of a man is completed by the coming of the Holy Spirit, as gift.

The Holy Spirit is spiritual fruit given by Jesus. Therefore, if we want to receive the Holy Spirit, we should first meet Jesus and undergo the process of healing by Jesus. We cannot receive the Holy Spirit without the experience of having met Jesus in advance. Having gone through this process, we will receive the Holy Spirit, and this is called baptism with the Holy Spirit.

Therefore, baptism with the Holy Spirit is intrinsically different from the gifts of the Holy Spirit such as prophesying, speaking with tongues, conversing with the Holy Spirit, or experiencing the Holy Spirit several times. This kind of experience of the Holy Spirit can be given to anyone, regardless of who he is, sinner or otherwise. However, baptism with the Holy Spirit will only be given when a man meets Jesus and is changed by Him. Naturally, it is essentially different from the gifts of the Holy Spirit, presence of the Holy Spirit, fullness with the Holy Spirit, and leading by the Holy Spirit.

However, since the gifts of the Holy Spirit, presence of the Holy Spirit, and fullness with the Holy Spirit can be shown as external phenomena when one is baptized with the Holy Spirit, the baptism with the Holy Spirit includes all these phenomena. Receiving the Holy Spirit in the Scripture means baptism with the Holy Spirit.

We can believe in Jesus and go to church without receiving the Holy Spirit. It is not a big problem that we attend church without the Holy Spirit, but it is reasonable to go to church so as to receive Him. The disciples did not receive the Holy Spirit as soon as they met Jesus, and it was some years before they received the Holy Spirit at Pentecost (Jhn 7:39).

The problem is that some have no idea of the Holy Spirit, even though they go to church. Many believers just lead a Christians' life, not knowing whether they have already received the Holy Spirit or if they still have to receive Him. If we do not know the Holy Spirit, it means that we have lost our direction in faith, and it means also that we do not know whether our faith is right or wrong.

If you have followed me up to here, some of you may say that you have never heard that there exists such a Holy Spirit and baptism with the Holy Spirit through Jesus. This passage describes the case of such believers:

He said unto them, Have ye received the Holy Ghost since ye

> believed? And they said unto him, We have not so much as heard whether there be any Holy Ghost. [Acts 19:2]

So far for these Ephesians, there had been no light shed on baptism with the Holy Spirit, so when spoken to about baptism with the Holy Spirit, some said that they had not even heard of such a Holy Spirit that comes after purification by Jesus.

However, blessed are those who can hear it now because they will have guidance to true faith.

Biblical Teaching about Baptism with the Holy Spirit

I will explain through Scripture that baptism with the Holy Spirit is not merely limited to experiences or gifts of the Holy Spirit, which is a shadow, but the essential change of men, which is the body or the essence.

The next verses are the words John the Baptist said concerning baptism by Jesus:

> I indeed baptize you with water unto repentance: but he that cometh after me is mightier than I, whose shoes I am not worthy to bear: he shall baptize you with the Holy Ghost, and with fire. [Matthew 3:11]

> And I knew him not: but he that sent me to baptize with water, the same said unto me, Upon whom thou shalt see the Spirit descending, and remaining on him, the same is he which baptizeth with the Holy Ghost. [John 1:33]

On the other hand, Jesus, just before ascending to heaven after crucifixion and resurrection, spoke to His disciples:

> For John truly baptized with water; but ye shall be baptized with the Holy Ghost not many days hence. [Acts 1:5]

John the Baptist said Jesus would baptize with the Holy Spirit, and as He ascended into heaven, He said to the disciples that they would be baptized with the Holy Spirit. As He had said, they were baptized with the Holy Spirit on the day of Pentecost. The baptism with the Holy Spirit was the essence of all efforts and sacrifice given by Jesus through His public life and crucifixion. Jesus was incarnated in order to realize this result. Baptism with the Holy Spirit is not given by our desire and prayer, but it is given only to those who have passed through the right faith-growing process with Jesus.

We can find two noticeable changes in the lives of the disciples who followed Jesus. The first life change came when they met Him and forsook all to follow Him. The second change occurred when they were baptized with the Holy Spirit on the day of Pentecost. As we know, the disciples were perfectly changed to be witnesses of Jesus, not at the time when they first met and followed Him, but after baptism with the Holy Spirit at Pentecost. This baptism with the Holy Spirit is the point where the promises in Scripture are fulfilled, and it is the goal we should always have in our hearts and should covet earnestly.

With the baptism with the Holy Spirit as the starting point, Jesus takes our bodies as His temple to be with us forever as the Holy Spirit. The kingdom of God has come on us individually when we are baptized with the Holy Spirit.

You may have lived your life as king of your own life in the past, but the new king Jesus Christ has come to change this kingship from now on. The kingdoms of this world have gone and the kingdom of God has come. Following this meaning, preaching the kingdom of God matches preaching the baptism with the Holy Spirit. The apostle Paul preached this kingdom of God. It is the key message of the gospel to be baptized with the Holy Spirit in this very world, rather than going to the kingdom of God after death.

But by the Holy Spirit

> Wherefore I give you to understand, that no man speaking by the Spirit of God calleth Jesus accursed: and that no man can say that Jesus is the Lord, but by the Holy Ghost. [I Corinthians 12:3]

The part we most frequently quote in this passage is "No man can say that Jesus is the Lord, but by the Holy Ghost."

Here, we will think about Paul's true meaning and confirm that the Holy Spirit is given by Jesus only. The traditional interpretation of this message is that if a person says, "Jesus is the Lord," then the Holy Spirit has come on him already. The logic here is that the Holy Spirit has come upon him, he is moved by Him, and he can confess Jesus is Lord.

Based on this understanding, when a newcomer gets to church, the church encourages him to confess this statement with his mouth. The church says that he who has confessed in this manner has been saved. They say the spirit of the confessed person is now saved to enter heaven, and he is to fight against the lust of the flesh for sanctification throughout the rest of his life.

However, this verse is not as easy as that. A single word of confession saying, "Jesus is my Savior," cannot be a proof that the Holy Spirit has come on him.

🗁 The Holy Spirit

To help understand this verse, I shall explain the Holy Spirit first. The Holy Spirit we generally know is the Holy Ghost in the Trinity.

According to the Scriptures, the Holy Spirit also came upon the people who lived in the Old Testament era:

> And the Spirit of the LORD will come upon thee *(i.e., Saul)*, and thou shalt prophesy with them, and shalt be turned into another man. [I Samuel 10:6]

> And when they came thither to the hill, behold, a company of prophets met him; and the Spirit of God came upon him, and he prophesied among them. [1 Samuel 10:10]

The Spirit of the LORD in the Old Testament period was not always with men. One feature of the Holy Spirit coming on the people in the Old Testament period was that the Spirit came upon a man who obeyed, but departed from him when he disobeyed (1Sa 16:14).

However, the Holy Spirit in the New Testament is forever with a person and never leaves him once He has come on him: "Cast me not away from thy presence; and take not thy holy spirit from me" (Psa 51:11).

The writer of this Psalm is David. He entreated God not to take the Holy Spirit from him, which does not mean he is earnestly hoping that God may not change His mind and withdraw the Holy Spirit He previously gave to him. He wishes for the Holy Spirit, which God never takes away.

The ever-staying Holy Spirit, which David wanted, was the figure of the Holy Spirit to be given by Jesus. This is the fulfillment of Immanuel by Jesus.

🗁 The Holy Spirit of Immanuel

There are many verses about the Holy Spirit found in the New Testament. However, what God ultimately wants to give us is the very Holy Spirit whom God will give to each of us through the cross of Jesus.

> In the last day, that great day of the feast, Jesus stood and cried, saying, If any man thirst, let him come unto me, and drink. He that believeth on me, as the scripture hath said, out of his belly shall flow rivers of living water. (But this spake he of the Spirit, which they that believe on him should receive: for the Holy Ghost was not yet given; because that Jesus was

> not yet glorified.) [John 7:37-39]

> And I will pray the Father, and he shall give you another Comforter, that he may abide with you for ever. [John 14:16]

> Nevertheless I tell you the truth; It is expedient for you that I go away: for if I go not away, the Comforter will not come unto you; but if I depart, I will send him unto you. [John 16:7]

In John, Jesus says He will give His disciples another Comforter, the Holy Spirit, after He is crucified. Only Jesus can give Himself up for crucifixion and then give them the Holy Spirit. The Holy Spirit in this instance represents the Holy Spirit of Immanuel who is with them forever. Immanuel means "God is with us:"

> Therefore the Lord himself shall give you a sign; Behold, a virgin shall conceive, and bear a son, and shall call his name Immanuel. [Isaiah 7:14]

> Behold, a virgin shall be with child, and shall bring forth a son, and they shall call his name Emmanuel, which being interpreted is, God with us. [Matthew 1:23]

In Matthew, the prophecy by Isaiah is applied to Jesus' conception by a virgin and his birth. When Jesus is conceived by a virgin and is born, this is the fulfillment of the Immanuel prophecy.

When a person is conceived through the word and brings forth a son, his salvation is achieved. According to the prophecy of Isaiah, the name of the son will be Immanuel. There is no need to argue whether the name of the son is Jesus or Immanuel because these two have the same meaning. The name Jesus means the Savior. The Savior brings oneness with God to man who was separated from Him because of sin. Consequently, the name Jesus essentially has the same meaning as Immanuel: God is with us.

The only one who can give us the Holy Spirit of Immanuel is Jesus. Therefore, the statement that a person has received the Holy Spirit is the same as his being born again by Jesus. If he received the Holy Spirit, Jesus is certainly behind it.

🗁 Meaning of Confession

"No man can say that Jesus is the Lord, but by the Holy Ghost" means that no one can confess Jesus as the Savior but by the Holy Spirit (1Co 12:3). To confess a certain thing means for a person to agree with the truth of that statement and admit it. However, if the certain event is in the future, he cannot fundamentally confess it since things may change in unexpected ways. Therefore, if he can confess it, he can only do so after the event has taken place.

I would like to explain one of my experiences that will help you understand this. One night, I finished my job in a place distant from my home. While driving home the warning light on my fuel gage started signaling that my fuel was running low. It was late at night, and I was crossing a bridge. The bridge had only recently opened to traffic and I was not familiar with the neighborhood. I had no idea where the gas stations were.

I prayed to God, "Please let the gas remain until I reach the gas station. I don't know where it is." The Lord told me in my heart, "It's OK. Don't worry."

However, the red warning signal kept on blinking. I wanted to trust Lord's reply, but I could not. I wondered if there was any reason why it would be the will of the Lord to give me trouble, and I also wondered if I had misinterpreted His response.

Anyway, I drove the car with great anxiety. I could only believe what He had told me after I had arrived at the gas station. I could confess, "So it is, to be sure," in response to His answer. However, before arrival, even if I tried very hard to trust His word, "You'll be safe," I could not do so. It is not a matter of how hard I tried to believe, but it is the matter of natural law.

The matter of confessing Jesus as the Savior is like this. When we are perfectly saved by Jesus, we can then say or confess, "Jesus is my Savior." "No man can say that Jesus is the Lord, but by the Holy Ghost" means that when the Holy Spirit has come on us, we, each of us, can know we are saved by Jesus, and we at the same time confess that He is the Lord (1Co 12:3).

If the Holy Spirit has come on a person, he has confessed Jesus as his Savior. When seeing the Holy Spirit on a man, we know Jesus has made him undergo his own cross. The Holy Spirit proves that Jesus worked for a man and made him born again:

> That if thou shalt confess with thy mouth the Lord Jesus, and shalt believe in thine heart that God hath raised him from the dead, thou shalt be saved. [Romans 10:9]

The above verse says that if you confess the Lord Jesus, you will be saved. We can only confess in this way when we have been saved by Jesus. Therefore, if a man has confessed Jesus as his Savior, it means he has met Jesus and Jesus has completed the salvation process and come on him as the Holy Spirit. Naturally, this person has already confessed the Lord Jesus as his Savior, and hence, he has been saved. The coming of Holy Spirit on a man is the token and evidence of his salvation. Therefore, "Jesus - Savior - salvation" explained here corresponds to "Jesus - Savior - Holy Spirit" in 1 Corinthians 12:3.

This concludes my clarification of the major topics covering the Holy Spirit and baptism with the Holy Spirit.

In the next section, I will explain the Second Coming of Jesus in the light of the stage of Acts in the faith-growing process.

Second Coming

The stage of Acts in the faith-growing process represents the time when Jesus who came comes again on our bodies as the Holy Spirit. So, the stage of Acts indicates the state in which Jesus has come on the individual again as the Holy Spirit at Pentecost.

The second coming of Jesus signifies baptism with the Holy Spirit for each person. It is the glory selectively given to each person who is healed and purified by Jesus, figuratively speaking, for three and half years.

Misguided Second Coming

Many of us might disagree that the Holy Spirit on the day of Pentecost is the second coming of Jesus because we learned that the second coming of Jesus would be visible and concurrent in the universe so that all mankind may see His coming. Also, we are expecting that Jesus will judge the whole world at that time. He will remove all unclean things, and then He will lead the good and peaceful world. However, this is misguided thinking.

Although the external world is clean and righteous, if I, myself, am not purified and righteous, then I am the one who will be judged by Jesus because of my uncleanness and unrighteousness. So the Scripture speaks of the cleansing of ourselves, not the whole world. Do not misunderstand this.

Biblically the second coming is as follows:

When Jesus comes to meet us after our true repentance, this is the first coming of Jesus to us individually. While we are following Jesus, Jesus will heal and purify us, and forgive us our sin on the cross finally. After that, Jesus will come again inside of us as the Holy Spirit to become one with us. This is Jesus' second coming.

So when we welcome the second coming of Jesus, it means that our sins are forgiven, and we are saved and born again. The Scripture does not speak of the concurrent and visible second coming but the Lords' second coming into us.

Jesus' first coming is the coming as the Lord of suffering, and His second coming is as the Lord of glory. The first coming is the time when a seed is sown in us, and the second coming is the time when the seed bears fruit and is harvested in us.

Thus, Jesus' second coming can be compared to the principle of the harvest. For example, when we gather persimmons from a persimmon tree, we only pick those that are ripe. We leave those that are not ripe so that we may reap them when they have later fully ripened. If we choose a specific time and reap all of them together, we then pick the unripe fruit and ruin them. In due course, they could possibly have ripened. Therefore, no experienced reaper will harvest them at the same time as ripe fruit.

In the same way, the Lord does not come again at a single time to judge all of us simultaneously. He only comes on the born again man individually with glory. This is a harvest of the soul. That is, He harvests soul by soul.

Wheat and Tares

The principle of reaping the persimmon matches the principle of harvest expressed in the parable of the wheat and tares. Let's consider what the harvest means in this parable:

> Another parable put he forth unto them, saying, The kingdom of heaven is likened unto a man which sowed good seed in his field: But while men slept, his enemy came and sowed tares among the wheat, and went his way. But when the blade was sprung up, and brought forth fruit, then appeared the tares also. So the servants of the householder came and said unto him, Sir, didst not thou sow good seed in thy field? from whence then hath it tares? He said unto them, An enemy hath done this. The servants said unto him, Wilt thou then that we go and gather them up? But he said, Nay; lest while ye gather up the tares, ye root up also the wheat with them. Let

> both grow together until the harvest: and in the time of harvest I will say to the reapers, Gather ye together first the tares, and bind them in bundles to burn them: but gather the wheat into my barn. [Matthew 13:24-30]

The wheat corresponds to the ripe persimmon, and the tares correspond to the unripe persimmon.

Why Not Now?

When the servants enquired whether they should pull up the tares, the householder told them to let the wheat and the tares grow together until the harvest. If we follow the servants' suggestion in this farming analogy we would pluck out the tares from time to time as the servants recommended. However, the kingdom of heaven is not like this.

We are to wait for the harvest time of each individual. It is because the tare might be changed into wheat. We should not pluck up the tare because the tare of today might be changed into wheat some day. This is why the householder told them to wait. If it were true that a tare is forever tare, he would not need to say to wait. In this case, they should pick the tares as often as they find them.

Some people insist that the householder said not to gather up the tares because it is difficult to distinguish the wheat and the tares when their blades are young. Others say the tares look very similar to the wheat when they have grown up.

However, we can find this interpretation is not true if we read the text more carefully. Verse twenty-six says, "But when the blade was sprung up, and brought forth fruit, then appeared the tares also." The tares and the wheat are judged depending on the fruit. Accordingly, in the time of harvest, it is a tare if it bears no fruit desired by the householder, and it is wheat if it bears the desired fruit. The tares and the wheat are finally identified at harvest time.

The tares are clearly revealed as tares, but the householder told the servants not to gather them up because there are some tares that will be changed into the wheat.

After this, Jesus interpreted the parable to the disciples, saying the tares are the children of the wicked one (Mat 13:38). Who are the children of the wicked one? Jesus says that the Jews who disputed with Him are the children of the devil (Jhn 8:44). That is, these kinds of Jews are the children of the devil. Did God gather them up at once? No. God is waiting until they repent to become children of the kingdom of heaven.

🗁 Respective Harvest Time

Here, the harvest does not represent a single moment in time, but the different harvest times of the respective wheat and tares. I think I need to explain the next passage for those who think that, in the harvest, the wheat and the tares are gathered at the same time. Re-read Matthew 13:30:

"Let both grow together until the harvest: and in the time of harvest I will say to the reapers, Gather ye together first the tares, and bind them in bundles to burn them: but gather the wheat into my barn."

Jesus says the harvest is the end of the world in verse thirty-nine: "The enemy that sowed them is the devil; the harvest is the end of the world; and the reapers are the angels."

The end of the world is the end of time for the old man of each individual. So there are two cases for the tares; the first case is that tares meet Jesus and are born again as wheat. This is the time of their harvest and the end for their old men. The second case is that the tares miss the chance to meet Jesus, so their harvest time and end time will be the time of their physical death.

The tares are not plucked out; they are allowed to live together with the wheat, which is to give the tares the opportunity to repent and to be changed into wheat. The meaning of the tares being left amongst the wheat is that the wheat will guide them to be wheat while living together. The stalks of wheat are reapers and angels themselves in this world. They have the life of Jesus within them so they can give life to the tares.

To sum up, this parable is about the reaping of our souls. Tares are sinful men, and the wheat represents born again, righteous men. Again, Jesus living within reapers and angels comes to the tares individually, and He heals the man and comes into him to stay forever. Through this step, the tares become the wheat and are thus harvested.

This is the life-giving process of Jesus to each of us, so harvest time is an individual experience, not a single moment in time.

Hope of Single Moment Second Coming is Self-Righteousness

I will give you a good method for checking whether your faith of today is the gift of God as the Bible says or if it is the work of the law (Eph 2:8). Check to see whether you are waiting for the second coming of Jesus as a single moment in time. If we are waiting for Jesus' concurrent second Advent, it proves that our faith is not the gift of God but the deeds of the law. We think we have done righteous deeds that will allow us to avoid the judgment of Jesus, so we desire Him to come again and judge this world.

Our human minds are very wicked. Why? I will give an example. We sometimes bring along an umbrella, although it is troublesome, after hearing that rain is forecasted for the afternoon. Of course, not all the people go out with an umbrella. Many people leave home without it for many reasons, despite the weather forecast.

Those who take an umbrella hope that it will rain in the afternoon as the weatherman said because then their labor of taking an umbrella will be rewarded. Further, they will feel happier when other people without an umbrella get wet in the rain. It is natural for those carrying an umbrella to wait for the rain to begin falling, based on their efforts of having taken an umbrella, which, however, assumes misfortune for those who had not prepared.

This scenario matches the mental state of those who are waiting for the concurrent second coming. Such waiting is fundamentally evil because it is based on the hope that the other people will be judged.

Not knowing this evil in their mind, they think they are on the Jesus' side and will not be judged but will join the heavenly wedding in the sky with Jesus. However, how can the second coming be the day of glory for them? In fact, it will be the judgment day of their faith:

> Woe unto you that desire the day of the LORD! to what end is it for you? the day of the LORD is darkness, and not light. As if a man did flee from a lion, and a bear met him; or went into the house, and leaned his hand on the wall, and a serpent bit him. [Amos 5:18-19]

If a person has received the right faith of God as a gift, he will not wait for such a concurrent Advent, the time when Jesus will come and defeat the world, because he already walks with Him now.

If a person additionally waits for Jesus to judge the world in the future, this waiting states that his current faith has been formed without Jesus. Since he does not walk with Jesus here now, he is waiting for Jesus who will come again to reward him and judge others. This kind of faith is the faith formed without Jesus in him and is dead faith. Such people wait with anticipation for the concurrent second coming of Jesus, without knowing what will happen to them on that day.

It would be wrong if Jesus had not yet come again as some two thousand years have passed since He said He would come quickly. Jesus has already come again, He is coming again, and He will come again. He has already come on a person who is born again; He is coming again now on those who are just being born again; He will come on others who will be born again. Jesus surely comes again.

Group View of the Second Coming?

> And then shall appear the sign of the Son of man in heaven: and then shall all the tribes of the earth mourn, and they shall see the Son of man coming in the clouds of heaven with power and great glory. [Matthew 24:30]

Some people assert, according to this verse, that the Lord will come visibly to all people in a single moment in time. They guess literally that all the tribes of the earth will mourn, seeing the Son of man coming in the clouds of heaven. However, this verse means each person, without exception, will receive Jesus' second coming with tears and deep emotion. It speaks of the individual experience, which is applicable to all mankind.

In "the Son of man coming in the clouds of heaven," the clouds are not the clouds in the sky, but they symbolize the human body. One of the prophetic verses about the Lord's coming in the Old Testament says:

> The burden of Egypt. Behold, the LORD rideth upon a swift cloud, and shall come into Egypt: and the idols of Egypt shall be moved at his presence, and the heart of Egypt shall melt in the midst of it. [Isaiah 19:1]

In this verse, the incarnation of Jesus Christ is prophesied. Here, Egypt is the symbol of the world, and the swift cloud is the symbol of the body of Jesus. The verse means that Jesus will come to the world and break down idols to make people know the right God, and He will melt the hearts of the people of the world to save them as a heavenly people. So, the cloud indicates the human body, especially the born again man's body.

The Lord will come again into individuals who are purified,

and those who receive Him will all mourn bitterly. This is because they will realize that they left God and brought the time of hardships on themselves as sinners in the past.

Accordingly, the second coming indicates Jesus' coming again as the Holy Spirit, and it is another expression of the baptism with the Holy Spirit. It also corresponds to the stage of Acts in the faith-growing steps.

In the next section, we will examine the End Times in the light of the stage of Acts of the faith-growing steps.

End Times

The end times also denote faith in the stage of Acts. Let's go further. People frequently cite Daniel or Revelation when they talk about the end times. I will explain it with Acts as the text. If we rightly understand the words of Acts, it will be clear that the end times we have heard about are not the end of the world literally.

The end times, according to Scripture, indicate the point where the end of old things and the beginning of the new things meet. Therefore, the end times could also be the turning point for dividing the old and the new. We generally think of the end times, in a negative manner, as the end of all things. However, the end times in Scripture indicate the beginning of new things. Thus, the end times are not something to fear or avoid. Rather, the end times should be met with gladness because the old things are passing away and the new things come.

The Great and the Terrible Day of the LORD

> For these are not drunken, as ye suppose, seeing it is but the third hour of the day. But this is that which was spoken by the prophet Joel; And it shall come to pass in the last days, saith God, I will pour out of my Spirit upon all flesh: and your sons and your daughters shall prophesy, and your young men shall see visions, and your old men shall dream dreams: And on my servants and on my handmaidens I will pour out in those days of my Spirit; and they shall prophesy: And I will shew wonders in heaven above, and signs in the earth beneath; blood, and fire, and vapour of smoke: The sun shall be turned into darkness, and the moon into blood, before that great and notable day of the Lord come: And it shall come to pass, that whosoever shall call on the name of the Lord shall be saved. [Acts 2:15-21]

When the disciples were baptized with the Holy Spirit on the day of Pentecost, people around them were amazed, Peter explained the situation by quoting some verses from Joel. This has very important meanings. Peter cited the prophecy (Joe 2:28-32) by the prophet Joel almost as it is, but Peter's words are slightly different. Read Joel 2:31:

"The sun shall be turned into darkness, and the moon into blood, before the great and terrible day of the LORD come."

We used to think the great and the terrible day of the LORD in Joel was the judgment day or end times, that is, the end of the world. However, when others said to Peter that he had had too much wine while he was baptized with the Holy Spirit on Pentecost, he cited Joel to plead against their mockery. In other words, Peter applies the great and the terrible day of the LORD not to the end time of the earth but to what the baptism with the Holy Spirit had done to him.

What does this mean? We can understand that the great and the terrible day of the LORD is not the end time of the earth but the time of baptism with the Holy Spirit.

🗁 Fear and Love

The fear mentioned in the 'great and the terrible day of the LORD' is not something general. It means fear towards God. We have this fear in us, and it came into us after Adam ate of the tree of knowledge of good and evil. Read Genesis 3:10:

"And he said, I heard thy voice in the garden, and I was afraid, because I was naked; and I hid myself."

The fear came after the human being was depraved. Hence, fear is a feature of sinners. Even while believing in God, praying to Him, and requesting Him earnestly, we have certain fears in us. Whilst we believe in God, we often think that God will punish us for our sins and praise us for our good works. If we see God in this way, we see Him with fears. When we believe in God based on these fears, it's legalistic faith, which is under the law. Those who have this kind of legalistic faith should meet the true Jesus and receive the Holy Spirit to be born again. Unless they eliminate these fears, they cannot enter the kingdom of God:

> But the fearful, and unbelieving, and the abominable, and murderers, and whoremongers, and sorcerers, and idolaters, and all liars, shall have their part in the lake which burneth with fire and brimstone: which is the second death. [Revelation 21:8]

Before receiving the Holy Spirit at Pentecost, Peter was seeing the 'great and the terrible day of the LORD' with fear. It proves that he was a sinner whose sin was not perfectly forgiven up to that time. This fear was cast out when he was perfectly reconciled to God through Jesus by receiving the Holy Spirit. The Holy Spirit is the love of God, and when the love of God is received, fears are cast out at the same time.

Consider 1 John 4:18: "There is no fear in love; but perfect love casteth out fear: because fear hath torment. He that feareth is not made perfect in love."

Love is not the gerund of 'loving.' It is the noun meaning 'the person who is born again.' Love comes to us from God through Jesus, and it is the Holy Spirit who comes on us in the days of Pentecost in our own lives. When the Holy Spirit comes on us, the old man, who was the base of the fear, is cast out. Therefore, we on whom this love has come have no fear.

Read Romans 8:15: "For ye have not received the spirit of bondage again to fear; but ye have received the Spirit of adoption, whereby we cry, Abba, Father."

Then, we are the beings of love. This love loves always and forever. For we are love itself; we do not require to love, but our life itself is love.

🗁 Great and Notable Day of the Lord

Citing Joel, Peter slightly changed a part of the quote. It is written in Joel "before the great and the terrible day of the LORD come," but Peter changed it into "before the great and notable day of the Lord come" (Joe 2:31; Act 2:20). This change is crucial, as it is quite opposite to the original meaning.

Why so? Before the day of Pentecost of Peter, Peter thought the end times would be the great and terrible day as Joel said. He also worried much and trembled with fear at first to think about that day. That was his old man's view. However, through Jesus, his old man finally died, and he received the Holy Spirit.

He originally thought that a terrible thing would happen at the end times, but when he had passed through it, a new world had been opened to him and nothing could be better. He realized the 'great and the terrible day of the LORD' in Joel means the 'great and notable day of the Lord.' So, he changed the phrase into the great and notable day of the Lord.

The end times will be a terrible day from the viewpoint of the old self, which dies, on that day, but it will be glorious from the viewpoint of him who is born again in the Holy Spirit. Peter confessed the words of Joel very accurately according to his experience. The prophecy of Joel has been individually fulfilled in Peter at Pentecost, the end times. Further, the prophecy of Joel should be fulfilled in us individually.

We can check our current positions of faith depending on how God looks to us. If someone thinks the judgment day of God is a terrible day, it proves that he is still under the control of the old man. It is because the old man in us fears God. On the contrary, if someone confesses that the day of the Lord is the glorious day based on his experience, he is already born again.

The Last Days Mean the End Times

And it shall come to pass in the last days, saith God, I will pour

> out of my Spirit upon all flesh... [Acts 2:17]

The 'last days' is the translation of the Greek *eschatos*. It also could be translated into the 'end times.'

Peter gives his evidence that the Spirit of God is poured out on him in his last days by quoting Joel. God poured out His Spirit on the 120 disciples, including Peter, on the day of Pentecost. Since the last days of the 120 disciples were at Pentecost, God gave them the Holy Spirit at that time.

It is the same nowadays. Anyone having met his personal last days will receive the baptism with the Holy Spirit, and those having not yet met their personal last days will not be able to receive Him. The last days in this instance do not mean the end times or the last days of the earth. They mean the last days of the old man of individuals or the end of the old world that the old man sees.

We are under the control of the old man as soon as we are born, and we then start to live in the world that the old man sees. When Jesus appears in this world and crucifies our old man together with Him, our old world will come to an end. This time is the last days. God promised to pour out His Spirit at this time to each individual.

Peter met Jesus and walked this way. He was baptized with the Holy Spirit in the last days of his old man. He cites Joel because it was the word for those who are in that right situation:

"It shall come to pass in the last days, and I will pour out of my Spirit upon all flesh."

Here, all flesh means all of those who have met the last days of their old men without exception. It does not mean the end of all mankind on earth.

Time of Salvation

> And it shall come to pass, that whosoever shall call on the name of the Lord shall be saved. [Acts 2:21]

Why is Peter mentioning salvation at the time of baptism in the Holy Spirit at Pentecost? The Scripture says, "Believe on the Lord Jesus Christ, and thou shalt be saved, and thy house" (Act 16:31).

When did Peter believe in Jesus and when was he saved then? Peters says he believed in Him and was saved when he was baptized with the Holy Spirit on the day of Pentecost. Since he realized it, he said whosoever shall call on the name of the Lord shall be saved.

In fact, the disciples, including Peter, did not know who Jesus was even while following Him. They realized and knew Jesus was the Savior after their salvation. It stands to reason. It is because we cannot know Jesus as our Savior before He saves us, no matter how firmly we agree to that. I already explained this matter in the previous section "Meaning of Confession."

We now gather in church in agreement that Jesus is the Savior, which is, however, the agreement that Jesus is the Savior of Peter or the disciples who lived in the past. Such agreement does not mean that we know Him as our personal Savior. When we are saved after passing through all the process like Peter, Jesus will be our Savior.

Peter, in his earlier time, made the famous confession: "You are the Christ, the Son of the living God"(Mat 16:16). He said many things and acted in many ways to show off his faith, but he knew nothing at all without experiences. By the baptism of the Holy Spirit on the day of Pentecost, he confessed Jesus is the Christ on the basis of his experience.

Therefore, "You are the Christ" in Matthew 16:16 was the confession only with lips and without experience, and the true confession of Peter is in Acts 2:21: "Whosoever shall call on the name of the Lord shall be saved." This word means that only the man who knows who the Lord is will call on the Lord correctly, and he will then be saved. The only way to correctly know the Lord is to be saved by Jesus. Therefore, 'calling on the name of the Lord' is equal to 'salvation.' They are the same in meaning.

The last days represent the time of baptism with the Holy Spirit. It shows that one's faith has reached the stage of Acts.

Next, we will touch on the issue of the Lord's Coming and the End of the World, which corresponds to the stage of Acts.

Lord's Coming and the End of the World

Faith in the stage of Acts represents the state in which the world is over and the Lord has come. I will describe what "Thy coming and the end of the world" means with reference to the words of Jesus (Mat 24:3).

The Background of the Chapter of the End Times

In Matthew Chapter 24, known as the "End Times Chapter," Jesus answers the question about the end times. We can read many expressions about the end times: "And woe unto them that are with child, and to them that give suck in those days! But pray ye that your flight be not in the winter, neither on the Sabbath day," and "For then shall be great tribulation, such as was not since the beginning of the world to this time, no, nor ever shall be." In addition to them, "the abomination of desolation," "there shall be famines, pestilences, and earthquakes in diverse places," and "the love of many shall grow cold." We may think these phrases describe the day when Jesus really comes again and judges the earth. However, by studying the background for why Jesus said these things, we will establish whether Jesus really meant the end times of the earth around us.

Matthew Chapter 24 begins as follows:

> And Jesus went out, and departed from the temple: and his disciples came to him for to shew him the buildings of the temple. And Jesus said unto them, See ye not all these things? verily I say unto you, There shall not be left here one stone upon another, that shall not be thrown down. And as he sat upon the mount of Olives, the disciples came unto him privately, saying, Tell us, when shall these things be? and what shall be the sign of thy coming, and of the end of the world? [Matthew 24:1-3]

When Jesus goes out of the temple, His disciples come to Him to show Him the buildings of the temple. Jesus then says not a single stone will be left on another but all will be thrown down. They ask Him privately on the Mount of Olives, "When will these things be?" and "What shall be the sign of your coming, and of the end of the world?"

To answer their questions, Jesus begins to talk about the great tribulation. The disciples asked Him when the end times would come, recognizing His coming and the end of the world as the end of the earth. We, as well as the disciples, also think of the second coming and the end times in such way.

However, Jesus' coming again and the end of the world do not mean the period of the end of the earth. The temple was completely and thoroughly destroyed by Roman General Titus in about 70 A.D. If we accept His word literally, the great tribulation must have broken out when the temple fell to pieces, and the Advent should have come. However, Jesus did not come again physically at that time. And the world did not end at that time.

This shows we are totally misunderstanding the Scripture. Since we are mistaken in interpreting the correct meaning and while the end times did not indicate the end of the earth, our understanding does not reflect reality.

Some people say the end times Jesus spoke of include both the destruction of the temple in 70 A.D. and the end times to come. However, this is nothing but a poor excuse. If they interpret that there will be a second coming when the temple is destroyed, the second coming should happen when the temple is thrown down. The interpretation that there will be a second coming when the temple will be destroyed in the future, whereas there was no second coming when the same was destroyed in the past, does not stand to reason.

The Scriptures are not written to describe historical facts. Although they are recorded based on history, they have spiritual meanings. The spiritual meanings are hidden and will only be only revealed by the Spirit. And the meanings are words of truth that apply to all mankind, transcending time and space.

Those who take pains to study the Scriptures may memorize verses well or find them easily in the Scripture. However, they can miss the true spiritual meanings. If I say to them that they must realize the spiritual meanings of the Scripture, they will oppose me by saying it will be dangerous to attempt to interpret the Scripture subjectively. However, if they do not know the spiritual meanings of the Scripture, they are inclined to insist on their own opinions, anytime and anywhere, like here in this instance.

Here, Jesus tried to transfer the spiritual message to the disciples through the destruction of the temple, the physical phenomenon. However, they kept on thinking about the physical destruction of the temple. We will misapprehend the Scripture if we only try to hear and understand the words of Jesus literally. However, carnal Christians may not avoid this confusion.

🗁 Meaning of the Destruction of the Temple

The temple is the place where God dwells. The place in which God dwells was the tabernacle in the wilderness in the Old Testament time, and it was developed to be the temple in the days of Solomon. When the tabernacle or the temple was built completely, the LORD was abiding there and the temple was filled with the glory of the LORD. As Jesus came to this world, the tabernacle and the temple as buildings were substituted with a man because He Himself was the temple. God abided in him, the temple, and He was full of the glory of God. This issue will be touched on in further detail in the section "The Place of God and Its glory."

What does the destruction of the temple that Jesus spoke of mean?

Mankind is born into this world, separated from God, and are identified as born sinners. We are sinners not because we have committed some crimes but because we are separated from God. Due to this separation, we do not know what God wants, and as such, our lives are being led by non-God beings.

We, under this circumstance, go to church to believe in Jesus and God. So we help the poor, do good things, attend church regularly, join church activities, fast, and pray to please God. We earnestly lay up this kind of righteousness to be shown to God later at the Day of Judgment, and we expect that we will finally go to heaven to live with God happily ever after. Most of us think that this will happen in the afterlife.

However, it is wrong for us to attempt to do good works whilst we are separated from God. Therefore, our hope to be with God afterwards by doing good works now is fundamentally wrong. If we walk with God and do what He accepts, it is good. The human being can do no good if he has left God who is the author of good. Therefore, in church, we should focus on being one with God through Jesus, not on doing self-righteousness.

However, without knowing this, we lay up self-righteousness again and again with the sweet expectation of being with God later. That is, we are building the temple in us in order to invite God in. However, God does not come into the temple built with self-righteousness. If we are like this, we are in the Old Testament period in our faith-growing process, and such faith is called 'legalistic faith' in this book.

When the time is ripe, God will thoroughly destroy the temples of those who built them with their self-righteousness. God will do so through Jesus Christ. In other words, when they start the New Testament period of their faith by meeting Jesus, these things will happen to them. God intentionally makes a moment, and when their self-righteousness has reached a climax, He will defeat the tall city and the tower of their self-righteousness. They will then be in utter confusion and will bear a grudge and cry bitterly:

> The great day of the LORD is near, it is near, and hasteth greatly, even the voice of the day of the LORD: the mighty man shall cry there bitterly. That day is a day of wrath, a day of trouble and distress, a day of wasteness and desolation, a day

> of darkness and gloominess, a day of clouds and thick darkness, A day of the trumpet and alarm against the fenced cities, and against the high towers. [Zephaniah 1:14-16]

Since the faith they laid up for years with great effort crumbles in an instant, the anguish at that time cannot be expressed with words. So, this word of Zephaniah is not an exaggerated expression. The more eagerly and the more wholeheartedly one has led a believer's life, the far more bitterly he will cry because he ventured all his life upon his faith.

However, self-righteousness should be demolished, regardless of enthusiasm and devotion, because it is not true righteousness. After that he will live. He should rejoice in that his self-righteousness fell down while he was still alive. He has a new opportunity to re-start. If he passes away, having self-righteousness in him, he will show them off before God, then God will say, "You did it for your own good, and you were rewarded at that time!" Then, he will be too late.

Accordingly, the time when the temple the old man laid up with eagerness is thoroughly destroyed is the last day. In this instance, since the old man's values are destroyed together with it, it is the last day of the old man. From that time on, he will not depend on the old man any longer and will learn to walk with God.

Matthew 24 describes the tribulation of a man during the process in which the old man is destroyed. It is not universal tribulation. The end of the world represents the end of the old world he used to see through the eyes of the old man.

It can also be called a process through which the old man dies to be born again as a new man: "All these are the beginning of sorrows" (Mat 24:8).

Here, the word *sorrows* is translated from the Greek *odin*, which is accurately translated as 'birth pangs'. All sorrow and tribulation are birth pangs occurring in the process through which a man is born again as a new man. His coming and the end of the world represents Jesus' ending of the 'old world' as He comes again as the Holy Spirit to an individual.

He who has undergone this process will be baptized with the Holy Spirit to have faith in the stage of Acts.

I will explain the Seventy Weeks of Daniel in the next section, which also represents the stage of Acts of the faith-growing steps.

Seventy Sevens

The seventy weeks in Daniel represent one man's being born again and the coming of the Holy Spirit to him. So it also represents faith of the stage of Acts.

Seventy Weeks

Let us look at the verse of Daniel, which is widely known as the description of the end times:

> Seventy weeks are determined upon thy people and upon thy holy city, to finish the transgression, and to make an end of sins, and to make reconciliation for iniquity, and to bring in everlasting righteousness, and to seal up the vision and prophecy, and to anoint the most Holy. [Daniel 9:24]

Here, many scholars interpret the seventy weeks in Daniel historically. So they calculate 490 years from the time when the temple was built in Jerusalem according to the history, and they figure out the time when Jesus is born in the land of Israel. If we understand the seventy weeks as merely an historical event, it will be a word having no connection with us who are alive now.

The seventy weeks represents neither the end of the earth nor a page in the history of Israel. Spiritually it denotes the acceptable year when Jesus comes inside of each of us with a new life. In that day, all our transgressions, sins, and iniquities will be forgiven forever and everlasting righteousness will be manifested in us. Therefore, seventy weeks refers to the end of the old man and the birth of the new man, that is, being born again or baptized with the Holy Spirit. It does not refer to the end of the physical world.

This will become quite evident if we read the dialogue between Jesus and Peter in Matthew.

Forgiveness of Seventy Sevens

> Then came Peter to him, and said, Lord, how oft shall my brother sin against me, and I forgive him? till seven times? Jesus saith unto him, I say not unto thee, Until seven times: but, Until seventy times seven. [Matthew 18:21-22]

When you read this, please substitute you own name for *Peter* because Peter's problem is ours. He asked the question we all want to ask. Peter asked Jesus, "How many times shall I forgive my brother when he sins against me? Until seven times?" Peter asked Him, thinking he would be regarded as righteous if he forgave his brother up to seven times. In other words, his question is, "How many times shall I forgive my brother if I would be considered righteous? Until seven times?"

Seven times for him has great meaning. He had seen many miracles and observed the powers of Jesus. Peter even confessed he was ready to die for Him. Forgiveness until seven times for him, therefore, is the forgiveness with all his life. It was the maximum value which men could reach.

Like Peter, our old man inside would ask, "How many times must I forgive my brother so that I will get a passing grade as a righteous man?" We estimate righteousness according to the number of times forgiveness is given to brothers.

Jesus answered in response to Peter's question, "Until seventy times seven." He said to forgive until seventy times seven.

What would seventy times seven mean? We, of course, know forgiveness until seventy times seven does not mean forgiving until 490 times and refusing to forgive at the 491st time. Some people think of seventy times seven as endlessly or without limit. This is not a correct understanding because Peter set the number of forgiveness to seven for the purpose of currying favor with Jesus, whom he followed at the risk of his life. So the request over seven times is meaningless as long as Peter is concerned. Surely, Jesus did not mean by seventy times seven to ask Peter to forgive

490 times or without end.

He meant the forgiveness of 'seventy times seven.' The seventy times seven (70x7) here matches seventy weeks (70x7) in Daniel. What then is the forgiveness of seventy sevens? This forgiveness is not of this world but of the kingdom of God. So if we wish to forgive in this manner, our old man should end and be born again, which is the process of seventy weeks as in Daniel.

Only such a born again man would be able to forgive brothers seventy times seven. He has come out of the world of the 'law of sin and death,' and now is in the world of the 'law of the Spirit of life' through the forgiveness of Jesus (Rom 8:2). The former is the world and the latter is the kingdom of God. If we are in the world, we are counting how many times we have forgiven brothers. Such forgiveness of seven times reflects the trivial thinking of the sinful world itself. We should get out of such a world by receiving the forgiveness of seventy times seven from Jesus.

In this passage of Scripture, Jesus is in the process of forgiving Peter and the disciples. After about three years, Jesus is crucified and resurrected in them, the disciples. Thus, the disciples were being forgiven seventy times seven from Jesus and were born again with His life.

Jesus appeared to the disciples after His resurrection and breathed the Holy Spirit on them:

> And when he had said this, he breathed on them, and saith unto them, Receive ye the Holy Ghost: Whose soever sins ye remit, they are remitted unto them; and whose soever sins ye retain, they are retained. [John 20:22-23]

Jesus saved the disciples. He gave the once and for all forgiveness to them and sent them out to give such forgiveness to their 'neighbors'. Likewise, when we receive the forgiveness of seventy times seven, we also can forgive our brother seventy times seven. This is the forgiveness until seventy times seven that Jesus wanted to give to Peter. Surely, such forgiveness cannot be compared to seven times of forgiveness.

If we speak of this from the point of view of salvation, we are to be saved first and are to save others in the same manner. We can do this because the life of Jesus has manifested in us.

In Matthew 18, after telling Peter to forgive his brother until seventy times seven, Jesus speaks a parable. This is the parable in which a man who owed his master ten thousand talents receives forgiveness of that debt (Mat 18:23-35). This is an important parable relating to the seventy weeks, so it will be touched on in the following chapter concerning faith in the Stage of the Epistles.

Now you will know the seventy weeks indicates baptism with the Holy Spirit. The man having attained the seventy weeks has faith in the stage of Acts.

Next, we will consider the Place of God and Its Glory in connection with the stage of Acts of the faith-growing process.

The Place of God and Its Glory

Now, I will explain the faith in the Stage of Acts in relation to the completion of God's dwelling place and its glory.

The Place of God

Where is the place of God? He dwells anywhere and anytime since He is omnipresent. Nevertheless, He hopes to settle at a particular place. He commanded Moses to let the Israelites make the tabernacle in the wilderness. He says He will dwell in it (Exd 25:8-9). After Moses finished building it, God came into it, and the tabernacle was filled with the glory of the LORD (Exd 40:34-35). The tabernacle was God's place in the wilderness.

After the Israelites entered Canaan, King David wished to make a temple in which God would abide. David says, "I dwell in a house of cedar, but the ark of God dwells under curtains" (2Sa 7:2). However, He does not allow him to build it. Rather, He let it be built in the time of Solomon. When Solomon finished building the temple, he brought in the Ark of the Covenant to the most holy place. And the glory of the LORD filled the temple (1Ki 8:11).

One thing we find in common here is that when the tabernacle or the temple was built, God came in there and the place was filled with the glory of God. During Old Testament times, God came to the tabernacle and the temple, and accordingly, the places were filled with His glory.

What about in the New Testament times then? Referring to John Chapter 2, Jesus drove the oxen, sheep, and doves out of the temple and overthrew the tables of the money changers. The Jews said to Him, "What sign will You show to us, seeing that You do these things?" (Jhn 2:18).

He then answers as follows:

Jesus answered and said unto them, Destroy this temple,

> and in three days I will raise it up. Then said the Jews, Forty and six years was this temple in building, and wilt thou rear it up in three days? But he spake of the temple of his body. [John 2:19-21]

According to this verse, His body is the temple. If we define the temple as the place where God abides, it is really so. Because God dwells in Jesus, Jesus is the first man who is the temple of God (Jhn 14:10). God dwelled in the temple of the Old Testament times and the temple was filled with glory. Therefore, it follows that God dwells in Jesus, so Jesus is full of His glory. Jesus was the first 'man temple' in which God dwelled, so He was full of the glory and grace of God.

However, after He was crucified, Jesus extended the ability to become a temple of the Holy Spirit to the 120 disciples on the day of Pentecost. After having finished His public life, Jesus spoke as follows to His disciples before crucifixion:

> In my Father's house are many mansions: if it were not so, I would have told you. I go to prepare a place for you. And if I go and prepare a place for you, I will come again, and receive you unto myself; that where I am, there ye may be also. [John 14:2-3]

This word sounds as if Jesus will ascend to heaven, build the temple, come again to bring the disciples there, and be with them. However, if this understanding is to be correct, then all of them should have died after the crucifixion of Jesus to go to heaven in order to live there happily ever after with Him. However, no man died with Him and went to heaven. They lived their own lives individually on the earth, and they went to heaven later. So, it is wrong to think that Jesus would come again for the purpose of bringing the disciples to heaven after finishing the mansions' construction in the kingdom.

The true meaning is that Jesus will make the bodies of the

disciples as temples and will dwell in them as the Holy Spirit. Jesus is to leave so that the Holy Spirit may come. Metaphorically speaking, Jesus is the flower and the Holy Spirit is the fruit. The flower should wither in order to bring the fruit, and the flower will be included in the fruit. So withering of the flower is to prepare and make the fruit.

The time of fulfillment is the day of Pentecost, and the place where He came is the individual bodies of the disciples. He prepared the dwelling place through His public life. In this case, the bodies of the disciples were the temples. After the Holy Spirit comes on them, they, the temples, are full of grace and truth to testify and preach the word of the Lord with great power.

Further, the apostle Paul says our bodies are the temple of God:

> Know ye not that ye are the temple of God, and that the Spirit of God dwelleth in you? [1 Corinthians 3:16]

> What? know ye not that your body is the temple of the Holy Ghost which is in you, which ye have of God, and ye are not your own? [1 Corinthians 6:19]

The place in which God dwells is gradually revealed in the order of the tabernacle, the temple, the body of Jesus, the bodies of the disciples, and the bodies of church members. Our bodies will also be God's dwelling temple when we have undergone the same process as the disciples. The principle for God to change us is to make us a temple and come into us. Thus, we can be full of grace and truth because of God inside us.

Let's Build a Temple

The spiritual meaning of building the temple is that our old man gradually becomes extinct and our new man grows in inverse proportion. When this process for building the temple is completed, our bodies will be the place in which God dwells. When this temple building process is fulfilled in us by Jesus, then God can be with us. There is no other way for God to dwell in us.

God is working now so that He may make a place in us and abide with us forever.

In Haggai, God speaks to the Jews who put off the time for rebuilding the temple by saying, "The time to build the LORD's house is not come" (Hag 1:2). Read the following verses from Haggai:

> Ye have sown much, and bring in little; ye eat, but ye have not enough; ye drink, but ye are not filled with drink; ye clothe you, but there is none warm; and he that earneth wages earneth wages to put it into a bag with holes. [Haggai 1:6]

This message makes us realize the misguided faith that we have. We pray to God to earn much money, increase the farm produce, eat much, and dress ourselves well whilst we are not very much concerned about building God's temple within us. As long as we have this sort of faith, we will not get full even if we eat. We will not feel warm even if we put on clothes, and we will not be well off even if we work hard and make money. Accordingly, we will find no satisfaction in the least in our whole life.

However, what is really miserable is that we are often unaware of our state, even though it is pointed out to us. We might ask, "When did I disobey the Lord and prevent Him from coming into my heart?" Or, "When did I say I would not build the temple in my mind?" These questions occur to us because we are utterly incapable of seeing who we are. The time will come when we realize our state, if God permits.

I have explained faith in the stage of Acts in many aspects. These include the Baptism with the Holy Spirit, Second Coming, Last Days, Seventy Weeks, and the perfection of building the temple. All these signify Jesus Christ who comes into us as the Holy Spirit. If they are fulfilled in us, we are the blessed who have faith in the stage of Acts.

Acts Stage Is Always Open to Us

Those having reached the stage of Acts can preach Jesus Christ with power like the apostles in the Scripture. Some people insist that the power and miracles recorded in Acts were given only once because they were needed to write the Scripture. That reasoning is not true. The things in the Scriptures are open to all men and all generations, and they are to be repeated for each person.

As Peter met Jesus and became a man of power two thousand years ago, we will be men of power like Peter when we personally meet Jesus. The Apostle Paul was changed, not by meeting the incarnated Jesus, but by meeting Jesus after the resurrection and ascension. As Paul did, we can meet Jesus who is resurrected and ascended into heaven. We can be His disciples; we can be His apostles and prophets. All good things in the Scriptures are possible for us, only if we would meet Jesus in our life now.

7

STAGE OF THE EPISTLES — LIFE OF THE BORN AGAIN

Faith in the stage of the Epistles is a continuation of the stage of Acts. It represents the faith that will be possessed by those who are baptized with the Holy Spirit, for the rest of their lives. During this process, they extend the life of Jesus Christ to others. True love for neighbors naturally flows from those who have this faith.

Twenty-one books from Romans to Jude are in the form of epistles in which the born again preach the words of life to the respective churches. These books show how those who have faith in the stage of the Epistles proclaim the same kingdom of God to other people.

During this period, we belong to the kingdom of God while living in this world. Once we go to heaven, all people there will already know about heaven, so there will be no need to preach the gospel. Therefore, if we have faith in the stage of Epistles, we can enjoy our lives to the utmost. This enjoyment also becomes the driving force for us in spreading the kingdom of God.

Faith in the stage of the Epistles will be the most meaningful and glorious period of their lives for believers. If we believe in Jesus, our goal should be reaching the faith stage of the Epistles. The apostles Peter and Paul also lived lives of such faith.

Man in the Stage of the Epistles Cannot Sin

You may ask, "Can the born again man commit sin again?" This is one of the most difficult issues that no one has resolved accurately according to the Scriptures as of yet. One could also ask, "Can those who have reached the faith stage of the Epistles commit sin?"

Regarding this issue, the traditional viewpoint is that they can commit sin, but they will be forgiven if they confess their sins. Further, the existing doctrine states that we will be perfectly sanctified only when we have passed away. It is not so. If a man is rightly born again, he is perfected and sanctified, and he cannot sin any longer. It cannot be said that we will commit sin no longer only after we have died and put off our fleshly bodies.

🗁 Whosoever Is Born of God

> Whosoever is born of God doth not commit sin; for his seed remaineth in him: and he cannot sin, because he is born of God. [I John 3:9]

The Scripture clearly says that born again man cannot commit sin because God's seed remains in him.

Yes. As the Scripture says, those having faith in the stage of the Epistles cannot commit sin any more. They will live the life of preaching the gospel until death. However, most people cannot understand that born again men do not sin. They think this state is unattainable. They think so probably because their sins are forgiven, yet they are still sinning. So they justify their sinning by saying, "We will be sinless only when we pass away."

However, the Scriptures say that the born again do not sin. This leaves us in the situation whether the Scripture is wrong, or we are wrongfully born again. The Scripture can never be wrong, so if there is something wrong; it is we who are mistaken in terms of being born again. That is, we commit sin because we mistakenly think we are born again. Actually, we are not. That's why we sin.

If a man is forgiven by Jesus, all his sins have been forgiven once and forever. It does not mean some sins are forgiven and others are not.

People often argue saying, "What about the sins the forgiven man will commit in the future?" However, if he has been forgiven rightly, he has been already changed into a man who will have nothing to do with sin in the future. Being forgiven does not simply mean that each of the sinful acts of the past, the present, and the future are and will be forgiven one by one. Forgiveness by Jesus represents the fundamental change of man.

Before forgiveness, he is sinner, and after forgiveness, he is a righteous man. The sinner has the nature of committing sins, and the righteous has the nature of committing no sins. As the sinner cannot do righteous things, the righteous cannot do sinful acts. We are to think deeply on this matter. In this regard, Jesus says,

> Even so every good tree bringeth forth good fruit; but a corrupt tree bringeth forth evil fruit. A good tree cannot bring forth evil fruit, neither can a corrupt tree bring forth good fruit. [Matthew 7:17-18]

A good tree brings forth good fruit, and an evil tree brings forth evil fruit. Forgiveness and being born again mean that the evil tree is born again as a good tree. Naturally, good trees bear only good fruit. Likewise, the righteous man will only do righteous acts, not sins.

Therefore, if a righteous man commits a sin, he does it because he is not truly a righteous man. The truly righteous man does not sin.

🗁 As Far as the East Is from the West

We will consider another verse below:

> As far as the east is from the west, so far hath he removed our transgressions from us. [Psalms 103:12]

This passage says God will separate our transgressions from us as the east is split from the west. The east cannot be united with the west fundamentally. For example, if the East Sea of Korea is moved to the West Sea, it will no longer be the East Sea. Accordingly, the east cannot be joined with the west. They are supposed to be separated by nature and definition.

Likewise, if we are separated from our transgressions, we cannot be combined with them any longer as the east cannot be combined with the west. This is the forgiveness by Jesus. We will be forgiven once and forever, rather than being forgiven each time when we commit a sin.

🗁 The Wind Blows Where It Pleases

It is difficult to understand the statement that the born again do not commit sin because we hardly believe that the born again man will no longer get angry or look on a woman with lust. We guess it will only be possible after we have put off our flesh and have gone on to the next world. Existing doctrines are established based on this idea.

However, what we should first know is that he who does not commit sin is not a man who does not get angry, and he is not a man who does not look on a woman with lust. These are natural emotions of men and cannot be transgressions. It is impossible for those who are not born again to comprehend what born again men are like, even if I explain it again and again. This explanation may sound like a useless excuse to them. It may be natural that the carnal men can find no big difference from the spiritually born again men.

Failing to see the difference, the Jews had Jesus crucified, and they persecuted Paul the apostle. If Jesus or Paul had shown the manners of a very gentle and dignified personality without a hint of anger, the Jews might not have persecuted them that much.

The carnal cannot recognize the spiritually born again. Nicodemus was surprised at Jesus' saying "You must be born again." Jesus further says to him,

> The wind bloweth where it listeth, and thou hearest the sound thereof, but canst not tell whence it cometh, and whither it goeth: so is every one that is born of the Spirit. [John 3:8]

In this dialogue, Jesus says to Nicodemus, who knows nothing about being born again, "You cannot recognize the born again man." It is natural. Having no experience of being born again, he cannot recognize the born again men and cannot grasp what being born again is.

What Is Sin?

If we are to understand that the born again do not sin again, we should first think of what sin is. The definition of sin is 'men's separation from God.' The book of Isaiah speaks of this separation:

> Behold, the LORD's hand is not shortened, that it cannot save; neither his ear heavy, that it cannot hear: But your iniquities have separated between you and your God, and your sins have hid his face from you, that he will not hear. [Isaiah 59:1-2]

We can notice here the separation between mankind and God due to iniquity, which is sin. Sin is the separation. And the actual separation is that we do not want to acknowledge God in our mind. Paul said in Romans as follows:

> And even as they did not like to retain God in their knowl-

> edge, God gave them over to a reprobate mind, to do those things which are not convenient. [Romans 1:28]

We are separated from God in our minds, and under such circumstances, we are living as the slaves of sin. God is omnipresent, but He does not exist in our mind. Actually, He exists in our mind, but we refuse to retain God in our knowledge. This is the separation. We are living everyday life with this separation. Naturally, we sin with every breath we take and with every move we make. That's why Jesus says that "the evil tree brings forth only evil fruits."

When Jesus comes to us, He gives us God, the Holy Spirit, in our mind. If that is accomplished in us, our sins are forgiven forever. In this case, we are good trees, which will bring forth only good fruits. Likewise, the born again would not sin again forever. This means that they will not be separated from God again, and also means that born again man, who is in the stage of the Epistles, will not sin again.

If we fail to understand the concept of being born again with regard to sin, we accept the human doctrine that man cannot be set free from the sin as long as he lives in the flesh. Such a statement denies that redemption by Jesus is once and forever.

Sin That Cannot Be Repented

In fact, we can find many Scripture passages leading us to misunderstand the forgiveness of sin. The representative verse of these is in Hebrews. However, reading deeply, no verses in the Scripture, including this one, deny once and for all forgiveness. We only misinterpret them.

Let's think through Hebrews:

> For if we sin wilfully after that we have received the knowledge of the truth, there remaineth no more sacrifice for sins, But a certain fearful looking for of judgment and fiery indigna-

> tion, which shall devour the adversaries. He that despised Moses' law died without mercy under two or three witnesses: Of how much sorer punishment, suppose ye, shall he be thought worthy, who hath trodden under foot the Son of God, and hath counted the blood of the covenant, wherewith he was sanctified, an unholy thing, and hath done despite unto the Spirit of grace? [Hebrews 10:26-29]

Here, "if we sin willfully after that we have received the knowledge of the truth" means sinning after knowing Jesus Christ and believing in Him. There remains no more sacrifice for sins because the sinner has treated the blood of the covenant as unholy and insulted the Spirit of grace.

At first glance, this word seems to state that the born again man can commit sin as a settled fact. So, they understand the verses as a strong warning to apostates who believed in God but backslid. However, this word does not mean we can fall while believing in Him, but it does say we can never fall if we believed rightly.

Here, believing in Jesus is expressed as "receiving the knowledge of the truth." Both expressions convey the same meaning. He who rightly received the knowledge of the truth cannot be depraved and cannot commit sin willfully. If he knew the truth but committed sin, then he knew the truth wrongfully from the beginning. In other words, he who fails to grasp the truth in the right way backslides and commits sins.

For example, if a man buys a regular movie ticket, he can naturally enter the theater. If he bought one but was refused entrance, then the ticket must be a fake one. It would be quite ridiculous if someone, to justify the situation, says, "You may not enter the theater even with a legitimate ticket. You must buy another one." Why do we need to buy another ticket? One ticket is more than enough.

It is the same with the forgiveness of Jesus. If a man commits sin again, even though he has been forgiven forever, he has been forgiven falsely. If he continues to insist that he has been truly forgiven, he despises the blood of Jesus as an unholy thing. He is insisting, by his word of mouth, that the blood of Jesus cannot forgive us once and for all.

He Who Cannot Believe in Jesus Because He Believes in Jesus

"For if we sin wilfully after that we have received the knowledge of the truth, there remaineth no more sacrifice for sins" (Hbr 10:26).

For those who are forgiven falsely in the manner mentioned above, no more sacrifice for sins is left. Why not? Such people justify their contradictory situation, in which their sins are forgiven but they stay in the sin, by saying, "This is the right way to believe in Jesus. All people follow this way!" Or, "The famous apostle Paul also said he was chief of sinners." And, "We must fight sin to the finish. We can completely break with sin only after we die." All these sayings are justifications based on misunderstandings.

The reason why there is no more sacrifice for sins for them is because they are deadly sure of believing in Him even if the sky falls. They firmly believe that they are perfectly forgiven by the blood of Jesus.

> For it is impossible for those who were once enlightened, and have tasted of the heavenly gift, and were made partakers of the Holy Ghost, And have tasted the good word of God, and the powers of the world to come, If they shall fall away, to renew them again unto repentance; seeing they crucify to themselves the Son of God afresh, and put him to an open shame. [Hebrews 6:4-6]

The writer of Hebrews says it is impossible for those who believed in Jesus and then fall away, to be renewed again to repentance because they crucify the Son of God again and make a spectacle of Him. This does not mean it is the will of God that He will not crucify Jesus again, but it means those who wrongfully believe in Jesus think in this way. They think that they crucified Jesus when believing in Him first, and when we tell them to have true sacrifice, they will fall into the situation of crucifying Him again if they follow our words. They meet this problem because they failed to realize that they had misguided and legalistic faith in Jesus from the beginning.

Anyway, if they do not realize they have such a legalistic faith, they will have to refuse the true sacrifice for sins and will subsequently have to keep the legalistic faith. Naturally, they still remain as sinners, so they will have to wait for the fiery indignation that will devour sinners.

This is the very miserable case in which they cannot believe in the true Jesus because they believed in another Jesus. True Jesus is the only way to salvation, and hence, to those who refuse it, there is no salvation. They cannot be renewed again to repentance. They are those who cannot believe in Jesus because they believe in Jesus.

As we can see from what was explained so far, the born again do not sin. However, as I said, there are many other passages that can be interpreted so as to make one think that being born again can be canceled or that the born again man can commit sin. But, such interpretation is caused by confusing the state of not being born again with the state of being born again.

I say once again that salvation in the Scripture has the same meaning as being born again. If we define salvation as the state in which we will go to heaven when we die, and define being born again as some changes in our actions, we are totally mistaken in terms of salvation and being born again.

Let us look at the parable of the servant who owed ten thousand talents in Matthew 18.

Parable of the Servant Who Owed Ten Thousand Talents

The verses related to this parable follow the verses cited for the seventy sevens (Mat 18:21-22). It will be helpful if you read this parable following the issue of seventy sevens. Read the following passage:

> Therefore is the kingdom of heaven likened unto a certain king, which would take account of his servants. And when he had begun to reckon, one was brought unto him, which owed him ten thousand talents. But forasmuch as he had not to pay, his lord commanded him to be sold, and his wife, and children, and all that he had, and payment to be made. The servant therefore fell down, and worshipped him, saying, Lord, have patience with me, and I will pay thee all. Then the lord of that servant was moved with compassion, and loosed him, and forgave him the debt. But the same servant went out, and found one of his fellowservants, which owed him an hundred pence: and he laid hands on him, and took him by the throat, saying, Pay me that thou owest. And his fellowservant fell down at his feet, and besought him, saying, Have patience with me, and I will pay thee all. And he would not: but went and cast him into prison, till he should pay the debt. So when his fellowservants saw what was done, they were very sorry, and came and told unto their lord all that was done. Then his lord, after that he had called him, said unto him, O thou wicked servant, I forgave thee all that debt, because thou desiredst me: Shouldest not thou also have had compassion on thy fellowservant, even as I had pity on thee? And his lord was wroth, and delivered him to the tormentors, till he should pay all that was due unto him. So likewise shall my heavenly Father do also unto you, if ye from your hearts forgive not every one his brother their trespasses. [Matthew 18:23-35]

There was a servant who owed his king ten thousand talents

and would have had to sell his body, his wife, children, and all that he had to repay it. His lord was moved with compassion and forgave him the debt. The servant went out and found one of his fellow servants who owed him a hundred *denarii*, demanded him to pay him the debt, and cast him into prison. Hearing this, the lord got angry at the servant, canceled forgiveness for the debt, and delivered him to the tormentors.

At the end of this parable, Jesus says, "So likewise shall my heavenly Father do also unto you, if ye from your hearts forgive not every one his brother their trespasses."

🗁 Misinterpretation of this Parable

After reading this parable, we may think our forgiveness might be canceled as in this servant's case. But it is not so. I will now explain the true meaning of the parable.

Jesus spoke this parable after He told Peter to forgive his brother seventy times seven when Peter asked Him if he should forgive him seven times. So, it is clear this parable is connected to forgiveness, that is, the remission of sins.

In contrast with our conventional thoughts, it is not a warning against the wicked servant's excessive, covetous desire. If we read this parable with this traditional idea, we will respond by saying, "Yes, I will forgive my brother with all my heart, not like the silly servant."

However, after reading this parable if we have that kind of understanding of the parable, then we will ask the next question as Peter did of Jesus: "How many times should I forgive my brother? Until seven times?" Then, Jesus will answer to us, "Until seventy times seven." And Jesus will then speak this parable to us again.

To repeat, Jesus preached the parable in answer to the question. Even after hearing the answer, if we ask the same question again, then it shows that we understood nothing about the parable. Therefore, if we simply say, "I'll forgive my brother with all my heart," after having read the parable, we have failed to understand it.

What conclusion have you reached after having read the parable? Have you made a resolution to forgive your brother sincerely from now on? Then, you have missed the point.

Very Odd Servant

Now, we shall find from where we started to misunderstand this parable. The forgiven debt of this servant was ten thousand *talents*, and the debt he will receive was a hundred *denarii*. Since one *talent* is equivalent to six thousand *denarii*, ten thousand *talents* are converted into sixty million *denarii*. I will convert the money into the present monetary unit in order to roughly estimate the difference between the two sums of money, although this conversion has no great meaning.

One *denarion* matches the one-day wage of a worker. Roughly estimating that wage as fifty dollars, ten thousand *talents* are equivalent three billion dollars, and one hundred *denarii* are equivalent to five thousand dollars.

Strangely enough, this servant whose debt of three billion dollars is forgiven tried to receive five thousand dollars from his fellow worker. Because of this, his forgiveness of debt was canceled.

In general, if our debt of three billion dollars was forgiven, we would not cast our fellow worker into prison so as to punish him for five thousand dollars. We would generally forgive the debt of this fellow, rather than cast him into prison.

Therefore, the act by the servant in the parable is unexpected. Is he therefore very unusual? Is he a rare, wicked man who will cast his brother into prison in order to receive five thousand dollars while his debt of three billion dollars is forgiven? If the Lord used as an example such a rare and extreme case, this parable would not be applicable to us, losing its worth as the word of truth.

However, the servant does not represent a few cases; on the contrary, he is a representation of all believers. That is why Jesus gives us this parable; He reveals ourselves to make us true believers.

🗁 Misunderstanding of the Servant

The key to realizing what the parable truly means is to see that the servant misunderstood forgiveness. He thought he was forgiven, but in fact, he was not. Therefore he acts as a man who is not forgiven.

Consider what the servant must have been thinking: The servant thought that the debt of ten thousand talents and the debt of one hundred *denarii* had the same nature, even though the amounts were different. So, he thought it was reasonable to prepare some money at each moment and return it to the lord. Naturally, he tried to acquire the debt from his fellow servant, and he finally cast him into prison.

However, the difference between ten thousand talents and one hundred *denarii* does not indicate a simple difference between much money and little money. Both of them are monetary units, but he cannot reach ten thousand talents by saving one hundred *denarii* one time and two hundred *denarii* another time. These two monetary units represent two fundamentally different values. Also, for the lord who forgave the debts, he does not need one hundred or two hundred *denarii*, which he does not value. If he valued money substantially, he would not have forgiven ten thousand talents. The lord, having forgiven ten thousand talents, never meant to receive one hundred or two hundred *denarii* back again. If he expected money back, he would be cheapening the grace he offered.

The servant may have knowledge of forgiveness, but not through experience; accordingly, he could not live the life of a forgiven man. In reality, he was not forgiven, but he misunderstood that he was forgiven. He represents a man who is under the law.

🗁 Grace That Cannot Be Repaid

Well now! Does this story reflect a special case or situation?

No, as I already explained, it does not. This servant symbolizes all who believe in Jesus. Jesus tells the story to try to awaken us. We have sinned in God's sight, and we owe Him. Because of our debt to God, we should sell our body, wife, children, all that we have, and our life as this parable says. In fact, the wages of sin is death (Rom 6:23).

However, God forgave all of our sins when we came to church, repented, and confessed Jesus as our Savior. It was said that we were forgiven at that time and the church proclaimed it. Ever since then, we think within ourselves, "The Lord forgave me my sins, and I will not commit sin, and I will love my neighbors as a new man. I will give tithes and do church activities, thanking God for His grace of forgiving me. I will never commit adultery, and I will never steal and kill."

Of course, we do or do not do these things because we are forgiven. We do so in compensation for the forgiveness with thanks. Most of us think in this manner, and we lead the life of believers according to this principle. However, this is the life of the servant whose debt of ten thousand talents was forgiven but who was delivered to the tormentors.

Let us bear in mind that the forgiveness of Jesus is not a matter of knowledge; something that could be ours through mere acceptance. But it is the transfer of the life of Jesus into us, which is life itself. This transfer of life is not possible by merely accepting it in our brain or mind.

We have been forgiven, but we have not been truly forgiven like this servant. Since we have not *experienced* true forgiveness, we have no idea of the great grace and joy forgiveness brings. As a result, we see it as something that is achievable by our own good works.

However, the grace and forgiveness that the Lord gives to us cannot be repaid by our good deeds. If we attempt to do so, it shows we do not fully understand and grasp the full implications of the Lord's precious death and His blood of redemption. Nevertheless, we are hoping to do good works at the first opportunity so that we can please God in return for His grace. So, we try to redeem *ourselves* by gathering one hundred or two hundred *denarii* every day.

This is the natural reaction of those who think that they are forgiven but actually are not. They do not know that what they are doing is dishonoring the grace of the Lord.

🗁 Real Forgiveness Is Being Born Again

In the parable, the forgiveness given to the servant is another expression of being born again through Jesus.

> Ye shall know them by their fruits. Do men gather grapes of thorns, or figs of thistles? Even so every good tree bringeth forth good fruit; but a corrupt tree bringeth forth evil fruit. A good tree cannot bring forth evil fruit, neither can a corrupt tree bring forth good fruit. [Matthew 7:16-18]

Before forgiveness, a man is corrupt tree, and after forgiveness, if it is true one, he is born again as a good tree. Good trees bring forth good fruit, and corrupt trees bring forth evil fruit. In fact, good trees do not pour effort into bringing forth fruit; they can do so naturally, without extra effort. But a corrupt tree requires a lot of effort against his nature to bring forth good fruit. Even so, he can never bring forth good fruit. This is the case of the servant in the parable. All his efforts I mentioned are the efforts of a corrupt tree to bear good fruits.

Did I say that the servant represents us?

🗁 How Can Gathering One Hundred *Denarii* Signify Casting the Fellow Servant into Prison?

How can gathering one hundred *denarii* imply casting his fellow servant into prison?

We normally think in the following way: We are already saved, and we will go to heaven when we die. However, the rewards in heaven will vary for each believer. So we are to carry out righteous acts as much as possible to get better rewards. Therefore we are eager to do good works.

However, such works have a fundamental problem; our doing good leads to the judgment and accusation of others automatically. For instance, if we are attending church service, being charitable, giving tithes, fasting, and believing in Jesus, we become proud of having done such things. We then begin to watch brothers around us. Seeing them, we judge based on the works we have done. You might think, "I attended the service, gave tithes, and joined church activities, but that brother does not. I am fasting and giving donations, but that guy doesn't." Thus, we accuse brothers, whether openly or secretly. But Jesus said to us, "Do not judge."

In addition, we may even condemn our brothers before Jesus, saying, "Lord, they don't come to the service. Lord, he doesn't give tithes, but I am doing all these things." If we think deep, even believing in Jesus is a kind of good work to us. So when we see unbelievers, we bring them in front of the Lord, saying in our minds, "See Lord, they are doing wrong. They do not believe in Jesus, but I believe."

In a spiritual sense, we are accusing these brothers, driving them into darkness, and casting them into prison. Consequently, those who work according to the law see the brothers who did not do so as those who owe them one hundred *denarii*. For example, the brothers owe the debt of not attending the service and the debt of not doing charity as many times as they did.

The traditional teaching that we know (and are taught) is that we are saved through faith, and good works are connected to rewards in heaven. So, we try to forgive brothers and love neighbors to accumulate rewards in heaven. However, this teaching is the law wrapped in the name of the gospel. If we follow this teaching, we will have to labor, being heavily laden, in the vicious circle of the law.

In order to love neighbors, we must be born again, and then we will be able to love neighbors naturally, not for getting rewards in heaven. The basic mistake of our faith is that we do not know exactly what forgiveness and being born again is. The forgiveness we currently understand is not the right one. We digressed from the truth, as we can see in the case of this servant.

🗁 What Brought the Servant to the Tormentors?

The parable says the servant cast the fellow servant into prison until he could repay the debt, and the lord got angry with this servant and thus delivered him to the tormentors.

Now, we will consider what brought the servant to the tormentors. The answer is his unforgiven debt. If the debtor fails to pay off the debt, he will be delivered to the tormentors. Since the servant did not clear his debt, he is finally turned over to them. Superficially, it is because he had the fellow servant thrown into prison. However, if he has cast his fellow servant to prison, it shows that his debts have not been forgiven from the very outset. The lord had forgiven him his debts, but on his side, he took the forgiveness of debts wrongly, and actually, he was not forgiven.

It is natural that he whose debts were not forgiven would want to collect the one hundred *denarii*. It is because he has something uneasy and nervous in his mind since his debts were not forgiven fully. He collects one hundred and two hundred *denarii*, rationalizing it in his mind by thinking, "This is for the purpose of receiving a reward in heaven, and it will show thanks for the grace of His having forgiven my debts."

If we act like the servant, our acts reveal that we are the debtor, and we will be delivered to the tormentors.

I am saying this out of kindness. Hearing this story, we are apt to resolve in our heart, "I will never behave like that servant." If we think further, we will know that he had to be delivered to the tormentors eventually because he did not liquidate his own debts at the start, so it is not because he cast his fellow servant into prison to receive his one hundred *denarii*. Please read this section carefully again.

To do good works, let the living Lord be with you first, then the good works will flow from you naturally. This is the way of truth. Don't try to do the good works by yourself to show them to the Lord. This is not the right way.

Likewise the Father Shall Do to Us.

Matthew 18:35 reads, "So likewise shall my heavenly Father do also unto you, if ye from your hearts forgive not every one his brother their trespasses."

Jesus concludes the parable of the unmerciful servant with the above verse, which looks like a severe warning. Yes, it is to those who live under the law.

However, what Jesus really meant by 'forgiveness from your heart' is the forgiveness of Jesus, i.e., forgiveness until seventy time seven. So, in order to exercise this forgiveness, we have to be truly forgiven first by meeting Jesus and by becoming one with God, receiving the Holy Spirit. Jesus is not mentioning seven or eight times or even 490 times of forgiveness.

If we cannot forgive as Jesus does, then we will do what the servant did. Accordingly, we will be treated as such. There is no other way. Jesus is illustrating a natural principle.

Forgiveness/Salvation Cannot Be Canceled

This parable also reveals the matter of cancellation of salvation mentioned in this chapter. That is, "Can the born again man commit sin?" At a glance, we may easily conclude salvation can be canceled and the born again man can commit sin. This conclusion may be reached when considering that the servant in the parable, once forgiven, was eventually delivered to the tormentors. However, that is not the right reading. The servant was not forgiven from the start; he misunderstood that his debts were forgiven. As a result, he was given to the tormentors to whom the unforgiven ought to go.

This parable is also a spiritual illumination for us. If we have no *experience* of being perfectly forgiven, we are to go where we ought to go. The perfectly forgiven do not commit sin again. They cannot sin because they have moved their positions from this world to heaven. The law of the world is no longer applied to them, and they are only under the control of the law of heaven. If someone's forgiveness from Jesus seems canceled, he actually was not forgiven, but he mistakenly thought he was forgiven.

Nothing can separate those in Christ from Christ: "Nor height, nor depth, nor any other creature, shall be able to separate us from the love of God, which is in Christ Jesus our Lord" (Rom 8:39).

The remaining life of those in the stage of the Epistles is the life of loving their neighbors as themselves. It will end in the stage of Revelation. In the Revelation stage, their life will finish in glory.

8

STAGE OF REVELATION — CONFIRMATION OF BORN AGAIN

Life of loving neighbors by those in the stage of the Epistles ends with their physical death. Their death represents a final confirmation about gloriously closing life in the stage of the Epistles. When those in the stage of the Epistles keep their faith until they die and are then confirmed as the truly born again men, they have reached the faith stage of Revelation.

Confirmation of Being Born Again

Once a man is born again, his born again life will be continued until his death. At the point of death, his born again experience will be confirmed as a true one. I will now explain this matter more accurately using the case of Jesus.

Being born again is a private matter for the man himself, but the confirmation of being born again is related to his neighbors because he, the born again, preaches the gospel to his neighbors until death. Read Matthew.

> Jesus said unto him, Thou shalt love the Lord thy God with all thy heart, and with all thy soul, and with all thy mind. This is the first and great commandment. And the second is like

> unto it, Thou shalt love thy neighbour as thyself. On these two commandments hang all the law and the prophets. [Mat 22:37-40]

Thus as stated, all the law and the prophets hang or depend upon our being born again (love God) and its confirmation (love neighbor).

Salvation and being born again have the same meaning. The apostle Paul describes salvation as follows:

> Not as though I had already attained, either were already perfect: but I follow after, if that I may apprehend that for which also I am apprehended of Christ Jesus. [Philippians 3:12]

Here, Paul is already born again and saved by Jesus Christ, but he says that he has not already attained. He is saying this, because he has the life to live after being born again, that is, the confirmation of being born again, which is to come.

🗁 Forgiveness of My Trespasses and My Brother's Trespasses

Please refer to the next verses that will help you understand what I am saying:

> For if ye forgive men their trespasses, your heavenly Father will also forgive you: But if ye forgive not men their trespasses, neither will your Father forgive your trespasses. [Matthew 6:14-15]

If this Scripture reads to you as a commandment then you have most probably failed to grasp its true meaning. God does not give us the law for us to keep through the Scripture. He gives us Jesus Christ, the Gospel through the Scripture.

If we read the above-quoted verse as "If you do not forgive men their trespasses, God will not forgive your trespasses," then there is no other stronger commandment than this verse. We must unavoidably forgive our brother so that we may be forgiven. Of course, there will be no problem if we can forgive brothers, but we have to take pains to do so. If we fail, we must repent to God and try again to do so. Indeed, the expression "all you who labor and are heavy laden" is an adequate word for us in this circumstance (Mat 11:28).

However, as I have already said, the Scripture is not the law that forces us to do something in this manner. The above passage is not a commandment but a simple description, meaning, "As I see you can forgive men their trespasses, you have been forgiven by God. Also, as I see you cannot forgive men their trespasses, you have not been forgiven by God." What I describe above does not tell us to forgive our brother, but it does suggest one bright way to those who labor to forgive brothers. That is, "Let God forgive you your sin first." Many people will wonder how this verse can be interpreted in that way.

I will use an illustration to help you understand this.

🗁 The Former Is Confirmed by the Latter

Imagine a man learns Taekwondo, the martial art, and he wins the first level. His winning the first level proves that he has successfully applied the martial skill of the first level to others. He won the first level, but his acquisition of the first level will be proved and confirmed depending on whether he can use the skill on others. If he cannot apply the skill to others, he has not really won it. In other words, he cannot show the skill of the first level because he did not win it.

This can be rewritten according to the description style of Matthew: "If you can exercise the first-level skill on others, the Taekwondo authority has qualified you for the first-level skill, but if you cannot practice the first-level skill on others, the Taekwondo authority has not qualified you for the first-level skill."

Since the first level and the first-level skill are inevitably connected, there is no loss of meaning if we say, "If you can make full use of the first-level skill, the Taekwondo authority will qualify you for the first level, but if you cannot make full use of the first-level skill, the Taekwondo authority will not qualify you for the first level." Therefore, if you can use the first-level skill on others, it proves that you are qualified with the first level.

Jesus also speaks in this way: "For if ye forgive men their trespasses, your heavenly Father will also forgive you: But if ye forgive not men their trespasses, neither will your Father forgive your trespasses." Paraphrased, it is as if Jesus is saying, "As I see you forgive your brother, you are rightly forgiven by God, and as I see you cannot forgive your brother, you are not yet rightly forgiven by God."

The point is that we should realize we are first to be forgiven by God if we are to forgive our brother. Anyway, His word about forgiving our brother represents an example in which the former is confirmed by the latter.

I am talking about the confirmation of being born again according to the same principle. We will be born again at a certain point of our life. He who is born again will live the born again life. In this instance, being born again and leading the born again life are connected as one, and when a man has lived the born again life without any problem, his being born again will be confirmed as perfect.

🗁 The Example of Jesus Christ

Jesus Christ, who is the model of all born again men, lived a life as the Son of God. While He was alive, He was the Son of God. However, He was confirmed forever to be the Son of God after He was dead. That is, He was confirmed forever to be the Son of God through death:

> And Jesus cried with a loud voice, and gave up the ghost. And the veil of the temple was rent in twain from the top to the

bottom. And when the centurion, which stood over against him, saw that he so cried out, and gave up the ghost, he said, Truly this man was the Son of God. [Mark 15:37-39]

In this scene, the centurion, having seen Jesus' death, accepted that He was the Son of God. There were many variables before Jesus was crucified. That is, He may have been tempted by devil and may not have been crucified. Of course, there was never such a possibility for God who sees the past, the present, and the future.

However, we, who are living in the world limited by time, always have variables. It was also applicable to Jesus who had come to the time-based world in which we are living now. Therefore, the agonies that He suffered when He was tempted by the devil in the wilderness or when He said, "If it be possible, let this cup pass from me" (Mat 26:39), were not a piece of cake, even though He was the Son of God. Since the history of the universe could be changed depending on what He decided in His heart, the temptation and the agonies were substantial and important.

The thing that made all these variables powerless is His death. After His death, there are no worries about Jesus being tempted by the devil or escaping the affliction of the cross as He has already completed it. No more variables whatsoever. All the situations are as fixed as His triumph. So, He said, "It is finished," just before He died.

Also, the writer of Hebrews described the death of Jesus using similar logic:

And for this cause he is the mediator of the new testament, that by means of death, for the redemption of the transgressions that were under the first testament, they which are called might receive the promise of eternal inheritance. For where a testament is, there must also of necessity be the death of the testator. For a testament is of force after men are

> dead: otherwise it is of no strength at all while the testator liveth. [Hebrews 9:15-17]

Accordingly, death confirms the life of a man, allowing no further changes. Being born again is confirmed in a man through his death.

By What Death?

I would like to talk a little more about the relationship between life and death. The death of a man puts an end to his life in this world. One malefactor who is hung on the cross beside Jesus lived an evil life, but he repented at the final moment before his death so that he could live in paradise with the Lord (Luk 23:40-43). The entire life of the malefactor was confirmed as good through this.

In addition, King Saul was approved by God in his earlier time, but he left God, and he finally took his sword and fell on it. The whole life of King Saul was finally confirmed as evil through such a death.

Therefore, a man's life, whether he lived a good life or an evil life, is confirmed by his death. The death of one malefactor was a good death and that of King Saul was an evil death. A good death represents that his life was good, and an evil death signifies that his life was evil. So, life matches death. "By what death does he die?" corresponds to the question, "What life did he live?"

Before ascension, the Lord says to Peter,

> Verily, verily, I say unto thee, When thou wast young, thou girdedst thyself, and walkedst whither thou wouldest: but when thou shalt be old, thou shalt stretch forth thy hands, and another shall gird thee, and carry thee whither thou wouldest not. This spake he, signifying by what death he should glorify God. And when he had spoken this, he saith unto him, Follow me. [John 21:18-19]

According to tradition, Peter is said to have died upside down on the cross. However, the word of by what death he should glorify God does not mean how he died, such as death from disease, death in prison, or death in a foreign land. These kinds of death have no relation to believing in Jesus.

Here, by what death Peter should glorify God means that he will glorify God with a new and changed life. This is the life of stretching forth hands and living a life as the Lord leads. Peter was young, in a spiritual sense, before meeting Jesus, and he walked the way he wanted. After having received Him, he finished his past life and started a new life. After the baptism with the Holy Spirit in the day of Pentecost, Peter began living a life in which he walked with the Holy Spirit, which is the life of glorifying God.

Since Peter's glorious life was finally confirmed by his death, the Scripture said by what death he should glorify God. "By what death will Peter glorify God?" means, "By what life will Peter glorify God?"

From the viewpoint of the faith-growing steps of an individual, the stage of Revelation represents the time when a man ends his entire life through death to confirm his life whether it is good or evil.

In this stage, after he who was born of the flesh is born again of the spirit, he lives the born again life, and then he actually goes to heaven. Naturally, faith of this stage is only applicable to those who are perfectly born again. Those who are not born again still remain in the Old Testament period when their lives of the flesh die. Such death cannot glorify God. A good death of a man glorifying God signifies that he meets Jesus Christ to be born again and ends life in the stage of Revelation. This is the death of glorifying God, and it is also the life of glorifying Him.

Our faith should grow to the stage of Revelation.

Epilogue

Our life begins in the stage of Genesis, and we are born in this world as sinners in the stage of Exodus. We live as sinners in the dark world of the Old Testament period, and when we feel exhausted and tired, we meet Jesus in our lives to start the New Testament period. When we undergo the stage of the Synoptic Gospels, according to His teaching and leading, Jesus comes on us as the Holy Spirit, and we are changed to be righteous. This is the stage of John in our faith. When the Holy Spirit is poured on us as happened at Pentecost, this time represents the stage of Acts in our faith. Now we begin to live the born again life which is the stage of the Epistles in our faith. When we have reached the stage of Revelation, we will finish our lives here. Thus, the Scripture has been perfected in us within our lifetime. God says such a life glorifies God.

Let your faith grow to reach the stage of Revelation. It is the only way for us to glorify God. And it is the way we should live our life in Christ.

May the grace of our Lord Jesus Christ be with you all.
Amen.

Table of Biblical Steps for Growing in Faith

	Eternity	Time and Space							Eternity
2 Parts		Old Testament Period-Law		New Testament Period-Grace					
3 Parts		Time of God		Time of Jesus	Time of Holy Spirit				
Bible	Genesis	Exodus	Laws / Prophets	Synoptic Gospels	John	Acts	Epistles	Revelation	
Salvation Steps	Creation	Birth	Legalistic Faith	Following Jesus	Born again /Salvation	Baptism by Holy Spirit	Born Again Life	Confirm'n of Born Again	
Life	in Eden	Life in this world →			Life in the Kingdom of God				
Points		▲ Eat the Fruit		▲ Ture Repentance	▲ Cross (Free from Law)			Death ▲	
Delivery			Pregnancy by Word ▲		▲ Delivery (Giving Birth to Jesus)				
	Eternity	Time and Space							Eternity

* This table summarizes the contents of the book. It might be of great help to understand the book if the reader refers to the table while reading it.

Additional Order

To order additional copies of this title, please contact one of the following distributors: Ingram, Amazon.com, Barnes & Noble or visit our website at haggaibooks.com

Forthcoming Titles

Haggai Books plans to publish the author's titles in English one after another. The forthcoming titles are:

Fresh Eyes to Read the Bible II: The Real Jesus
This title will reveal the real Jesus by exploring the true spiritual meanings of Scripture, which are quite different from the morals and ethics of the world.

Fresh Eyes to Read the Bible III: Good, Evil, and the Resurrection
This title will touch on such subjects as fellowship with God, tithes and offerings, the true nature of devil/Satan/demons, and the Word and resurrection.

A Spiritual Reading of First, Second, and Third John
This title will reveal a fresh way to have no sin during your lifetime through once-for-all forgiveness by Jesus Christ.

Other titles from the author will be published as and when they are made available.

FaSS Seminar

FaSS Evangelists (FaSS) stands for ***Fa***ther, ***S***on, and Holy ***S***pirit, and the name references Matthew 28:19: "Go ye therefore, and teach all nations, baptizing them in the name of the Father, and of the Son, and of the Holy Ghost."

Baptism in the name of the Father, the Son, and the Holy Spirit represents the steps for growing in faith. Our faith grows from Father stage to Son stage, and finally we reach the Holy Spirit stage. Those who have undergone these stages will receive the life of Jesus, becoming one with God.

FaSS Evangelists organizes seminars focusing on the "Biblical Steps for Growing in Faith" emphasized in this book, Fresh Eyes to Read the Bible. The seminar will be led by the author.

Those lost sons who are exhausted in the existing faith system are very well welcome. Having read this title, if you wish to know the real Jesus, true faith, and hidden meanings of the Scriptures, please contact us by email : seminar@fass.kr or visit us at our website www.fass.kr.

FaSS Evangelists
www.fass.kr

www.ingramcontent.com/pod-product-compliance
Lightning Source LLC
LaVergne TN
LVHW091028080826
845145LV00002B/400

* 9 7 8 8 9 9 5 3 8 8 5 4 9 *